Praise for W

Wisdom that comes from the heart ... ... n I
say both Linda and Dalene have w... ... ... :ly
precious hearts that have embraced li... ... ... well
pleasing to the Lord. I could not more highly recommend this book to you.

Dr. Don Wilton, Pastor, First Baptist Church, Spartanburg, SC

Words to Live By is no mere flip-calendar advice. It propels readers into proactive living using action verbs as launch pads. Focusing on one transformative word per week allows for soaking when we are accustomed to sipping truth.

Cynthia Ruchti, Speaker and Author of *Tattered and Mended:*
The Art of Healing the Wounded Soul

Knowledge is plentiful. It's what we do with what we know that equips us to grow. Through God's Word, relatable stories, and practical helps, *Words to Live By*, will help the reader put into action the things we think we know. Caution: you may never be the same again.

Brenda Blankenship, Bible Teacher, Speaker, Author

The prelude to the Gospel of John declares that "In the beginning was the Word . . . and the Word became flesh and dwelt among us." That Word is Jesus Christ. Linda Gilden and Dalene Parker have discovered gospel truth in fifty-two ordinary words that become, through the lens of faith, words to live by for all of us. Take these words to heart. Ponder and reflect upon them and these words will reveal, again, the one Word made flesh.

Kirk H. Neely, Pastor, Author, and Counselor

The concept [of focusing on one word a week] suggested by Linda Gilden and Dalene Parker intrigues me. Since I believe an abundant life is balancing who I am with what I do, examining one action verb a week gives just the right amount of time for absorption and application. I like the five subdivisions for each week, which provide a variety of reflective perspectives. *Words to Live By* can be a terrific catalyst for spiritual growth all year long.

Ginger Cox, Writer, Speaker, and Nature Photographer

Words to Live By directly connects readers to the Word from one simple word. The heartfelt stories of each chapter prompt the reader to meditate on God's presence in *their* lives and embrace His truths from everyday events. Linda and Dalene have written a wonderful resource to support believers in their walk with Christ.

Vanessa R. Chandler, Educator

The average person hears about 50,000 words a day. It's no wonder we are overwhelmed in finding clear direction in our lives. Dalene and Linda cut through our word-cluttered world, providing one word a week to capture our focus. Clearly, a simplified, needed devotion delivering a powerful impact in any reader's life.

Veneal Williams, Author and Blogger

Words—can bring life, and that life more abundantly. Words can introduce hope to a dark place, encouragement to the down-trodden. Words also have the power to destroy. A careless or unkind word spoken can damage a person for years. What words will you share with those whom you love? This book will cause you to pause and consider the power and importance of the words you choose.

Tama Westman, Author of *Why You Do What You Do*

Are you looking for a resource that can help change your life, improve your mood, and help you gain a deeper understanding of God's Word? Linda and Dalene have done just that in this wonderful book that is filled with practical, memorable ways to incorporate biblical principles into your life. I can guarantee that if you take the time to dig into this resource you will be encouraged, strengthened, and blessed with the insight and application that *Words to Live By* contains.

John Thurman, M.Div., M.A., LCHMC, Therapist, Speaker,
Author, and International Crisis Response Specialist

Taking a simple, everyday action word and embedding that word into one's memory bank, causing an immediate connection to a profound truth is exactly what *Words to Live By* does for the reader. Linda Gilden and Dalene Parker have brought together God's Word and its application to our lives in a unique and unforgettable way.

Kathy M. Howard, Author of *From Dishes to Snow* and
From Driftwood to Sapphire

Linda and Dalene write from the heart with wisdom and insight relevant for today's challenges. The weekly focus on one word, from The Word, is a great way to reinforce spiritual truth.

Candy Arrington, Author, Editor, and Speaker

Dive into this terrific work of art and immerse yourself in these engaging stories to broaden your walk with God. *Words to Live By* provides stunning examples of positive, godly responses to daily challenges through active resolution and causes one to ponder the deeper questions of life, the ones we often hurry past or outright ignore. Find comfort, peace, joy, and abundant wisdom here that will revolutionize your life.

Aaron M. Zook, Jr., Author, Speaker, and
ZookBooks CEO

In this fast-paced world, it is very calming and refreshing to discover this "devotional" book that forces you to slow down, digest, and savor the guidance offered up a week at a time. Fifty-two weeks, fifty-two critical *Words to Live By*, and time to connect, think, and apply simple words of action and the promptings of the Holy Spirit. Thank you, Linda and Dalene, for this inspirational book and its unique concept!

Christine Phillips, Retired Teaching Veteran and
Alpha Delta Kappa Member

Words to Live By is a clarion call to practice our faith. The devotions give new meaning to action words we often forget or ignore. *Words to Live By* will encourage and instruct you as you strive to serve the Lord.

Gloria Penwell, Mentor and Encourager of Writers

As a marriage and family therapist, I see how powerful words can be in restoring relationships and changing perceptions. *Words to Live By* is perfect for helping individuals, couples, and families tap into the power of words acted on and influenced by God's Word.

Marie F. Duncan, LMFT, Ed.D.

Rippling with apt metaphors and real-life illustrations that flesh out each word offered for reflection, *Words to Live By* sheds fresh light on the Scriptures selected for meditation. Spot-on.

Nikki Grimes, Award-winning Children's Author,
Artist, and Speaker

Mind-opening *Words to Live By* offers refreshing, thought-provoking, practical stories and anecdotes to help us continuously learn more from the Creator of the Word.

Cindy W. Haggerty, School Library Media Specialist and
Teacher Librarian

Though by no means exclusively for educators, the many classroom anecdotes in *Words to Live By* will encourage teachers to apply God's Word in practical, focused ways as they concentrate on the application of one word per week in their personal and professional lives.

Eric Buehrer, Founder and President,
Gateways to Better Education

52 ORDINARY WORDS THAT LEAD TO AN EXTRAORDINARY LIFE

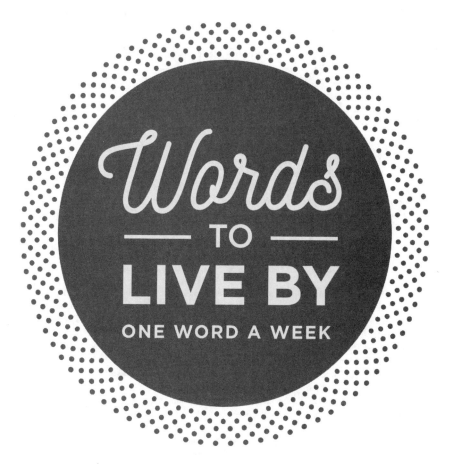

Words
— TO —
LIVE BY
ONE WORD A WEEK

LINDA J. GILDEN AND DALENE V. PARKER

WORTHY®
Inspired

• • • • • • • • • • • • • • •

To Pamela Clements and the Worthy Publishing family, thank you.
We are blessed to have you share our excitement and belief in this book.
Your words of encouragement and partnership continue to be a treasure.

• • • • • • • • • • • • • • •

Published by Worthy Inspired, an imprint of Worthy Publishing Group, a division of Worthy Media, Inc., One Franklin Park, 6100 Tower Circle, Suite 210, Franklin, TN 37067.

WORTHY is a registered trademark of Worthy Media, Inc.

Helping people experience the heart of God

Library of Congress Cataloging-in-Publication Data

Names: Gilden, Linda Jeffords, author.
Title: Words to live by : 52 ordinary words that lead to an extraordinary
life / Linda J. Gilden and Dalene V. Parker.
Description: Franklin, TN : Worthy Pub., 2016.
Identifiers: LCCN 2016011303 | ISBN 9781617957222 (tradepaper)
Subjects: LCSH: Language and languages--Religious aspects--Christianity. |
Devotional literature.
Classification: LCC BR115 .L25 G55 2016 | DDC 242/.2--dc23
LC record available at http://lccn.loc.gov/2016011303

ISBN: 978-1-61795-722-2

For foreign and subsidiary rights, contact rights@worthypublishing.com

Cover Design: Brian Bobel

Printed in the United States of America
16 17 18 19 20 LBM 10 9 8 7 6 5 4 3 2 1

To my family, your words of encouragement
and love fill my heart. Thank you.
To my friends, you are great cheerleaders!
To the God of all words, thank You for Your Word,
which blesses me every week.
To my writing partner, Dalene, you never cease to amaze me.
You exude the spirit of Jesus and speak His words
in everything you do. You are an inspiration and a joy
to write with. I am so thankful you are my friend.

Linda

• • • • • • • • • • • • • •

With gratitude for the gift of words that optimize our lives—
words from Him, from family and friends, and from
the most encouraging coauthor I could ever hope
to partner with—I dedicate this labor of love.
May our readers find blessing, encouragement,
and hope for their lives in these pages.

Dalene

INTRODUCTION

*W*ords are powerful. They have the ability to hurt, condemn, and disappoint. They may also encourage, uplift, and effect positive changes in our thinking and our speaking. That is our goal for *Words to Live By*—to focus on 52 ordinary words that when considered and applied creatively and consistently in fresh new ways may reap extraordinary benefits.

The average person uses over 7,000 (men)—20,000 (women) words every day, words that can make a difference and help people grow in their faith, improve their mental capacity, and enrich their relationships. In the midst of those thousands of words, can you imagine what would happen if you truly concentrated on incorporating one positive, powerful word each week into your faith, your mind, and your relationships?

We are word lovers who especially like to find new ways to use words. That love propelled us to write *Words to Live By*. But more than that, we are friends who have seen the power of words work in our own lives and the lives of others. In our various roles as wives, mothers, daughters, sisters, friends, grandmother, and teacher, we have used words to bless those around us and each other. We would love to see you do the same.

The most important words of all are those God has spoken to us. You will find each of the words or concepts in *Words to Live By* referenced in the Bible. Each week we look at one word in several different ways. Focus on that word. Pray that word. Watch for ways God brings that word to mind during the week. Ask Him to help you apply the weekly word to your daily life.

May the words of our pens and the prayers of our hearts be pleasing in your sight, Lord, our Rock and our Redeemer (Psalm 19:14, authors' paraphrase).

Linda and Dalene

LISTEN

$\mathcal{C}$ommunication is important but we sometimes forget it involves two elements—speaking and listening. We become so focused on what we want to say that we don't listen for a reply. Jesus challenged people to really listen to those around them, to Him, and to God.

This week observe the listening styles of those you are communicating with. Look at your own listening styles as well. Be intentional about being a good listener. Recognize the gift of listening is important to developing close relationships and meeting the needs of others.

ARE YOU LISTENING?

"He wakens me morning by morning,
wakens my ear to listen like one being taught."
Isaiah 50:4

The Bible is full of examples of important listening: Mary listened to Gabriel's announcement about being chosen as the mother of Christ. She accepted what she heard and made herself available. The shepherds listened to the angels proclaim Jesus' birth. They began to worship long before they ever saw His face. Joseph listened to the dream which warned him of impending danger for baby Jesus; he fled with his new family to Egypt until it was safe to return. Of course, every writer of the Old and New Testament listened to God before setting His words in ink.

New learning standards emphasize the importance of active listening. Teachers and students alike need practice developing these skills in the classroom. Too often teachers do not allow students enough time to collaborate and listen to each other's ideas. Too often students do not really listen for instructions.

Two methods I use to encourage listening when I'm communicating essential content to my students:

1. (Interrupting their conversation) "You'll have to forgive me. I have this ridiculous notion that what I say might be important. Please humor me and listen."

2. (Whispering) "I hope you can hear me because what I'm about to say will be on the test tomorrow." This method I learned from my high school teacher who refused to talk over her students. Instead, she reduced her voice to a whisper as she communicated essential information.

Whether through a dream, angelic proclamation, or a whisper, may our ears be "wakened" today to listen like one being taught!

SIGHT OR SOUND?

"My sheep listen to my voice;
I know them, and they follow me."
John 10:27–28

*N*ancy and Gary consider their blindness a nuisance, not a disability. They compensate for lack of sight by listening well. Gary determines a coin's value by listening to it plink when thrown onto a hard surface. When asked if they could choose between sight or hearing, Nancy and Gary quickly reply: "Hearing!"

Listening helps them imagine all the faces, places, and details they cannot see. Hearing means being able to sing beautifully. For this couple, it would be a shame not to hear the nuances of music, nature, and voices.

In contrast, my husband's cousin Tomi, blinded in an automobile accident, would choose sight over hearing. Fiercely independent and determined, Tomi finds her blindness creates "layers of complication" in situations. Because she had sight until her late twenties, Tomi remembers how people and places looked decades later. The first time I drove to her house, I got lost and called Tomi for help.

"Where are you?" she asked.

I gave her the street name and nearby landmarks.

Plugging that information into her memory, Tomi directed me to her house where I sheepishly admitted that her sense of direction was much keener than mine, even though I could see.

Nancy, Gary, and Tomi are inspirations and reminders to soak up all the sight and sound we can—and never to take either for granted. What do you see or hear today that you want to thank God for?

LISTENING IN THE STORMS

"Hear my cry, O God; listen to my prayer.
From the ends of the earth I call to you, I call as my heart grows faint;
lead me to the rock that is higher than I."
Psalm 61:1–2

The beautiful set of wind chimes my husband gave me ranks as my "best ever" present from him—it calms my soul and makes me smile to listen to their melodious harmony.

Of course the harder the wind blows, or the greater the storm, the more likely I will be to hear those chimes. Since emotional "storms" have been threatening my relationships lately, that means now is a very good time for listening to the wild, sweet harmony of the wind chimes—and listening for the wild, sweet harmony of understanding that often comes after the storm.

After all, it's in the storms that we are forced to listen more closely. It's also when we need the most assurance that we are being heard.

Today my friend Pam asked me how I was doing, and I told her— all of it. It wasn't pretty. It wasn't uplifting. It wasn't what I meant to come out of my mouth. But I needed someone to listen, and she did.

And guess what? Pam told me she had promised to do one thing each day that would show God's love to someone else. Today it was listening.

Thank You, Lord. Now I'm ready to hear what You are trying to teach me through this storm.

Is there someone or something you need to listen more carefully to today? May you find that listening helps you hear the harmony your soul longs for.

THE LESS YOU SAY, THE MORE YOU HEAR

"I said, 'I will watch my ways and keep my tongue from sin;
I will put a muzzle on my mouth while in the presence of the wicked.'"
Psalm 39:1

*R*emember how Jesus responded to his accusers? With silence. No pretending. No defending. He just listened to what they had to say and said nothing in return. Although saying nothing might be the very best response, saying as little as possible is the next best.

Dr. Kirk Neely, pastor and counselor, gives excellent advice regarding how to deal with critical, negative people. When confronted by an undeserved tirade or caught up in a blame game, he suggests using this simple response: "I'm sorry you feel that way." Most arguments and accusations are built—and sustained—on feelings rather than facts. By using this verbal response, you acknowledge the accuser's feelings, but do not agree with his interpretation—or misinterpretation—of the facts.

Acknowledgment does not imply agreement and usually ends an argument swiftly. There's nothing in that statement that can be disputed or that requires further discussion. Basically, it shows you were listening, that you heard what the other person had to say, but not that you agree. It's a great way to honor someone's feelings without compromising your own. When the conflict dissipates, chances are you can work together to reach a mutual agreement. If not, at least no lasting damage has been inflicted.

Next time you find yourself confronted with someone who strongly disagrees with you, try saying, "I'm sorry you feel that way." Then listen for what that person and the Holy Spirit really need to communicate.

LISTENING WITH THE HEART

*"Let the wise listen and add to their learning,
and let the discerning get guidance."*

Proverbs 1:5

The lady sitting on a bench as I exited the airport undoubtedly noticed my tear-stained face and wobbly smile. My daughter had just left for another long stay overseas. Without knowing or asking the reason for my sadness, she listened with her heart and her eyes. Her only communication was a smile and "God bless you." But that was enough to make me smile, too, this time with no wobbles.

Annette is a single mom who listened with her heart instead of her head and adopted two boys with multiple learning disabilities. She did not listen to those who foresaw trouble for her. Instead, she did her best to provide a stable home filled with love and laughter for precious but unwanted children.

Listening with the heart is an art. It requires a deliberate disciplining of the tongue and a training of the mind and eyes to search, sense, and supply other people's needs. That's what the lady at the airport did for me. That's what Annette did for the sons she adopted.

One of the ways I get my students to think about the importance of listening is by posting this pun on the board: Here to learn? Then learn to hear! But paying attention with our ears is only part of listening.

Today let's focus on listening not only with our ears, but also with our hearts.

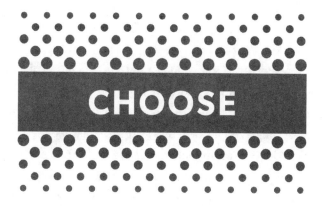

CHOOSE

$\mathcal{L}$ife requires many choices. Some easy and some not so easy. But all require some degree of thought and many a great deal of prayer. Be attentive this week to the number of times you must make a choice and commit to asking God's guidance as you weigh one thing against another.

YOUR NAME HAS BEEN CALLED

"You did not choose me, but I chose you and appointed you to go
and bear fruit—fruit that will last. Then the Father
will give you whatever you ask in my name."
John 15:16

*R*ed rover, red rover, send Linda right over!" One of my favorite recess games at school was Red Rover.

Red Rover requires two teams. It doesn't matter how large the teams are as long as each side has at least three players.

The children on a team hold hands to form a human chain. Then they call out a friend's name on the other team to be "sent over." They chant, "Red Rover, Red Rover, send Sara right over." The chosen person runs as fast as possible to try to break through the chain. If the defenders' hands separate, the one who has come over chooses a person to take back to his team with him. If the defense holds, the challenger joins that team.

The excitement and anticipation of waiting to hear whose name would be called was tremendous. I remember the thrill of hearing my name called and being chosen to represent my team.

Each of us has been called by name by the One who created us.

He has left the choice up to you as to whether or not you will serve him. What will your response be when you hear him say, "Send [your name] right over?"

LIFE'S CHOICES

*"Because of the LORD's great love we are not consumed,
for his compassions never fail. They are new every morning;
great is your faithfulness."*

Lamentations 3:22–23

Life is full of choices. Some are easy. Some are hard and many are in between. But no matter what your choice, it requires weighing two or more options and committing to one of them.

The easy choices are fun. Would you like chocolate cake or pecan pie for dessert? Should I wear my black or brown pants today? Should I sit at the front or the back of the room in my club meeting? Which movie shall we see on Friday night?

The hard choices are just that—hard. They are life-changing. Whom should I marry? Do I choose eternal life with Jesus or a life in hell with no hope? Should we add another round of chemotherapy or enjoy the remaining time without enduring more side effects? When something bad happens, do I choose to be a victim or an overcomer?

Everyday choices affect our lives. Every morning when we wake up, there is a choice. Are we going to live this day in a good way or a bad way? God gives us new perspective when each day begins.

Each day provides a clean slate, full of the Lord's compassions. So if you have a bad day, when your head hits the pillow, thank God the day is over and wake up with a fresh, new start.

WALK POSITIVELY

*"May the Lord make your love increase and overflow
for each other and for everyone else, just as ours does for you."*

1 Thessalonians 3:12

"Oops! I am so sorry!" Shara looked at the contents of her coffee cup, now all over the front of Wesley's formerly clean, crisply starched, white shirt. "Are you all right? Did this hot coffee burn you?"

Stunned, Wesley looked down at his shirt. He took the napkin Shara offered and blotted the spreading stain. "No, I'm fine. I think the shirt caught most of it."

"I feel terrible," Shara said. "Please let me take your shirt to the cleaners for you."

"No problem," said Wesley. "I have a pile of things to drop off on my way home. I'll just add one more! This should be a good conversation starter at my board meeting in a few minutes."

Instead of letting the incident ruin his day, Wesley made a choice. He chose to react in a positive way to a negative situation, which blessed Shara and turned what could have been a downhill day for her into one that was blessed from the start.

When the mailman doesn't bring your much-anticipated acceptance for admission into college or rebate from a high-priced item, do you thank God that you haven't received a "no" or does it become a dark cloud over everything you do that day?

Regardless of what life spills on you or fails to fulfill for you, choose to walk positively through your day.

DECISIONS, DECISIONS

"I will instruct you and teach you in the way you should go;
I will counsel you with my eye on you."

Psalm 32:8

ccording to a recent blog, the average person makes around 35,000 decisions a day. It's hard to imagine having time for that many decisions in 24 hours, isn't it? Of course, this includes all decisions large and small—Should I get out of bed? What should I eat for breakfast? Scrambled eggs or fried? The list goes on and on.

Often we make decisions without even thinking about what we are doing. But making a choice not only affects us. Many times there are far reaching and sometimes serious consequences. For every important decision, weigh carefully the options and try these action steps:

- Seek God. Pray about your decision. Read your Bible and observe God's direction. Listen to what God has to say to you. Get a notebook, and journal His answers; record your choices to see God's hand at work.
- Seek godly counsel. This may come from friends, counselors, or family members. Remember, however, the best counsel comes from God.
- Seek information to make the best decision. Gather all the pros and cons of your choice and pray through them.

Ask your praying friends to pray with you. If your decision is really big, form a team to lift you up in prayer.

JUMP OFF THE FENCE

"But if serving the LORD seems undesirable to you,
then choose for yourselves this day whom you will serve. . . .
But as for me and my household, we will serve the LORD."

Joshua 24:15

The greatest choice of all comes when we are confronted by our sin and we must choose whether or not to accept Jesus into our lives. The course of our lives can be changed in an instant: assurance of our eternity is just one simple choice.

In playing Red Rover, the thrill of hearing your name called is great. But greater is the thrill that comes in knowing that for life, the game that really matters, your name has already been called. You don't have to wait and see if it is your turn. God has called each one of us, by name, to come to Him. He loves us from the moment we are born. We need only to choose to respond to His calling to immediately become part of His family. Once you make that decision, all your other choices are made based on the values you hold as a Christian.

You can't sit on the fence. Life is filled with choices and you are in control. Choose to commit. Make good, solid choices. And if you haven't ever dealt with the choice of God's calling you to be part of His family, put that first on your list for prayer and consideration today. Jump off the fence!

BELIEVE

*T*hose who know Jesus and trust in Him understand that total, unwavering belief is the key to living life. John 10:10 states that is why Jesus came, so that we could live it "to the full."

Are there days when your level of belief seems to be more fragile than others? Perhaps a fresh look at this word will bring new understanding and depth of commitment. We have been given the ultimate reward for our belief—eternal life. This week work on taking your belief to an even deeper level.

I DO BELIEVE

"I do believe; help me overcome my unbelief!"
Mark 9:24

"What's wrong with your mom?" concerned friends asked. Confined to a hospital bed, hooked to oxygen, wired to a heart monitor, linked to an IV, and tethered to a catheter, Mother's hospital stay stretched well over a month.

"It would be easier to say what's NOT wrong with her," I replied. Congestive heart failure, three surgeries, a skin graft, staph infection, unstable blood pressure, diabetes—at 81 years of age, Mother was battling for her life. Several times we thought she might lose the battle. Her only living sister died during this tension-filled time, yet we dared not tell Mother. We didn't want sorrow added to her list of woes.

I claimed Psalm 41:3: "The Lord will sustain [her] on [her] sickbed and restore [her] from [her] bed of illness." Though I knew this might mean spiritual sustenance and heavenly restoration, I believed God could help Mother overcome physically as well. Little by little, she improved. Every day we prayed and personalized Psalm 91. Reading verse 16 about the Lord satisfying with long life, I asked Mother what she considered a long life.

"Well, Dad lived to be 92. That's a pretty long life."

"So, is that your goal?" I asked.

"No, I want to make it to 102!" She replied.

Do I dare to believe she will?

If it's His sovereign will, then yes!

Today, why not ask the Lord to sustain or restore your faith and help you believe His promises.

DON'T YOU BELIEVE?

"Cast all your anxiety on him because he cares for you."
1 Peter 5:7

When it's time to send a loved one away for a year, what's the best way to handle that inevitable sense of loss and longing that makes you simultaneously happy (for the one leaving) and sad (for those left behind)? How do you NOT worry or wonder about the health, welfare, and happiness of someone you care about deeply, but cannot get to in a hurry?

Ask Morgan. My daughter's college roommate and I were chatting about my daughter, Susanne's impending departure overseas. Susanne had landed a teaching assistant's position in a local high school on the island of Corsica, France. After acknowledging how much I would miss her, but how excited I was for her, I said, "I sure hope she will call or Skype often. At least we can stay in touch that way."

That's when Morgan socked it to me (gently, of course): "Don't you think that when we have to hear from our loved ones so often just to know they are okay, it's kind of like telling God you don't believe He will take care of them?"

ZING! Was that a prick of the conscience I just felt?

Yes, I believe it was.

Will He take care of my darling daughter?

Yes, I believe He will. After all, she's His daughter, too!

Thank You, Lord, for reminding us to believe in Your loving care!

JUST BELIEVE

"I remain confident of this: I will see the goodness of the LORD in the land of the living."

Psalm 27:13

*M*argo had been praying almost constantly since yesterday. The news wasn't good. She had neglected her health, and her doctor told her that she had to make some serious changes. She needed to take better care of herself. Margo was discouraged.

As she prayed, the phone rang. It was her friend Joyce. "How are you?" Joyce asked.

Margo replied, "I'm okay."

"You don't sound too okay," Joyce said. "Anything I can do?"

"No. Just pray for me. I'm just trying to process my morning conversation with my doctor."

"I pray for you every day anyway. Whatever it is just hang on to God's promises. You can believe every single one of them!"

"Thanks."

Margo searched her Bible for scriptures that would increase her faith.

She took a break from her search to go get the mail. A small package was among the bills and letters.

She opened it and took out a beautiful turquoise magnet from a friend. The note said, "I am giving these away at my ministry table. I thought of you and wanted to encourage you." The magnet had only one word on it—"Believe."

Margo also corresponded with a friend in another state. She felt safe confiding in her and told her of her doctor's report.

Her friend responded with Psalm 27:13. "Believe this verse," she wrote. "God is faithful."

Is there someone in your life that needs to be encouraged to believe?

TOUCH HIS CLOAK

"Just then a woman who had been subject to bleeding for twelve years
came up behind him and touched the edge of his cloak.
She said to herself, 'If I only touch his cloak, I will be healed.'
Jesus turned and saw her. 'Take heart, daughter,'
he said, 'your faith has healed you.'"
Matthew 9:20–22

Can't you see it? A crowded marketplace with people of all ages and stages clamoring to get to Jesus. To hear the voice of the One who performed miracles and look into the kind eyes of this gentle Savior was worth wading through crowds. Many had help getting to Jesus because of illness or infirmity.

In the crowd was a woman who had bled for twelve years with no relief. She was tired and weak. She pushed ahead because she believed more than anything that if she could just get to Jesus, she would be healed. Finding the crowds thick and almost unnavigable, she got close to the ground and reached between many legs to snag the hem of his garment. Only a touch of the edge of His robe. What amazing faith! What depth of belief!

Are you facing something that seems insurmountable? A health issue, a big decision, or a family relationship? You need enough faith to believe that even the slightest touch to His cloak will bring about a miracle in your life. Can you do it? Do you have the faith of the lady who reached through the crowd?

Believe and reach out to Jesus.

GOD, PLEASE SEND SNOW

*"Therefore, whoever takes the lowly position of this child
is the greatest in the kingdom of heaven."*
Matthew 18:4

*H*eading for the door after church, Mrs. Glen ran into Brooke, one of the four-year-olds in her choir. Brooke immediately wrapped her arms around Mrs. Glen's legs and said, "I love you, Mrs. Glen."

"I love you, too, Brooke. I'm so glad you are in my choir."

"Mrs. Glen, do you think it is going to snow tonight? I really want it to snow."

"Well, Brooke, God is the only one who can make it snow. Why don't we tell Him you would like some snow?"

Mrs. Glen knelt down by Brooke and took her hands. "Dear God, Brooke would really like to have some snow to play in. Snow is a beautiful part of winter and we would all enjoy looking at it. Please send some snow to us. Amen."

Brooke jumped up. She tugged on Mrs. Glen's hand and said, "C'mon."

"Where are we going?"

Brooke looked at her quizzically. "Outside to see the snow, of course!"

Mrs. Glen laughed. "Well, Brooke, I don't know if God will send snow that fast. But we'll keep praying."

"No, He will. Come on. Let's go!"

Often it is the words and faith of children that speak volumes to those much, much older. If everyone prayed, believing as Brooke did that without question God was going to answer her prayer, we could change the world.

Of course, it snowed that night!

WAIT

$\mathcal{W}$aiting is not easy, especially when you are waiting for something you really want. God answers our prayers in many ways but often that answer includes waiting. Be encouraged this week. You are not alone as you wait for His answer. Cling to His promises while you wait. Take this week's devos to heart and put them into practice. And hang on! God is faithful and will be with you through the wait.

WHILE YOU WAIT

"'For I know the plans I have for you,' declares the Lord,
'plans to prosper you and not to harm you,
plans to give you hope and a future.'"

Jeremiah 29:11

Jeremiah's words, often written on graduation cards and plaques, are interpreted to mean that God's children will prosper and be protected under God's plans. What a comfort. However, a closer look at the context shows God's people in captivity when they receive this declaration. King Nebuchadnezzar had carried them into exile from Jerusalem to Babylon. They had seventy long years before they could return. Forced into servitude, their situation hardly seemed conducive to prosperity.

Yet, as they waited for the hope and future God promised, He gave them specific instructions, which, by the way, sounded nothing like moving plans! God commanded them to build houses, plant gardens, get married, have children, increase in number.

To top it all off, God expected the exiles to "'Seek the peace and prosperity of the city to which I have carried you into exile. Pray to the LORD for it, because if it prospers, you too will prosper'" (Jeremiah 29:7). Say what? Do good, work hard, seek to prosper people I don't even like in a place I don't plan to stay?

That's right.

When you experience a time of waiting, purpose to look for the ways God is growing you—perhaps in patience, trust, flexibility, compassion, or understanding. Remember God's promises to give you a hope and a future. Ask Him to help you serve Him faithfully wherever He places you. Seek the peace and prosperity of those around you, even if you won't be neighbors for long.

WAIT FOR THE WHISPER

"Then a great and powerful wind tore the mountains apart . . .
but the LORD was not in the wind. After the wind there was
an earthquake, but the LORD was not in the earthquake.
After the earthquake came a fire, but the LORD was not in the fire.
And after the fire came a gentle whisper."

1 Kings 19:11–12

Rock-shattering wind? Devastating earthquake? Consuming fire? Gentle whisper.

Elijah, understandably exhausted from his showdown with the prophets of Baal, his call down of rain, and his chase down by Jezebel, who threatened his life, needed a word from the Lord. He literally had one mountaintop experience after another: first, Mount Carmel, where God sent fire to consume the water-soaked wood and offering, and then Mount Horeb, where God spoke directly to Elijah, showcasing His power and giving him further instructions. Though Elijah, exhausted, asked to die, God had more prophecies for him to deliver and a successor for him to train. But first, he had to wait.

Imagine the exhilaration of standing on a mountain as blasts of wind burst boulders apart, an earthquake splits open ravines, and a fire rages. These outward manifestations of God's power in nature mirrored the inner turmoil Elijah was feeling. And yet, it was not until after all the disasters desisted that God spoke, and then in a gentle whisper.

If you're feeling shattered, crushed, or consumed by a storm in your life right now, take heart. The storm will pass. Wait for His gentle whisper.

GOD'S WAITING ROOM

"But as for me, I watch in hope for the LORD,
I wait for God my Savior; my God will hear me."
Micah 7:7

*M*ary Catherine sent her college application to her top three choices. She asked God for favor with the universities. Every day after school she checked the mail on the way into the house. She wanted to be hopeful, but the longer she waited the more impatient she got. Her days were filled with trip after disappointing trip to the empty mailbox. Didn't God know her whole career depended on this? She wanted God to answer her prayers.

Often we feel the same way as Mary Catherine. We are asking God for what we want, and even though we don't say it aloud, we could add to our prayer, "And please answer it now!" We want to finish our prayer and say, "Amen!" and get up off our knees hoping to find an immediate answer. Many times God's answer is just not fast enough.

Waiting for answers to prayers is not easy. Like Mary Catherine, we feel the wait is far too long and the "empty mailboxes" become almost overwhelming. We need answers and we want them now because we think that is the best.

The one thing we don't take into consideration is that God sees the big picture, and He knows the best time for you to receive the answer to your prayer.

We can be at peace in God's waiting room knowing He loves us.

WAIT FOR FURTHER INSTRUCTIONS

*"You must wait seven days until I come to you
and tell you what you are to do."*

1 Samuel 10:8

The Bible describes Saul as "an impressive young man without equal among the Israelites—a head taller than any of the others" (1 Samuel 9:2). Saul was obedient; he followed his father's orders to find their missing donkeys. Yet, when Samuel the prophet began to pronounce blessings over Saul as Israel's first king, Saul protested his unworthy status—from the smallest tribe and least clan of Israel.

Samuel knew that did not matter, so he obeyed heavenly orders and poured oil over Saul's head, proclaiming him king. Then he told Saul specifically what to do and expect next: Meet two men near Rachel's tomb; they will inform you about your donkeys. Go to the great tree of Tabor. Three men carrying goats, bread, and wine will meet you there. Accept two loaves from them. Go to Gibeah and join a procession of prophets. There "the Spirit of the LORD will come upon you in power, and you will prophesy with them; and you will be changed into a different person" (1 Samuel 10:6). Then he was told to wait seven days until Samuel came to him again.

Imagine the awe and anticipation Saul must have felt. So much happening so fast, resulting in a changed mission, a changed person, and a changed nation.

Be willing to follow God's leading and wait when He is silent, knowing His plan will take place in His timing.

WHAT KIND OF
WAITER ARE YOU?

*"I wait for the LORD, my whole being waits,
and in his word I put my hope."*

Psalm 130:5

Rarely does our prayer time end and we immediately see the answer to our prayer. We would like that, but once we say "Amen!" we usually find ourselves waiting for the answers.

What does that process look like for you? Many times you will be one of three kinds of waiters.

1. Impatient. You think God is taking too much time to answer you. You think to yourself He's God. He can do anything. But because He is God, He knows the best time to answer. If you are waiting impatiently, ask yourself: *Is there something in my life that is hindering my relationship with God?*

2. Passive. You believe God answers prayers. But since you didn't hear an immediate answer, your faith that you will ever have an answer diminishes. If you are a passive waiter, you may ponder, *Was my prayer heartfelt?*

3. Hopeful. You are sure God will answer your prayer and are at peace knowing the answer will come at the right time for you. You know God heard your prayer and will answer.

A young father in the maternity waiting room has no doubt in his mind that a baby is coming. He may not know the exact hour or minute, but he knows meeting his son or daughter is imminent. The baby is coming!

Waiting for prayers to be answered is the same way. The answer is coming!

ACCEPT

$\mathcal{A}$cceptance is one thing that is easily talked about but not always easy to do. In Matthew 7 Jesus admonishes us to treat others as we would like to be treated. That includes accepting them for who they are. Sometimes that is really hard. But practicing acceptance in our lives, acceptance of others, of situations, and of God's grace in every relationship and situation, creates a foundation for a happy, peaceful life.

GLAD TO BE ME

*"Make every effort to live in peace with everyone and to be holy;
without holiness no one will see the Lord."*

Hebrews 12:14

"*M*om, I thought I'd go out with Vanessa tonight."

I looked at my daughter, knowing she expected me to forbid it. But I also knew she really didn't have plans with Vanessa. You see, my daughter was a teenager. One of her greatest pleasures was to see me upset over something that wasn't even going to happen.

I had just returned from a seminar on personalities. After studying the four personalities for three days, I realized my melancholy personality was prone to want things perfect in a way that caused me to stress prematurely over the smallest things. My daughter's personality was sanguine, and she loved to play a joke or do anything to excite me.

There are four distinct personalities or temperaments. Understanding the personalities and how they react to various situations helps us to allow people to be who they are. In other words, melancholies like me tend to judge others because of our perfectionism. But once we understand ourselves and know we have that tendency, we can cut other personalities a little slack, because we know how we are made.

God made each one of us unique. But He did not make us perfect. Understanding each other can deepen our relationships and help us enjoy them more.

Thank God for your uniqueness and ask Him how you can understand your family and friends better.

HARD WORK, NOT WORRY

"Do not worry about your life. . . . Who of you by worrying can add a single hour to his life?'"

Luke 12:22, 25

"My daddy should be getting out of jail soon," Terica confided to her teacher. "I went to see him last night, and he said the lawyer told him things looked good."

"What does that mean for you?" Mrs. Pickens asked gently. "Where will you live when he does get out?" She knew Terica lived in a hotel with her dad before his arrest, and with her aunt since.

"Well, we plan to stay with my aunt until my dad gets his job back and saves enough for a house. Right now Daddy needs the money I bring in—to pay the lawyer. That means I only have twelve dollars to last me the rest of the month. I don't want to ask anybody for help, but that's going to be difficult."

"I admire how hard you're working and how you're handling that responsibility, Terica. Here it is Friday afternoon and you've stayed to make up missing work. Plus, you were not satisfied until your essay made the 'A-Wall.'"

Terica just grinned. She was happy to improve her grade and did not appear worried about her future.

This teenager had accepted the things in her life she could not change and worked hard to improve what she could.

Let's choose today not to worry, but instead accept our circumstances and work hard to improve what we can. God will take care of the rest.

BE CHEERFUL, ANYWAY!

"An example of patience in the face of suffering . . . "
James 5:10

*M*iriam flexed the fingers on both her hands several times, then shook her head, and said, "I guess I'll have to accept the fact that some things just won't work like they used to."

The muscles in her hands had atrophied and arthritis had taken its toll. Miriam could no longer play the piano and most of the time, even the simple act of holding an eating utensil or a pen firmly enough to make them perform the task intended presented quite a challenge. The previous year, she underwent two surgeries recommended to improve her finger flexibility, and consequently, had a little more dexterity. But it was still nowhere what it used to be.

Many years prior, as a young woman whose health hung precariously in the balance for many months with a muscle disease that mysteriously manifested itself, Miriam learned to accept her limitations and be thankful for all she could still do. She found the positive in every situation and found a way to be cheerful and encouraging.

In spite of numerous hospital stays and health crises for herself and family members through the years, Miriam rarely complained. Even after being forced to make an assisted living facility her primary residence, she exuded patience and peacefulness. Everyone loved being around her.

Today, if you are suffering, ask the Lord to help you accept your limitations patiently. May He also grant you His peace, His power, and His comfort.

ACCEPT THE GIFT
AND THE GLUE

"He is before all things, and in him all things hold together."

Colossians 1:17

Marjorie beamed as she held out the pin she bought for her mom at the thrift store boutique. She couldn't wait until she got home or for a special occasion. She wanted to give it now—in the parking lot! The gold stick figure of a girl with wild frizzy copper hair, a blue heart, and a silver star in her hand reminded her of *Stargirl,* one of her mom's favorite books.

"It's perfect. Thank you so much. I'll wear it tomorrow." Smiling, Mom took the pin from her daughter and then, *kerplunk!* It landed on the asphalt and one of "Stargirl's" arms fell off.

"Oh, no. I didn't mean to drop it," Mom apologized.

"It's okay. We'll glue it back together when we get home," Marjorie said. And an hour later, Stargirl was good to go.

All of us have days when the gifts we give or the gifts we receive seem broken or inadequate. Whether an actual gift or something intangible like the gift of time or health, sometimes we need "glue" to hold it all together. Thank goodness, God is in the Super Glue business and will gladly take and repair our brokenness or inadequacy and make us whole again.

He goes before you today, giving you good gifts and ways to offer your gifts to others. Accept and offer these gifts with gladness, even when they need a little heavenly glue to hold them—and you—together!

NO EXCUSES

"'Ah, Sovereign LORD,' I said, 'I do not know how to speak;
I am only a child.' But the LORD said to me, 'Do not say,
I am only a child.' You must go to everyone I send you to and say
whatever I command you. Do not be afraid of them,
for I am with you and will rescue you,' declares the LORD."

Jeremiah 1:6–8

"*I* really don't deserve this."

"I don't know what I'm doing."

"I'm not the person for the job."

Have you ever heard or made excuses like these for something that seemed too difficult? Jeremiah must have felt the same. Often in danger from angry religious and political leaders, he admitted to God that he felt inadequate for the call on his life. The book by his name details the personal struggles he faced as he fulfilled his role as prophet. And yet, though often full of doubt and sometimes dread regarding the deeds he was told to do and the words he was told to speak, he knew God accepted no excuses. Whatever he needed to accomplish his assignment, God promised to provide. So Jeremiah accepted the mission and the provision.

What is it in your life that seems too difficult for you to do? What kind of excuses do you find yourself making? Today, let's dedicate our doubts to God and trust Him to be all that we need. Because He is able, we are able.

TRUST

$\mathcal{L}$ife involves a lot of trust—trust of your family, friends, and coworkers. But the greatest trust is the trust you put in God. He knows the big picture of your life, and you can trust His plan for the best for you.

JUMP TO ME!

"Those who know your name trust in you, for you, LORD,
have never forsaken those who seek you."

Psalm 9:10

"*D*addy, he'p!"

"I'm right here, sweetheart. Jump to me."

Kerry stood on the end of the diving board. She leaned forward, but her little three-year-old body shook with excitement, anticipation, and fear. Her desire was obvious as she reached out her hands to her father. But her tentativeness was equally obvious.

"Daddyeeee."

"You can do it, Kerry. Jump to Daddy and I will catch you."

Those sitting around the pool cheered, coaxed, and prodded Kerry to take the leap. More than once she retreated to the back of the board, afraid to jump. Finally, with much coaxing and encouragement, Kerry once more approached the end of the diving board.

"Daddy, he'p." Once more she pleaded for her daddy to help.

Daddy waited patiently in the water at the end of the board with his hands outstretched. "I'm right here to catch you."

Looking straight into her daddy's eyes, she leaped off the board and into his arms. When she bobbed back to the surface, her smile was as wide as could be. Applause and cheering followed.

Kerry's father hugged her and drew the beaming child close. "I knew you could do it!"

Are you standing on the "diving board" of an issue today? Do you trust your heavenly Father to catch you? Have you heard Him say, "I will catch you?" Then, jump!

KILLER JOBS

"Though he slay me, yet will I hope in him."
Job 13:15

*G*race glanced at the clock and groaned. Six-thirty already? Again? After working nearly twelve hours a day for three weeks straight, she still had not caught up. But home—and hopefully supper—were calling her name. She was not disappointed.

After polishing off the savory butternut squash soup and the spicy stewed apples prepared by her sweet daughter, Grace met her friend Ginny for a quick walk around the neighborhood. Ginny needed to talk, so three miles passed quickly. Ginny poured out her grievances about the challenges her job presented. When she was through, Grace prayed for God's supernatural provision and that Ginny would find joy, encouragement, and unexpected delight in the job she had been called to do. The two lifelong friends parted with a hug and a promise not to do any more work that evening. If God wanted them to get extra hours in before the next morning, surely He would awaken them early. But working harder and longer was not really the solution either woman craved. They both needed more rest and balance in their lives, but could not see a way for that to happen in the foreseeable future.

Killer jobs can consume us, dampen our spirits, sap our energy, and test our faith. We can even feel like God has abandoned us, just as Job felt when he suffered so many trials and losses. Even when everyone told him that God was not faithful, based on what was happening in his life, Job still trusted. If Job determined to trust God "though He slay me," then surely we can trust Him too.

Ask God to help you trust Him, knowing that He is present in every circumstance.

BEFORE AND AFTER

"'I prayed for this child, and the LORD has granted me
what I asked of him. So now I give him to the LORD.
For his whole life he will be given over to the LORD.'"
1 Samuel 1:27–28

*H*annah's story is remarkable. Not only did she keep her promise to God after the birth of her long-awaited son, but even more remarkably, Hannah trusted God before God answered her request for a son. For many years, Hannah endured the torment of not being able to conceive and countless provocations from rivals who could. Yet she didn't retaliate; she just wept, prayed, and worshipped. After Priest Eli's pronouncement, she must have felt more hopeful. Bottom line: Hannah trusted God, regardless of how or when He answered her prayers.

After Samuel's birth, Hannah weaned him and took him to the temple to live "young as he was" (1 Samuel 1:24). Oh, how her heart must have ached as she hugged him good-bye. But Hannah still worshiped. Immediately after dedicating Samuel to the Lord, she prayed: "My heart rejoices in the LORD. . . . There is no one holy like the LORD. . . . The LORD is a God who knows. . . . The LORD brings death and makes alive. . . . The LORD sends poverty and wealth" (1 Samuel 2:1–3, 6–7). After giving up her little boy and before God sent her five more children, Hannah trusted Him.

May we be more like Hannah as we seek God's favor, trusting Him before, after, and in between and praising Him and honoring Him with our very best.

EXERCISING YOUR TRUST MUSCLES

*"Trust in the LORD with all your heart and lean not
on your own understanding; in all your ways acknowledge him,
and he will make your paths straight."*

Proverbs 3:5–6

Sally desperately needed to get out of her contract for her old job. After many years of searching and praying, she finally procured a new job in her hometown instead of forty miles away. Two years earlier, a serious accident on the highway heading to work resulted in such physical and emotional trauma that her doctor suggested Sally not continue that drive. She needed to be closer to home. And yet, there was no one to take her old job. Even after interviewing seven candidates for the position, her supervisor could not find a replacement and refused to release her from her contract. If she broke the contract, her license could be revoked. Sally was stuck.

Prayer warriors committed to praying for the solution to Sally's dilemma. Her new boss promised to hold her job open until notified otherwise. Her old boss agreed to hire a substitute until a suitable replacement could be found. These things did not happen by accident. God was working in Sally's favor; she just had to acknowledge His sovereignty, exercise her trust muscles, and wait for Him to straighten out all the details on the path He directed her to follow.

Today, try flexing your trust muscles. If they've gotten a little flabby, perhaps it's time to exercise them more.

A RUNNING LEAP

"Do not let your hearts be troubled.
Trust in God; trust also in me."

John 14:1

*J*ustin toddled around the room playing with his older cousins while waiting for dinner. They were playing with cars, paying little attention to anything else.

Grandpa walked into the room to announce food was on the table. But before he said a word, two-year-old Justin hopped up and without warning, ran full speed ahead to Grandpa. When Justin was three feet away, he took a leap right into Grandpa's arms. It was a good thing Grandpa anticipated this or Justin might have not thought this was so much fun.

Grandma wasn't too fond of this game. She was always afraid Grandpa wouldn't be looking or wouldn't hear Justin coming. But every time Justin took a leap, Grandpa was ready, and once he swooped Justin up in his arms, they both laughed and laughed at each other. Neither ever seemed to tire of this game.

Watching Justin trust his grandfather to always be there for him is a perfect picture of how I should trust my heavenly Father. Every time I catch a glimpse of Him, I should just take off running to Him, knowing He will "catch" me.

I don't have trouble wanting Him to catch me when I have a problem or concern. But shouldn't I get up every morning and instead of turning on the television news, take a leap into His arms?

Today, dare to leap into the Father's arms, knowing that He will catch you.

APPRECIATE

*M*uch is taken for granted in our country. We live in freedom—freedom to worship as we choose, freedom to marry whom we would like, freedom to go to work each day at the job of our choice. Many of us have more than enough to eat. When we say our prayers at night, do we remember to tell God how much we really appreciate His care and provision? Look around you and this week make note of the blessings in your life. Remember to express your appreciation to God.

CLEANSING COP-OUT

*"No, in all these things we are more than
conquerors through him who loved us."*

Romans 8:37

 There is nothing quite like doing without to make you appreciate something. This rings true for food, especially. Trying to eliminate excess baggage on board my sleek physique, I decided to purchase a cleanse system. Worked great the first day and most of the next. Though my body felt weak, my spirit felt strong. My prayer life intensified, and when hunger pangs hit I prayed for those who needed to "hunger and thirst after righteousness." I thought of how difficult it must have been for prisoners in cattle cars or concentration camps to adjust to starvation. I felt like a wimp.

Two "cleanse days" back-to-back nearly wiped me out. Though I managed fine during the day, at night, I retired early. The first night at nine. The second at seven. But by ten p.m., I was awake again, headachy and wobbling into the kitchen searching for sustenance. Unfortunately, I scarfed down the next day's breakfast AND lunch before midnight.

If only I had pushed through a few more hours. Or slept more. The literature said achy feelings were just signs of detoxification, but I thought I would pass out before the toxins escaped. God's Word says we are more than conquerors. I need to try again.

Since I did not have the personal willpower to withstand my hunger, I should have called on God's strength to see me through. Next time, I will seek Him when it seems I can't go on.

Meanwhile, I really appreciate a normal plate of food!

TRUE APPRECIATION

"Therefore each of you must put off falsehood and speak
truthfully to his neighbor, for we are all members of one body."
Ephesians 4:25

"Would you like another block?" I asked, sitting on the floor with my granddaughter. Without waiting, I handed her the next block. I wasn't sure what she was building. So far she thought it was more fun to knock the blocks over than to finish the structure!

"Ta tu," she said.

Already Carly is learning to express gratitude. "Ta tu" is heard often—when she finishes eating and when her diaper is changed. Even though she doesn't understand why, Carly is learning to appreciate.

One of the first things parents teach their children is to appreciate things. Parents encourage children to say "thank you" even if they aren't ready to master all the social skills. In the beginning, children learn by example, simply mimicking the words of their parents. It becomes a game. Often parents respond with applause, smiles, and affirmation.

But though mastering the art of saying thank you is important, the art of feeling thankful should be our goal.

Genuine appreciation was modeled by the man who had been demon-possessed and told everyone what Jesus did for him (Mark 5), by the two blind men who were given sight (Matthew 9), by the crippled man healed by Peter right outside the temple (Acts 3), and many more biblical characters.

Look for opportunities to express gratitude from your heart. Tell God "thank You" for all He has done for you.

HE PINS HIS SOCKS

"Let them give thanks to the LORD for his unfailing love
and his wonderful deeds for men."
Psalm 107:15

$\mathcal{E}$very time I unload the dryer, I appreciate the fact that my husband pins his socks. After years of baskets of unmatched socks, Pat found a simple solution—now before he drops his dirty socks into the hamper, he safety-pins them together. Voilà!

That is only one small example of how my marvelous man makes life simpler. The aqueduct he constructed in the basement ranks as another personal favorite. Now after heavy rains, I no longer slog and slip through giant puddles on the floor. Instead, I watch with satisfaction as the water winds its way around the perimeter of the basement, channeled safely into a drain. Definitely appreciated!

Of course, lest I paint too perfect a picture, I'll admit there are things I do not appreciate. But when I start concentrating on the imperfections, I think back to a decision I made long ago to tune my mental radio station to WPDR (What Pat Does Right) instead of WPDW (What Pat Does Wrong). It makes an enormous difference in the amount of "static" I hear, the amount of satisfaction I feel, and the amount of appreciation I express.

If there's someone in your life whom you have not yet learned to appreciate, trying tuning in to W_DR (substitute his or her initial) and see what kind of reception you get!

PAPA'S GENEROSITY

"There will always be poor people in the land.
Therefore I command you to be openhanded toward
your fellow Israelites who are poor and needy in your land."
Deuteronomy 15:11

Papa loved helping people. Whether plowing gardens, painting houses, or giving them groceries, he was always ready to help.

Running a grocery store was his livelihood. He kept the small country store well-stocked and welcomed everyone who came by.

Ray, his grandson, helped him on weekends. Ray noticed some of the country folks came in and needed more than they could afford. Papa always said, "No problem. I'll put the ticket in the box until you get caught up."

When Papa died, Ray's dad, Clyde, cleaned out the store. He found an old cigar box full of unpaid invoices.

Hundreds of people came to Papa's funeral. Clyde was amazed. "Why are so many people here?"

One by one they came to Clyde and told him how generous his father was.

"Papa bought medicine for my daughter. I appreciate that so much."

"Because your dad was so kind, we made it through a hard time."

"Papa gave me milk when our cows went dry. He was a great man."

Words of appreciation flowed. Clyde discovered how generous his father had been. Almost everyone who came to the funeral hugged Clyde and gave him a story of Papa's generosity.

God provides our every need whether or not we can "pay" for anything. We can show our appreciation by returning His love and sharing it with others.

THANK GOD FOR SERVICE LEARNERS!

"I thank my God every time I remember you."

Philippians 1:3

$\mathcal{M}$ason and Bailey had no idea what they signed up for when they asked to be my service learners, students who earn elective credit for providing service to others in a work setting. Of course, the Lord knew exactly who I needed. Oh, how I appreciate them! However, I am not sure they feel the same gratification since service in my classroom often offers challenges.

When Mason tries to fold his long legs underneath his small work area, he encounters a few obstacles I've stored there. Now and then he manages to move away from the drudgery of typing and actually make some headway cleaning out a cabinet. Technical challenges and various errands occupy much of his time. Regardless of the tasks assigned, Mason's calmness and humor help level out the gamut of emotions that cavort about our classroom.

Bailey has an even bigger challenge as her shift with me includes helping attend to twenty-eight sophomores. Several of them clamor for her attention. After assisting struggling students, she files, organizes, and edits, including the school newspaper, usually on a tight deadline.

Both seniors have earned my admiration, appreciation, and gratitude. Without complaint, they daily offer ninety minutes of devoted service and get nothing in return but an elective credit they don't even need.

Today, let's take inventory of those who offer help when we need it most and find ways to express our gratitude to God and appreciation to them.

REJOICE

To some *rejoice* feels like a churchy word. But rejoicing is an emotion we should practice daily. True joy comes from deep within. Let your joy come out and make every day this week a joy-filled one.

I WILL REPAY YOU

"Be glad, O people of Zion, rejoice in the LORD your God,
for he has given you the autumn rains in righteousness.
He sends you abundant showers. . . .
I will repay you for the years the locusts have eaten."
Joel 2:23, 25

*G*od delights in restoring and replenishing. This applies to possessions and relationships. Remember Job? Without wrongdoing or bad choices, he lost everything simply because Satan desired to test him. Yet afterward, "The LORD made him prosperous again and gave him twice as much as he had before. . . . The LORD blessed the latter part of Job's life more than the first" (Job 42:10, 12).

Remember Joseph? His brothers sold him into slavery, costing him his youth and forcing him into a foreign culture and many trials. Years later, his loss turned to gain as he earned the Pharaoh's trust and was put in charge of all Egypt. When his brothers came searching for food to stave off the famine of their homeland, Joseph was in a position to help—and forgive. Instead of being bitter, he rejoiced that God honed a horrifying ordeal into glorifying generosity. To the brothers who betrayed him, he said: "'You intended to harm me, but God intended it for good to accomplish what is now being done, the saving of many lives'" (Genesis 50:20).

What difficulty, challenge, or trial are you facing that you need to trust God to turn into good? Rejoice, for God is still in the business of restoring and replenishing.

I WILL BE JOYFUL

"Though the fig tree does not bud and there are no grapes on the vines,
though the olive crop fails and the fields produce no food,
though there are no sheep in the pen and no cattle in the stalls,
yet I will rejoice in the LORD, I will be joyful in God my Savior."

Habakkuk 3:17–18

"Rejoice" implies a command to be happy, but feeling happy is not always natural or realistic. Given Habakkuk's desperate starvation-type conditions, it seems almost absurd to be joyful. Yet, the joy of the Lord cannot always be explained or limited to a certain set of circumstances. Look at the last clause of Habakkuk's sentence: "Yet I will rejoice in the LORD, I will be joyful in God my Savior" (3:18). He makes a firm, willful decision, unrelated to the situation and not from his emotions.

What if next time our bank statement dips into the red, cupboards are bare, and gas tanks are empty, we refuse to be negative and declare war on despair? Repeat Habakkuk's declarations of independence from circumstances and affirm your allegiance to the Lord: "I will be joyful in God my Savior." Habakkuk's last verse encourages us to look at our situation from a higher perspective: "The Sovereign LORD is my strength; he makes my feet like the feet of a deer, he enables me to go on the heights" (Habakkuk 3:19).

Lord, even when I don't feel joy, help me choose to rejoice in Your strength and Your faithful provision.

WITH GREAT JOY

"To him who is able to keep you from falling and to present you before his glorious presence without fault and with great joy."
Jude 24

"*W*ith great joy." This phrase almost always accompanies a new beginning: wedding announcements, baby births, salvation testimonies, job promotions, and healing proclamations. Unhappily, no matter how many of those situations we enjoy, our lives are certain to have trials and tragedy as well. Humanly speaking, there is no guarantee the joy can be sustained.

Earlier in the book of Jude, the author reminds us that among God's chosen people miraculously delivered from Egypt were many who did not believe. Consequently, they were destroyed. Even the angels "who did not keep their positions of authority but abandoned their own home—these he has kept in darkness, bound with everlasting chains for judgment on the great Day" (v. 6). It's a little scary to think those who had the greatest potential and reasons for trusting God fell—and were severely punished with lasting consequences.

And yet, Jude reminds us we have all the power we need to stay strong and true to Him who called us, because He is the One who is able. He is the One who will keep us from falling. He is the One who will present us faultless before His glorious presence. He is the One!

So let us magnify and glorify the One who has the majesty, power, and authority to convict us, correct us, and carry us through—with great joy!

ALWAYS PRAY WITH JOY

"In all my prayers for all of you, I always pray with joy."

Philippians 1:4

Sixteen times in Paul's letter to the Philippians, he mentions the word "joy" in one form or another. In fact, joy is the book's entire theme, in spite of the fact that Paul writes this letter from the confines of a Roman prison. Regardless of his circumstances, Paul speaks confidently and encouragingly. He also admonishes his readers to be more like Christ, warns of danger from inward and outward enemies of the Church, and shares the secret of contentment. Perhaps this is Philippians' greatest gift, an acknowledgment that God supplies all our needs, including contentment, even when circumstances do not seem conducive to joy.

It's almost as if Paul challenges us to choose contentment rather than to wait for it to settle in on its own. The *HBJ School Dictionary* defines the word *content* as being "happy enough not to complain" and equates *contentment* with "satisfaction or ease of mind."

Today I'm going to make a conscious effort to pray with joy, refuse to complain about anything, and be satisfied with what I have. I'll start by giving thanks for all the people who make life easier and perhaps even pen a note to show my gratitude. But will I also choose to thank God for those people and circumstances that make life more challenging? With His help, I'll try, for therein lies the secret of true contentment and joy.

REJOICE ANYWAY

"The LORD has done it this very day;
let us rejoice today and be glad."

Psalm 118:24

Do some days seem to lend themselves more to rejoicing than others? Most likely birthdays, weddings, graduations, job promotions, book launches, and holidays come to mind. Yes, those days are special.

But what about days that aren't calendar-specific? The day an icy wind is blowing, it's drizzling rain, your joints ache, you step outside, and your umbrella turns inside out. Can you rejoice in that day? Absolutely!

Regardless of the weather, your health, your finances, or the state of your umbrella, you can rejoice because God made this day for you. He is waiting to fill it with His special touches—a friend's hug, a coworker buying you a cup of coffee, or a child's note stuck in your briefcase or laundry basket. Or it may come from reading your favorite scripture over and over until you realize that, indeed, the greatest rejoicing comes from a personal relationship with the Author of all hope.

We all have days we don't feel like rejoicing. Purpose to rejoice anyway! You don't have to feel it; just will it. Ask God to show you how to reach out to someone else. Take cookies to a friend, make a meal for someone who broke his leg, call someone you haven't talked to in a long time.

Thank God for these people and His purpose in your life. You will find yourself rejoicing regardless of how you feel!

CHANGE

Change is not always easy. But it keeps us fresh and allows us to experience new things. Don't resist change; embrace it and learn from it.

THE DIFFERENCE
THREE DAYS CAN MAKE

"For as Jonah was three days and three nights in the belly
of a huge fish, so the Son of Man will be three days
and three nights in the heart of the earth."

Matthew 12:40

Lucille Godwin, beloved English professor at Mars Hill College, provided lifelong lessons that reached far beyond the classroom. Once when I entered her office to talk about an assignment, she could tell that something of far greater concern was troubling me. After hearing my tale of woe, she softly shared this priceless wisdom:

"When you are going through a difficult time or struggling to make a hard decision, just remember the three darkest days in the history of mankind. After Jesus' crucifixion, His disciples were so disillusioned, disappointed, and distraught they didn't know what to do. Everything looked dark and dismal. But then . . . three days later, look what a difference it made! All of a sudden, hope was restored. Life-giving, life-changing hope. So now, whenever anything distresses you, I challenge you just to give it three days. I guarantee that either your circumstances will change or you will change so you can handle those circumstances. Your hope will be restored, and your purpose defined."

Mrs. Godwin's counsel to "give it three days" has stayed with me from college days until now. Waiting and praying for three days can make a life-changing difference. It has stood the test of time. Why don't you try it too?

KAMATARA

"You will no longer be called Jacob; your name will be Israel."

Genesis 35:10

Kamatara. Her name tag caught my eye immediately. Intrigued, I inquired.

"That's an unusual name. Beautiful. Will you tell me about it?"

"It's my spiritual name in Sanskrit. It stands for 'Shining Love.' My birth name is Paula Veronica Victoria Ruth Ann Filipiak, now Johnson since I married. My birth name is still meaningful to me as representing my past, my formative years, my parents' love, and all that has led me to this moment in time. But I go by Kamatara because it represents who I am now and what I have become—what I'm growing into. Perhaps who I'm meant to be."

"Wow. That takes some kind of courage to make a change like that."

"Yes, and it really confused some people too. Especially my husband and my parents. They didn't understand what to make of it or why I felt the need to change. It's just that I wanted to have a more spiritual name because of what's important to me now. But I haven't lost any of who I was or what my birth name represents. In fact, I still use my legal name as my 'battle' name for those times when I have to be a good soldier and somehow fit into this cookie-cutter world."

Kamatara. Shining Love. Isn't that what we all should strive to represent? Maybe not in our names, but certainly in our actions and attitudes. What do you need to change today?

BYE, BYE, FLIPPER!
IT'S TIME TO CHANGE.

"There is a time for everything,
and a season for every activity under heaven."

Ecclesiastes 3:1

$\mathcal{I}$ used to love my "Flipper" (flip phone), especially its diminutive size and LACK of allure. It did not tempt me to surf the Internet or check messages. No dings or noisy notifications. Everything could wait.

Attempting to model self-control and hoping my teenage students would follow my example, I lectured:

"Let's talk about separating our personal and professional lives. At work, I concentrate on work. I turn my phone off when I arrive. I turn it back on when I leave. I might go ten hours without checking my phone. That way I can concentrate much better. My friends and family know I won't answer while at work. If there's a real emergency, someone will notify the front office and get in touch with me."

Unimpressed, Madison remarked: "No wonder you don't leave your phone on. You're probably embarrassed! How old is that thing, anyway?"

Hmmmph! Maybe I liked being one of the last hold-outs. So much for my influence!

However, when I could not receive messages containing any multimedia component, not even an emoji, I missed important conversations or meeting times. Still, I managed—until a 2,000-mile road trip made the smartphone's advantages irresistible: GPS, camera, Internet, e-mail, etcetera, all in one device. So I purchased the least expensive Android available. Of course, now I can't imagine changing back.

Lord, thank You that even when we are forced to change, You help us find value in the new while remaining true to our core values.

REARRANGE A CHANGE

"I will give you a new heart and put a new spirit in you."

Ezekiel 36:26

"*I* never know what your room is going to look like when I walk in," Sharon said as she and Carolynn joined me for our Friday lunch.

"You can count on it being messy," I quipped in reply.

"No, not that. You have it rearranged differently every few weeks. I like it. Wish I could do that in mine," Sharon said.

"Me too. I want you to come to my room and help me figure out something creative to do with my desks," Carolynn commented.

"I'll be glad to, but I have a better idea. If you ask some of your most reliable students to help you design a new seating chart and tell them your preferences, you may be pleasantly surprised by what they come up with. And it won't create more work for you."

Carolynn looked a little skeptical, but agreed to think about that option.

Change is often challenging because it can also be inconvenient or uncomfortable. However, sometimes someone else's perspective can help you see or do things differently and better. God revealed through Ezekiel His plan to give His people a new heart and a new spirit. That change would in turn result in more changes—for the better.

Trust God to reveal to you ways others can help you make the changes you are hoping will happen. Then be willing to accept their help and try something new!

NEVER BEFORE, BUT MAYBE AGAIN!

*"Every good and perfect gift is from above,
coming down from the Father of the heavenly lights,
who does not change like shifting shadows."*

James 1:17

*W*hat do roasted mushrooms, tropical pave, and bacon popcorn have in common?

Nothing at all, except they were all new to me, and offered on the same menu at a classy rooftop restaurant. Some people order the same item time and again to be certain of liking it. Not me. When I eat out, I scan the menu for something I don't recognize. Trying new dishes satisfies my curiosity, even when it doesn't "match." For the record, I may not always like it!

Case in point: the mammoth plate of mushrooms with its various shapes and textures intrigued me, but by the time I finished, I felt I had foraged through a forest for fungi. Next came a tropical concoction called "pave" (rhymes with *of*)—light layers of mango compote, pineapple curd, and coconut glaze. Splendid! I could have—should have—stopped there. But the last course of caramelized popcorn with bits of candied bacon tickled my taste buds as well. Though none of these foods went together, the change in routine and the surprise elements satisfied me.

Have you ever thought about how much variety God offers—in food, weather, personalities, appearance, or opportunities? And yet His character does not change. From the safety and security of His constant love, we can venture forth to make changes that challenge us.

CHERISH

Cherish is not a word you hear often in today's contemporary language. But to cherish something means to hold dear something you value above many other things. Family, friends, your mother's Bible, the time with family, and more are things to be cherished. Most of all this week, cherish your relationship with God.

GOOD THINGS

"But store up for yourselves treasures in heaven,
where moth and rust do not destroy,
and where thieves do not break in and steal."
Matthew 6:20

*C*arol traveled for business. Even though her grandchildren were small, she faithfully gathered postcards and mailed them back home.

In the beginning, Carol's daughters or daughter-in-law commented on receiving the postcards and how much the children enjoyed them. Sometimes when she visited, one of the children brought his or her card to Carol to show her they received it. After a while, no one ever even mentioned the card had been received, so Carol cut down on the cards she sent. For her, it was a way of letting the grandchildren know she was thinking about them while she was gone.

One morning her oldest granddaughter came to spend the day with Carol. She brought along a cute princess purse a friend of Carol's had made for her. The purse bulged!

Carol asked, "Shari, what's in your purse? It looks like it may pop wide open!"

"Oh, Grandma, this is where I keep all the postcards you send me."

Carol was so surprised. She had no idea Shari treasured those postcards and kept them all together.

Some people are savers and some throw everything away. In the end, those who are depositing things in the storehouse of heaven are keeping the things that really matter. God reminds us in Matthew 6:21, "For where your treasure is, there your heart will be also." Where is your treasure?

SPECIAL MOMENTS

"Blessed rather are those who hear the word of God and obey it."
Luke 11:28

Three-year-old Shannon loves to go to Grandma's house. When she goes, she walks straight to a dish where she finds two plastic eggs, one for herself and one for her sister. The eggs contain small pieces of chocolate.

The funny thing is Shannon goes straight to the eggs every time she walks through Grandma's door. And every time, she acts as surprised as if she had never seen the eggs before. She shakes the egg and says, "What's in it?" She smiles like she can't imagine what is in the egg. Then, when she has enjoyed the anticipation long enough, she goes to the porch and closes the door so the special moment of opening the egg is just for her.

Have you ever felt that way when you hear God speaking to you? His voice, while maybe not a surprise, comes to you in a way that is so fresh and brings such pleasure that you want to savor that moment. And like Shannon, you want to get in a room and close the door so you can cherish that time just between the two of you. Eventually, you may share what you have discovered with those you love, but not until you have enjoyed hearing God speak just to you.

Think back to one of those moments. Have you had one lately? Maybe you need to listen more carefully today to hear that still, small voice.

YOUR TRIALS

*"Consider it pure joy, my brothers, whenever you face trials
of many kinds, because you know that the testing of your faith
develops perseverance. Perseverance must finish its work
so that you may be mature and complete, not lacking anything.
If any of you lacks wisdom, he should ask God, who gives generously
to all without finding fault, and it will be given to him."*

James 1:2–5

How can the word *joy* and the word *trials* be linked together in the same scripture? Why is it that perseverance is a prerequisite for maturity? James has a logical explanation.

As Jesus' brother, James witnessed firsthand the mission and martyrdom of God's Son. No doubt, he saw or knew about what Jesus went through to fulfill His purpose as the sacrificial lamb to take away our sins. Although James, like many others close to Christ, may have misunderstood some of Jesus' actions and intentions, evidently he gained the wisdom, maturity, and perseverance he needed to grasp the gravity and the grace of the good news. Then he passed it on.

When someone signs up to follow Christ, James informs them of the prerequisites: trials come before joy; tests of faith come before perseverance; perseverance comes before maturity. And all of these character traits require wisdom. Thankfully, God waives those prerequisites and promises to provide all the wisdom we need.

When considered this way, perhaps we can learn to cherish and find joy in the trials we experience, knowing they make us complete. That makes it all worthwhile.

CHERISH YOUR PRAYER CIRCLES

*"Through these he has given us his very great
and precious promises."*

2 Peter 1:4

*Hope this book will mean as much to you as it did to me. It changed the
way I pray!*
Love, Martha

I could not know my lifelong friend Martha would change my life
with a simple, but priceless gift: *The Circle Maker* by Mark Batterson.
Even greater than the gift was the invitation that accompanied it:
"Come join our circle of women who meet monthly to pray with
and for each other: Amy, Elizabeth, Carla, Lesa, Wanda, and Cindy.
You'll feel at home and very welcome." How right she was. These
new friends became powerhouse prayer warriors and gave me a fresh
awareness of the personalized love and support system God provides
for His children so they need never feel alone. When we aren't meeting together, we keep up with each other through group texts, joining
spiritual forces to pray through serious concerns about family, home,
work, and health. But we share lots of laughs, too. Truly, I am blessed.

It's the same for me at work, in our Sunday School Life Group,
and with my professional sorority, Alpha Delta Kappa sisters, where
a precious group of friends too numerous to name actually love and
care for each other like family.

If you're blessed by the bounty of prayer warriors in your life,
cherish them. If you need someone to circle you in prayer, ask the
Lord to provide. He cherishes you enough to do just that.

MEMORIES

"For though I am absent from you in body,
I am present with you in spirit and delight to see
how orderly you are and how firm your faith in Christ is."

Colossians 2:5

The summer of 2015—and David Piacentini—mark some of my most cherished memories. From his native island of Corsica, France, David visited us for over three weeks. Together with my children, Daniel and Susanne, we toured the southeast United States. We bonded instantly, as though I had another son I'd never met before.

The words from a song I once heard applied perfectly to this young man whose orderly habits and faith in Christ refreshed and intrigued us all: "The Jesus in me loves the Jesus in you. You're so easy, so easy to love." From David's fervent prayers in French before each day's excursions, we could tell he loved Jesus. With his buoyant personality and eagerness to help, he found countless ways to please us and make us laugh. But when my mother-in-law died unexpectedly during his brief stay, he also found ways to comfort and offer quiet joy.

I pray daily this young man will realize his incredible worth and place in God's appointed service, following the dream God gave him. I also hope our paths will cross many more times in the future. Meanwhile, I am thankful for cherished memories.

Is there someone absent from you, yet close in your heart? Cherish the memories and offer the prayers that keep you ever present in spirit.

THINK

When we were children, our teachers often told us to "put on our thinking caps." Most of you reading are probably too old for your "thinking caps," but it is always a good idea to keep thinking about the things that are important. Spend some time this week pondering the blessings of God in your life.

DON'T FLOAT AWAY

"I can do all this through him who gives me strength."
Philippians 4:13

After days of heavy rains, the topic of conversation almost anywhere you go is water. Our area of the country endured torrential rains and flash floods. Cars and houses were submerged.

Did you know that a small car can float away in just twelve inches of water? A full-size car can float away in eighteen to twenty-four inches of water. Just a small amount of water under the wheels can pick a car up and move it from one spot to another. And once the car is moving, it can float quite a distance.

During a bad storm some people think they are as safe in their cars. But the truth is that high water can make even a big car become a moving danger for those in it and those in its path.

Sometimes it can take only a small amount of temptation to move us from a place of security in our faith to a destination way out of our comfort zones and a position of uncertainty.

When you are faced with a decision or temptation, think and pray about whether or not this is a good thing for you. How will it affect your family? How will it affect you personally? Most of all, how will it affect your witness and walk with God?

Think before you act. Don't let temptation "float" you into dangerous places.

BLESSED BARRICADES

"Build up, build up, prepare the road!
Remove the obstacles out of the way of my people."
Isaiah 57:14

Just above the road on Interstate 26 in South Carolina, there is an electronic banner that reads, "Caution: Do not go around barricades."

Isn't that kind of a no-brainer? Do you even need to think about it? A barricade is supposed to keep people and vehicles out. By definition a *barricade* is "a blockade, obstacle, barrier." Barricades are strategically placed to keep people out. Why would anyone think they shouldn't heed that directive?

Most people do not need a warning when they see a barricade. They surmise there is danger ahead. But a small percentage of others don't heed the warning and forge ahead, usually getting into trouble.

Isn't that what our relationships with God are like? We may hear Him say from time to time, "Caution: Do not go around barricades." When God says we can trust His wisdom in providing the barricade or obstacle, we don't need to know what is on the other side. We can trust we don't need to go there.

Have you ever asked God to give you wisdom in a situation and then did what you wanted to do anyway? You may have seen a "barricade" or felt some hesitance about moving through the obstacle but you went through it. The result? You were miserable.

God provides direction for our lives if we just ask Him. When you see an obstacle in your path, think about how much God loves you. He may have put the barricade there to protect you. Turn and go in another direction. You can trust Him.

THINGS ABOVE

"Since, then, you have been raised with Christ, set your hearts
on things above, where Christ is, seated at the right hand of God.
Set your minds on things above, not on earthly things."

Colossians 3:1–2

When you think of "things above," what comes to mind? God? Heaven? Blue skies? Rainbows? Airplanes? Birds? Lofty thoughts like love, generosity, praise, gratitude, and joy?

"High" things raise our thoughts to a place where we experience wonder and awe. In contrast, thinking about "earthly things" soon traps us in turmoil, twisting our thoughts and wreaking havoc on our health. Colossians implores us to rid ourselves of anger, malice, slander, and filthy language. Just holding a grudge against someone or rehashing a negative incident in our minds or to friends and family casts a gray pall over our mental landscape. Thoughts about things above get obscured by things below all too quickly.

However, the rest of Colossians 3 prescribes how to rid ourselves of the gravitational pull of earthly things. First, put on your "new self, which is being renewed in knowledge in the image of its Creator" (v. 10), and since your new self has likely lost a significant amount of weight by throwing off all the old things, you will need the new "clothes" described in verses 12–14: compassion, kindness, humility, gentleness, patience, forgiveness, and love. Once donned, you'll find matching accessories in the peace and gratitude department (v. 15).

Although this attire is available only in heavenly places, God has already prepared and purchased your wardrobe through the blood of His Son, Jesus. Why not try on some of the "things above" today and see if they make your time on earth more joyful?

TICK, TOCK

"How, then, can they call on the one they have not believed in?
And how can they believe in the one of whom they have not heard?
And how can they hear without someone preaching to them?"

Romans 10:14

Tick, tock, tick, tock, tick, tock! The metronome kept a steady beat. One beat every four seconds.

Our Sunday school speaker was a missionary from China. He began a slide show with pictures of the Chinese people and his ministry there.

The metronome continued to tick and tock. It became somewhat annoying.

The only thing you could think about was the sound of the metronome. The missionary continued talking about the needs of the Chinese people he worked with. Finally, the missionary came to the end of his presentation.

"Did you know that in China someone dies every four seconds without knowing Jesus?" he said. There was total silence in the room except for the tick-tocking of the metronome every four seconds. *Tick, tock, tick, tock, tick tock* continued to echo mentally.

A simple illustration but a really thought-provoking one.

How can so many people die without hearing the message of Christ? China is a big country with billions of people. And while over a hundred million of them know about Jesus, there are so many more who don't.

I will probably never go to China, but in our country, state, and neighborhood, there are people who need to hear the message of God's love. Can I be more intentional about sharing that love with them?

Can I ever forget the message of the tick-tocking? Perhaps every time I look at my watch or hear a clock strike the hour, I will be reminded to think of those in the world who don't know Christ and say a prayer for them.

THOUGHTS AND ATTITUDES

*"For the word of God is living and active. Sharper than
any double-edged sword, it penetrates even to dividing soul and spirit,
joints and marrow; it judges the thoughts and attitudes of the heart."*
Hebrews 4:12

"*A*ctions speak louder than words" is not always true! Too often I
hastily judge someone whose actions appear to be selfish, insolent,
apathetic, or arrogant. Recently, one of my hardest-working students
sat in the back of the room shaking her head every single time I spoke
or gave directions. *What's up with her?* I thought, irritated by her "defi-
ant" attitude. I had become accustomed to Adenia's many questions,
but not her insolence. I stepped closer and asked, "Adenia, what's
wrong? You keep shaking your head every time I say something."

"I'm cold," she replied. "I'm trying to get warm."

Ouch. I was wrong. Again. Blinded by her "actions," I mis-
interpreted Adenia's attitude and presumed to know her thoughts.
Silly, silly me. I apologized for getting irritated and turned up the
thermostat!

Oh, how I want to be so filled with God's Word and His wisdom that I see past others' actions and discern their true thoughts and
attitudes. Then my own thoughts and attitudes will more closely
match that of the only One who can truly judge the motives and
actions of those around me.

*Lord, forgive me for thinking ill of those whose actions I misinterpret.
Only You can know the intent of their hearts. Please keep my thoughts in
line with Yours today.*

GIVE

$\mathcal{B}$ecause of God's great gift to us of His Son, Jesus, we should be encouraged to give to others. Giving generously fills your life with happiness and love.

A VERY SPECIAL GIFT

"Thanks be to God for his indescribable gift!"
2 Corinthians 9:15

"*C*'mon, open this one. Open it first before we do anything else." My mother and younger sister were bouncing with excitement.

"But we always open presents at the same time," I protested.

Slowly I began to open the mystery package. Discarding the paper and opening the box, I stared in disbelief. There it was! My tablecloth. Totally finished with every cross perfectly stitched!

For months I had searched for my tablecloth kit. I knew I had put it in a safe place when Mother had given it to me. But despite cleaning out closets and storage boxes, I couldn't even find the kit to start stitching!

To make matters worse, my sister had already finished her tablecloth.

And now, Christmas Eve. The first present I opened was THE tablecloth. Ready to be placed on my dining room table. Mother and Sis had known where my tablecloth was the whole time I was searching for it!

Regardless of how surprising or extraordinary, no gift can compare with the most precious gift God gave us that first Christmas. He sent us His perfect love through a tiny baby, His Son, Jesus Christ. Jesus' life, death on the cross, and resurrection provided a way for us to come to the Father. And thousands of years later, His gift is still available to all who will receive or "open" it.

Make a special effort to share God's gift with someone today.

UNDESERVED GIFT

"If ye then, being evil, know how to give good gifts unto your children,
how much more shall your Father which is in heaven
give good things to them that ask him?"
Matthew 7:11 KJV

*M*arsha and Gabby often went on trips with each other's families. One weekend, Gabby accompanied Marsha and her family on a beach trip.

They had fun surfing, sunning, throwing horseshoes, and other things. On Friday night they decided to go to the mall and window shop. Marsha's mom was going to drive them and shop on her own.

Marsha and Gabby were in the kitchen deciding which stores to visit. Marsha's dad joined them. "What are you girls scheming about? Going shopping with Mom?"

"Not exactly. I mean, she is taking us to the mall, but then we are on our own," Marsha said.

"I get it." Dad winked. "You are too old to be seen on a Friday night with one of the parents."

"Aw, Dad . . ."

Dad walked to hug Marsha and pushed a twenty-dollar bill into her hand. "Have a great time."

Moving to Gabby, he did the same thing.

Gabby looked in her hand and a big tear escaped. "Oh, Mr. Mike, no one has ever done anything like this for me."

"Take it and spend it on something you would really like."

"Thank you," she said.

Have you ever had a totally unexpected surprise from God that moved you to tears? Just like Mr. Mike, God delights in giving us things we feel are undeserved.

GIVE ME WISDOM

"So give your servant a discerning heart to govern your people and to distinguish between right and wrong."

1 Kings 3:9

When the Lord appeared to Solomon in a dream and told him to ask for whatever he wanted God to give him, Solomon answered wisely even before receiving the gift of wisdom. He simply asked for the ability to administer justice wisely for the people he was appointed to lead. God was pleased that Solomon did not ask for longevity or wealth or the death of his enemies. As a result, He promised to grant Solomon's request and add to it riches and honor and long life, with the condition that Solomon obeyed God's commands.

Isn't wisdom the best gift we can ask of God too? With wisdom, we can make right decisions, avoid danger, counsel others, and be assured we are on the best path. It appears that one characteristic of wise people is that they do not think they already know everything and are humble enough to recognize that there is always more to learn.

If you haven't already asked for wisdom today, why not do so now?

Father, thank You that You stand ready to give good gifts to Your children when they ask. Like Solomon, we ask for wisdom in conducting our affairs, making decisions, and managing all You have entrusted to us. Help us please You with our choices and utilize the discernment You provide through the Holy Spirit. Thank You for this wonderful gift. In Jesus' name, amen.

TREASURED GIFTS

"There are different kinds of gifts, but the same Spirit."

1 Corinthians 12:4

"*H*ere's one!" My sister held up a perfect conch shell.

"Here's another one!" My brother pulled a whole sand dollar from the edge of the ocean.

As I continued to walk on the beach, I also found some wonderful treasures. By the time we returned to our hotel room, we had a bag full of impeccable and unusual shells. We carefully spread them out on the table to show them to our parents.

That time of "show and tell" is one of my favorite memories from our annual beach trip. Recently I shared that with my dad. He began to chuckle.

"What's so funny?" I asked. "We found some really good shells."

"I know you did." His smile got bigger. "Did you really think there were all those shells on the beach?"

"Did you . . ."

Dad nodded. "While you were taking a nap I went to the shell store and found a few I thought you'd like. Then before I came back to the room, I carefully placed them on the beach."

My daddy's naptime escapade at the beach was a great picture of our heavenly Father's method of giving us gifts. They are all around us. Sometimes He hides them and we have to discover them. Every discovery helps us to understand Him better and appreciate the things He has given us.

Are you constantly on the lookout for God's special gifts in your life?

THOUGH THEY ARE STRANGERS

"Dear friend, you are faithful in what you are doing for the brothers,
even though they are strangers to you."
3 John 5

*R*ains resulting from Hurricane Joaquin pummeled the southeast United States for several days, causing flooding in what some reporters called biblical proportions. Classes at the College of Charleston and the University of South Carolina were cancelled because of submerged houses, washed-out bridges, unnavigable roads, and unavailable drinking water. The governor declared a state of emergency.

In league with the Red Cross, schools, churches, and businesses many hours away from the affected areas collected bottled water, washcloths, soap, toothpaste and toothbrushes, and other basic necessities. It mattered not that the people in need were strangers; pictures and stories of the newly homeless sufficed to arouse compassion and rally assistance from those who could help.

We don't have to look far to find people in need. Our mailboxes and in-boxes overflow with continual pleas for money and prayers. Ask the Lord to help you discern which of these "strangers" He wants you to help with the resources He has provided. And as always, don't forget about the neighbor across the street, the coworker in the next cubicle, or your own family members. God commends us for being faithful to our brothers, regardless of whether we know them or not. Find a way to share with someone today.

EXERCISE

$\mathcal{M}$any people shy away from physical exercise. And as good as physical exercise is for the body, there are other areas of life that benefit from exercise as well. Why not exercise your faith this week and reach out to someone who does not have a relationship with God?

KEEP IN STEP

"Since we live by the Spirit, let us keep in step with the Spirit."
Galatians 5:25

New means of tracking exercise constantly hit the market, from basic step-counting pocket pedometers to high-tech personalized apps which monitor everything from heart rate to calories burned. At the same time, commercials for mammoth burgers and easy, greasy pick-up meals bombard the senses and entice the work-weary into quick, tasty meal solutions. Which side wins: exercise or eating? For those hooked on exercise, the lure of unhealthy eating cannot match the satisfaction of a lean, healthy body, so they choose wisely what goes in their mouths to avoid sabotaging their muscles' hard work.

The same battle rages in our spiritual walk. "The sinful nature desires what is contrary to the Spirit, and the Spirit what is contrary to the sinful nature" (Galatians 5:17). Which side wins: sin or Spirit? Paul commands us to live by the Spirit so we won't gratify the desires of our sinful nature. By aligning our priorities and schedules with Christ, we crucify the passions and desires of our sinful nature and build up "fitness" in the spiritual realm.

Today, choose to be fit for the King by exercising your spiritual muscles. See how many steps you can take toward love, joy, peace, patience, kindness, goodness, faithfulness, gentleness, and self-control. Keep in step with the Spirit and see how much better you feel at the end of the day!

EXERCISING GODLINESS

*"For physical training is of some value,
but godliness has value for all things, holding promise
for both the present life and the life to come."*
1 Timothy 4:8

Exercise profits the body, mind, and soul in countless ways. Any type of movement which promotes circulation, burns calories, or offers a break from one's routine can be beneficial. An hour's walk in a park or the woods refreshes and restores the weary or worried. There are also those who maintain the daily discipline of a rigorous workout regimen. All these forms of physical exercise have value.

But Paul's words to Timothy indicate that the exercise of godliness, which also requires training, holds a deeper and more eternal value. The Native Americans model an understanding of this principle. A Cheyenne warrior named Wooden Leg summed up how his people exercised both physical and spiritual discipline: "To 'make medicine' is to engage upon a special period of fasting, thanksgiving, prayer and self-denial. . . . The procedure is entirely a devotional exercise. The purpose is to subdue the passions of the flesh and to improve the spiritual self. The bodily abstinence and the mental concentration upon lofty thoughts cleanses both the body and the soul and puts them into or keeps them in health. Then the individual mind gets closer toward conformity with the mind of the Great Medicine above us."

Today, why not plan and purpose to add some physical and spiritual exercise to your routine?

NOT A WALKER OR A WHEELCHAIR

"Dear friend, I pray that you may enjoy good health
and that all may go well with you,
even as your soul is getting along well."

3 John 2

As she prayer-walked around the independent-living apartments her mom was preparing to move into, Lynn beseeched the Lord for several specific requests: "Lord, may Mother make new friends quickly and enjoy many outings with them. May she have a sense of adventure for this phase in her life. May she appear to be the youngest member of this retirement community, staying vivacious and offering encouragement and good cheer to those around her. May she not need a walker or a wheelchair for at least ten years. May she bring You honor and glory in this place."

A block away from the apartments, Lynn circled the on-site gym and outdoor recreation area and continued her prayer. "Lord, help Mother to make her way often to the gym, where she can keep her body healthy and strong. May she enjoy sweet fellowship with her neighbors and friends in this recreation area. Help her find ways to use her gifts of music to minister to others. Let her discover the sweetness of solitude or the delights of conversation in this hidden gazebo."

Is there someone in your family or circle of friends anticipating a change of location or occupation? Why not offer specific prayers for physical and spiritual well-being to ensure your loved one enjoys good health in all the ways that matter?

PUT ON YOUR TENNIS SHOES

"You, dear children, are from God and have overcome them,
because the one who is in you is greater than
the one who is in the world."

1 John 4:4

General, our dog, is seventy-seven years old humanly speaking. Yet when he spies anyone donning tennis shoes, he hardly acts his age. He smells a walk and can hardly contain himself. He nudges us with his nose, paws at the door, then barrels down the steps. It's as if going on a walk is the most glorious of all canine adventures. Oh, to be more like General and eagerly seek the exercise our bodies crave.

A prayer card published by a company called Forward Movement has on one side a beautiful prayer and on the other, "A Morning Resolve," which proposes a variety of "exercises": "I will try this day to live a simple, sincere, and serene life . . . exercising economy in expenditure, generosity in giving, carefulness in conversation, diligence in appointed service, fidelity to every trust, and a childlike faith in God. . . . I will try to be faithful in those habits of prayer, work, study, physical exercise, eating, and sleep which I believe the Holy Spirit has shown me to be right" (Anonymous).

Unfortunately, General has managed more discipline and consistency in these areas than any of his humans. And yet, God has promised His children overcoming power. Let's make a point of utilizing that power to exercise in all the ways the Holy Spirit nudges us.

First step? Put on your tennis shoes!

KEEP MOVING

*"But grow in the grace and knowledge of our Lord and Savior
Jesus Christ. To him be glory both now and forever! Amen."*
2 Peter 3:18

Dick Van Dyke is ninety years old. Many of us would consider that elderly. After a wonderful career in entertaining, you would think he could stop and rest now. But he has a new book called *Keep Moving*, full of advice for those of us who would like to reach ninety. The bottom line—keep moving. Go to the gym, take a walk, dance, just do whatever motion you can to keep your body moving.

That is actually pretty good advice for our spiritual lives.

When you are in toddler Sunday school, you learn your first Bible verse—"God is love." For sure, He is love. But if all we ever learn about God is that He is love, we are missing much of His faithfulness and character. Our relationship with Him will become stuck in one place, and that is not good. We need to keep moving and growing.

Develop a plan of daily Bible study. Bible study books are helpful, but I also read lots of God's Word. Pray. There is no substitute for spending time in God's presence. Serve others and share God's love as you serve. Attend church. Being with a community of believers strengthens your faith. You don't have to do everything at once; just keep moving along.

At any age, make sure you are in the best physical and spiritual shape you can be.

THANK

It is important to live in a constant state of thanksgiving. Even though things in the world might not be exactly as you think they should be, there are multiple blessings right in front you. How about the ability to read this book? Or the understanding God gives you as you read His Word? Take time today to thank Him for special blessings in your life.

P'AYMO'

"This is the confidence we have in approaching God:
that if we ask anything according to his will, he hears us."

1 John 5:14

*O*nce again the Brent family joined hands as they thanked God for their food. Two-year-old Shelly loved this part of the meal. As she grasped her brother's hand on one side and her mother's on the other, she smiled as she bowed her head.

"Lord, thank You for this food and use us to do Your will. Amen."

When Shelly's dad finished the blessing, everyone looked up with a hearty "Amen."

As was her custom, Shelly grinned and said, "P'aymo'?"

The family once again bowed their heads as a different family member thanked God for their meal. At the end of the second blessing, the family said, "Amen," and Shelly once again repeated her desire to have another blessing. "P'aymo'."

This continued until each family member had a turn to express their thanks. At the end of the last blessing, Dad said another "Amen" and suggested they eat. Shelly clapped her little hands and said again, "P'aymo'."

"Shelly, you are right. We should all pray more. God loves for us to talk to Him and thank Him for what He has given us. But it would make God very happy if you ate a good supper."

I think we would agree with Shelly. We should all p'aymo'. Whether at mealtime or during a moment during the day, God is always glad to hear from us.

We have so much to be thankful for. Why don't you p'ay a little mo' today?

THANK YOU

"One of them, when he saw he was healed, came back,
praising God in a loud voice. He threw himself at Jesus' feet
and thanked him—and he was a Samaritan.
Jesus asked, 'Were not all ten cleansed? Where are the other nine?
Has no one returned to give praise to God except this foreigner?'
Then he said to him, 'Rise and go; your faith has made you well.'"
Luke 17:15–19 NIV (2011)

When Jesus healed ten lepers, only one man returned to thank Jesus. Only one out of ten whose lives had been drastically changed by Jesus' healing touch.

The other nine men were so excited they forgot their manners. We can understand why they were so excited. After a lifetime of this horrible, debilitating disease, the joy of being healed had to be immense. But this one man's joy was so great he couldn't help but turn around to thank Jesus. After all, his life was changed forever.

Have you ever experienced a touch from God that was so amazing and so life-changing that you couldn't contain yourself? Did you call a friend? Did you do a happy dance in the solitude of your home? Did you cry or maybe laugh uncontrollably? Each of us responds differently to God's blessings, especially those that are answers to fervent prayers.

But let's take a lesson from the leper who returned to Jesus. Always remember to thank God for the specific blessings in your life. Has He healed you recently? Restored your family? Give Him thanks in all things. And above all, thank Him for the abundant life He has given you.

THANKFUL FOR THE FIRE

"For everything God created is good, and nothing
is to be rejected if it is received with thanksgiving."
1 Timothy 4:4

$\mathcal{F}$ran's dad gently shook her shoulders. "Honey, wake up. The church is on fire. We are going to be with the pastor. Everyone is gathering in the parking lot to pray."

Fran rubbed her eyes. "The church is on fire?"

"Yes."

When Fran and her family arrived at church, everyone was gathered in the parking lot. Many held hands. Some cried. None could take their eyes off the flaming building they loved so much.

The pastor began to speak. "This is a sad occasion. Our beautiful church is gone. We thank God no one was hurt. We are going to continue to thank God in the midst of this tragedy."

The pastor continued, "For years we have prayed about our need for a new sanctuary, but no one wanted to tear down the old one. The woodwork was all hand-done. Now we have no choice but to rebuild a larger space for ministry."

Because of the fire, this church was able to build a new sanctuary that allowed room for them to grow. Today the church is more than double the pre-fire size and is reaching out to people all over their community and the world. They thank God for the new facility that allows them to reach more people than ever before.

Have you ever had a circumstance in your life that seemed really bad, even tragic, but when you looked back you realized God had a hand in it all along? Thank God for it. Ask Him to show you His plan even when the times are hard.

A THANKFUL HEART

"Let the peace of Christ rule in your hearts, since as members
of one body you were called to peace. And be thankful."
Colossians 3:15

You live in your hometown. You married your high school sweet-heart, live a mile from your parents, and worship every Sunday with the same folks you have known for years. One day your husband comes home from work and says, "Guess what, honey? I've been transferred. We are going to the other side of the country. Won't that be fun?"

"Fun?" you would have said if you weren't speechless. *I was born here and thought I was going to die here.* "Are you serious?" you finally whisper.

"Sure," your husband says, adventure written all over his face.

When you finally recover from the shock, you can either become bitter and make this really hard on your family, or you can support your husband and face it with a positive attitude that will be conta-gious to your family.

Thanking God for your circumstances will change your attitude. What is good about this move? You will explore another part of the country, make new friends, and decorate a new home. The children will have opportunities to play different sports because of the differ-ence in the weather. Your family will grow stronger and closer together as you arrive at a new destination knowing only each other.

When God suddenly changes the direction of your life, do you whine about the change or thank Him for His provision in every area of your life?

YOUR PEOPLE DELIVERED

*"There will be a time of distress such as has not happened from
the beginning of nations until then. But at that time
your people—everyone whose name is found written
in the book—will be delivered. . . . Those who are wise will shine
like the brightness of the heavens, and those who lead many
to righteousness, like the stars for ever and ever."*

Daniel 12:1, 3

*H*uman nature causes us to cringe when we hear about horrific happenings or see evidence of the end times escalating. It can be scary to contemplate. Of course, we should be shining our lights to draw men to the Savior. It is our sacred responsibility to lead as many as we can to righteousness. But we can cancel the fear factor. When the Tribulation comes, we're going to be gone. Delivered. Out of here. Up there with Him. Thanks be to God!

How do we know? God's Word says so in Revelation 3:10: "Since you have kept my command to endure patiently, I will also keep you from the hour of trial that is going to come upon the whole world to test those who live on the earth." Thanks be to God!

Though there will still be challenges and trials, dangers and difficulties, we as believers need not fear the unspeakable disasters and righteous judgment that will befall those who rejected Christ. Thanks be to God!

We have work to do, yet we can also relax knowing God has already declared both the victory and our deliverance. Thanks be to God!

FOCUS

$\mathcal{F}$ocus is not an easy thing to do. Life is full of distractions that take our attention away from the things we should really focus on. This week ask God to direct your focus and help you not to miss the things He wants you to notice or prioritize.

IT ALWAYS GROWS OUT WELL

*"So we fix our eyes not on what is seen, but on what is unseen,
since what is seen is temporary, but what is unseen is eternal."*

2 Corinthians 4:18

*J*oy wrinkled her nose at her reflection, studying her new asymmetrical bob.

"If you don't like Helen's haircuts, why do you keep going back?" Beth asked.

"Good question," Joy replied. "Sometimes Helen doesn't focus the way I wish she would on my hair. But what she does focus on impresses me. Helen finds the good in other people. She focuses on trying to improve herself, help someone, or share a spiritual insight. I respect those qualities in her. Besides, she's quite interesting!"

"And you have an interesting haircut to prove it," Beth said, smiling.

Joy thought about her salon visit. Although she had taken a picture of the hairstyle she hoped for, Helen only glanced at it, nodded, and started trimming, talking animatedly the entire time. But when Helen suddenly gasped and said, "Uh-oh," Joy knew it had happened again. Helen got so caught up in conversation she failed to focus on the haircut. She apologized and said it was too late to fix that side, but she'd get the other one right.

"Besides, asymmetrical is in," Helen said hopefully.

"It will be fine," Joy responded. And it was. She had chosen Helen as her stylist for the things she did focus on, rather than the things she didn't. Besides, Joy liked surprises and her hair always grew out well!

Is there something in your life that has not turned out as you hoped or expected? Would changing your focus about what really matters help it seem less catastrophic? Why not try?

KEEP YOUR EYES ON HIM

*"You will keep in perfect peace those
whose minds are steadfast, because they trust in you."*

Isaiah 26:3

Several years ago there was a song about a plastic Jesus on the dashboard of a car. At the time I thought it was a bit sacrilegious and wondered how anyone could possibly think that was okay. How could you have a plastic replica of someone so special? Didn't that belittle Jesus' place as Lord of lords?

But years later, I went through a very difficult time. I was distraught and couldn't concentrate on anything. In fact, I could rarely do anything but sit and hold my Bible. But the one thing that got me through that time was focusing on Jesus and talking to Him. I think if I'd had a plastic Jesus to put on my dashboard or in my kitchen or anywhere I could see it, it might have helped to keep my focus where it should be.

Regardless of our current situations, focusing on Jesus is important. During the good times we need to focus on Him and praise Him for His provision and love. When things are not going well, focusing on Him is essential for everyday functionality. If things are rolling smoothly along, we probably have extra energy to focus on Him and praise Him for the amazing God He is.

Do you feel a little like you have lost your focus today? Focus on Jesus and allow Him to guide your steps.

ALLOT OR ALLOW?

"Teach us to number our days aright,
that we may gain a heart of wisdom."
Psalm 90:12

*H*ave you noticed that without allotting specific boundaries for work-related activities, they expand to whatever time you have, often bleeding into time you meant to save for and focus on family?

For the past several weeks, I had allowed myself to spend too many hours at work and once again, my job threatened to consume me. How could I focus on what really mattered?

First I prayed for wisdom about priorities. Then I created a schedule of the hours I would allow for work requirements—at work. Finally, I made a mental commitment not to treat every "requirement" as an emergency.

Of course, when my colleague Aaron called on Sunday afternoon with a work-related question just before my daughter and I left for a *Mary Poppins* play, he had no way of knowing how hard I was trying to focus on family time and keep it separate from work time.

My rude response surprised both of us as it tumbled out of my mouth: "Sorry, I'm not the right person to ask. Number one: I don't know. Number two: I don't care."

Aaron had every right to be miffed at me. Yet, the situation Aaron called about would not count until the following year. Today what counted was spending time with my daughter and enjoying a bit of light-hearted entertainment. Still, I could have at least offered a "spoonful of sugar to make the medicine go down" a little easier.

Monday morning, I will apologize to Aaron (again!) for my brusqueness. Together, we can ask God for wisdom and discipline to focus on what really matters.

FOCUS ON WHAT MATTERS

"Fixing our eyes on Jesus, the pioneer and perfecter of faith."
Hebrews 12:2

My husband and I went out for a quiet dinner at an area restaurant. Shortly after we were seated, a father and son were seated at the table next to us. With tables only a few feet apart, it was difficult to avoid interaction.

The two-year-old was in constant motion. He banged the flatware on the table. His father gently took the fork and spoon from his chubby little hands. The little boy played "peep eye!" with us. Horrified that he was interrupting our dinner, the father tried to turn the boy's attention away. When fries arrived, he began dipping them in ketchup then throwing them toward our table. The father scooted the plate away.

Earlier the father had propped his phone on the salt and pepper shakers. A movie played on the small device, a movie that looked perfect for a two-year-old with its animation and songs. The little boy paid no attention to the phone as he explored all the things on the table. Once the flatware, fries, and other things were removed from the table, the boy noticed the sounds coming from the phone and began to focus on the movie.

Life is full of distractions, not just for little boys. And sometimes they keep us from focusing on the things our Father wants us to focus on. What is it that keeps you from paying attention to those things that really matter, especially your relationship with God?

LITTLE BLESSINGS

*"Fix your thoughts on Jesus, whom we acknowledge
as our apostle and high priest."*

Hebrews 3:1

Janice smiled as she took her seat near the back. The concert had begun before she could get there from work. But she immediately felt drawn into the spirit of the beautiful music of the concert choir.

The choir was dressed in their singing outfits of green and white school colors. Flanked by red poinsettias and gold bows, they looked like they could have come straight from the front of a Christmas card. Quite a nice picture! But Janice didn't linger long on the big picture. Her focus went immediately to a lovely young girl in the middle of the back row. Halfway through the song their eyes met and both smiled. Without missing a note, Polly raised one eyebrow in a silent salute to her mother.

No one else in the auditorium knew what had transpired. But in those few seconds of connection, Janice had been intensely blessed by her daughter.

Most of us have overloaded calendars. Often just the smallest moment of blessing is enough to get us through the day. Connecting with a loved one or special friend can give us the courage to keep moving on.

Even brief moments of connection with God during a busy day keep us focused on what really makes a difference, and often it's just a little thing. Don't ever forget to thank God for the little things. Remember, sometimes it's the little things that mean the most.

FORGIVE

"*Father*, forgive them." Even on the cross Jesus knew how important forgiveness was. Unforgiveness can hold you back from living a life of freedom and love. Examine your life this week and see if there is a need for forgiveness. Don't wait any longer to restore a relationship and bless others.

WINNING THE PRIZE

"Brothers, I do not consider myself yet to have taken hold of it.
But one thing I do: Forgetting what is behind and straining toward
what is ahead, I press on toward the goal to win the prize
for which God has called me heavenward in Christ Jesus."
Philippians 3:13–14

ℒack of information and a misunderstanding fueled the conflict between us. Jamie saw no point in following my directions, and I saw no reason for him not to! Our wills clashed and our tempers tangled. After a few verbal volleys, I walked away. Still, my seething took too long to simmer down. Why did I let him push my buttons? Who was the adult in this situation? Obviously, I still had some growing up to do.

As the day wore on, things improved. Lilly, a former student who had quit school for a time her junior year, shared an essay about how that decision changed her perspective. During her months at home, she learned how difficult job seeking was without a high school diploma or a GED. Now she determined not to let "drama" or anything else stand in the way of her graduation goal. Evidently, she decided to forgive and look past the hurts so she could keep her eyes on the prize.

I needed to follow Lilly's example. I forgave Jamie and made a concerted effort to listen to him. Instead of resenting his moodiness and cynicism, I began to value his depth of thought and his incredible giftedness with words and music.

Father, help me be quick to forgive and forget what's behind so I don't miss what's ahead.

SHIPWRECKED OR SMOOTH SAILING?

*"May the Lord direct your hearts into
God's love and Christ's perseverance."*

2 Thessalonians 3:5

Shelley propped the picture of the shipwrecked sailboat in front of her students. They studied it curiously, and then listened to her story.

"A few years ago, I bought this painting for my son Rob. I thought he would like it since he likes boats. You know I try to support local artists and, of course, I got a bargain."

"No wonder it was a bargain. That boat is mired up, not going anywhere," Adam quipped.

"You're right," Shelley replied, smiling. "And for that reason, my son hated the painting."

"It's kind of drab too," Nathaniel stated. "I can see why he wouldn't like it."

"Wish I had seen it that way," Shelley replied. "I found a replacement picture, much brighter with several sailboats cruising along. My son is much happier with that picture. But the shipwreck made me think of our classroom. Yesterday that's what our class felt like to me. Some of you didn't follow the rules and we lost valuable work time. But I overreacted and got angry. I want to apologize for my behavior. Could we compromise and get our boats back in the water? I'm ready for some smooth sailing. How about you?"

"Aye, aye," Matthew and Kendrick chorused in unison.

"Ready when you are, Captain," said Nathaniel.

Do you need to get unstuck or navigate some choppy waters? Sometimes a genuine apology is all it takes to make the wind blow in your favor again.

YELLOW BALLOONS OF FORGIVENESS

"Forgive, and you will be forgiven."
Luke 6:37

"Annie. Mom, you forgot Annie!"

I stopped the car and turned toward the backseat. "Kim, why didn't you say something sooner?"

"I guess I didn't think about it!"

"Okay, well, the rest of you get out and go to school, and I'll go get Annie."

What was Annie's mom going to say?

We had carpooled with Annie since the beginning of the year. Everything had gone well until now.

Once I got Annie to school, I called her mom at work. "I am so, so sorry. Please forgive me. I love Annie. I just had too much on my mind and headed straight to school when we left our house. I won't let it happen again."

"Annie was fine. No harm done. Just please remember her tomorrow," she said with a chuckle.

"Oh, I will. Thank you."

The next morning when the children and I were ready for school, we headed out the door. Everyone stopped and started laughing.

"What's so funny?" I asked as I locked the door.

"Look at the van."

There was my big red van with a bunch of yellow balloons tied to the mirror. Written in big letters across the balloons was one word—A-N-N-I-E.

Annie's mom had not only forgiven me for yesterday's oversight, but my sweet friend had added humor to the whole situation. Forgiveness and a good laugh. What could be better?

Is there someone who needs to receive some yellow balloons from you today?

FORGIVE

*"'In your anger do not sin': Do not let the sun go down
while you are still angry."*

Ephesians 4:26

*R*achael held her head in her hands and sobbed. "I can't believe he is gone. I never had the chance to tell him that I forgave him. What am I going to do?"

Her friend put her arm around Rachael's shoulders. "I'm sure he knew you loved him."

"Yes, but how am I going to live with this guilt? I should have talked to him a long time ago."

"Well, you can tell him now." Kendra walked over and picked up an empty chair. She set it in front of Rachael. She patted the seat. "Pretend he is sitting right here in front of you. Tell him everything you wanted to say. Let him know you forgive him."

Kendra walked out of the room to give Rachael some privacy. Rachael spoke softly for a while then just sat with her head bowed.

Kendra returned. "Feel better?"

Rachael looked up. "Yes, I think I do."

You always feel better when you forgive another and let go of negative feelings. Sometimes those feelings grow for many years.

Fortunately, we serve a God who forgives right away. All we have to do is ask Him to forgive us. So don't hesitate. If there is something you need to say to Him, do it now. And if there is someone in your life who needs your forgiveness, don't wait. Forgive him or her today.

THROUGH HIS EYES

"Bear with each other and forgive whatever grievances
you may have against one another.
Forgive as the Lord forgave you."
Colossians 3:13

"*I* finally figured out how to forgive my brother," Lydia stated as she and her friend Lucy circled the mall on their Saturday morning walk.

"You're kidding. That's been bugging you for years," Lucy responded.

"Yep. But not anymore. I decided to look at the situation from his perspective, and all of a sudden, it made sense. He's not purposely trying to hurt me. He's just trying to protect himself from being hurt. What looks like selfishness to me is actually just fear of losing control."

"Wow. You've come a long way to get to that point."

"It's about time. All I really needed to do was put myself in his position and try to see things through his eyes. He's scared. He's lonely. He's out of his comfort zone. Now I don't blame him for his actions. I actually understand him a little better."

"Guess that feels pretty freeing."

"Forgiveness is always freeing, isn't it?" Lydia asked. "I just wish I had realized all this before."

Today, like Lydia, I need to step into someone else's shoes for a while to see things from a different perspective. Then, with the Lord's help, I will forgive. And by His grace, we will both be free.

Lord, help us to bear with each other and to forgive the people who grieve us, as You have forgiven us.

HONOR

Honor is one of those words you hear at wedding ceremonies. But just as we honor our spouses, we ought also to honor our parents, our loved ones, our friends, our government—and the list could go on. Honor is another way of showing our love to and respect for others.

EVERYTHING?

> *"Do everything without complaining or arguing, so that you may*
> *become blameless and pure, children of God without*
> *fault in a crooked and depraved generation,*
> *in which you shine like stars in the universe. "*
>
> *Philippians 2:14–15*

Jake and Maddie shuffled slowly into the kitchen reporting for chore duty. Mom handed them their assignments and began humming the jaunty little tune she taught them for the "Do everything without arguing or complaining" verse in Philippians 2:14.

"Awww, Mom! Pleeeeease! You can't really expect us to sing while we do chores, can you?"

"Maybe not. But I can expect you not to complain or argue."

"Not even about cleaning out the cat litter box?" Maddie asked.

"Not even that."

"Not even about swishing out the toilet?" Jake queried.

"Not even that."

"Might as well stop asking," Maddie interjected. "The Bible verse says everything. We can't win."

"Oh, but you can," Mom answered. "The next verse says you get to shine like stars. Plus, you know how happy it makes me when you honor God by obeying cheerfully."

"Excuse me, Mom, but I can't stand here talking. I've got a toilet to swish." Jake said.

"And I have some cat poop to scoop," Maddie said, smiling.

"That's the spirit. Proud of you two! Maybe I'll let you choose your chores for next week."

"Thanks, Mom."

What is there on your don't-want-to-do list today that you could do without arguing or complaining? Why not use this opportunity to shine like a star for Him?

HONORING FATHER AND MOTHER

"Honor your father and your mother, so that you may
live long in the land the LORD your God is giving you."
Exodus 20:12

"Mom, I'm not going to go on the trip to France."

"Why?" I asked. Doug had been planning this trip for months.

Sitting across the table from me, my college student son said, "You told me how you felt about the trip. There is a lot of unrest in that part of the world. You said you have strong reservations, but you would let me make that decision on my own."

"Yes, you are old enough to do that."

"Well, I trust your judgment. I have prayed about that trip. I want to honor you, respect your wishes, and not go. I'll see Paris someday."

My eyes and heart filled up. Doug made a smart decision in a way that blessed me and his dad. I was so proud of our son and thankful he was so mature in his decision-making.

On my drive home from college that day, I think I experienced a little of what God might feel when He gives us choices and we choose the one that honors Him most. Often I am "on the fence" about going one way or another. One option is what I know would be God's choice. The other might not be a bad choice, just not the best option.

What better way to honor God than to stay on the path He has chosen for you?

THE HOLY AND THE COMMON

*"They are to teach my people the difference
between the holy and the common."*
Ezekiel 44:23

*H*ow many times have you honored your family or guests by setting the table with your finest china, crystal, or silver? I'm ashamed to admit I average twice annually. Convenience usually wins over the special care required to hand-wash and store these "valuables." Of course, the fact that our china pattern went out of circulation shortly after we married and is now nearly impossible to replace sometimes puts the brakes on my desire to "be fancy." And yet it is so beautiful that its use ought not to be limited to display in a china case. Plus, when I think about all the people who went out of their way to find and purchase our selected wedding pattern, I realize I am not honoring them when I fail to use their gifts.

Ezekiel's mandate for the Levitical priests included teaching the Israelites to recognize what was sacred and what was common. Once instructed, the Israelites had no excuse for choosing the common when the holy was within reach. By acknowledging and following God's sacred decrees, they honored Him.

Obviously, this has little to do with dishes. Or does it? I want to honor Him too. One way I can do that is to start using the best I have to honor those I love and care about. That means the best of my time, my energy, my talents, my words, and yes, even my dishes!

Lord, show me how to recognize the difference between the holy and the common—and to choose what honors You, and those I love—most.

SHARE THE LIGHT

"You are the light of the world. A city on a hill cannot be hidden.
Neither do people light a lamp and put it under a bowl.
Instead they put it on its stand, and it gives light to everyone
in the house. In the same way, let your light shine before men,
that they may see your good deeds and praise your Father in heaven."

Matthew 5:14–16

*N*early a thousand people depend daily on Myra—as media specialist, teacher, problem-solver, communicator, encourager, and friend. She runs the library like a city on a hill—the centerpiece of the school. Here important meetings take place, resources are supplied, wisdom dispensed, training developed, and technology traumas treated in their own Tablet Emergency Room.

Of course, Myra would be quick to credit Carrie, her right-hand woman, and a few others who give her the support she needs to do her job. Still, it must be hard serving people who need help all day long. Too often the responsibilities extend way past closing time and into the weekends. Myra is like a candle, burning at both ends and sometimes in the middle, too, but always sharing illumination with those who need it most. The source of the Light within her is also the reason behind her hard work and good deeds. She exemplifies the words of Father James Keller: "A candle never loses anything by lighting another candle." Myra honors God through her many talents and selfless service to others.

Today let's let our lights shine so that others may see our Father more clearly and give Him the honor and praise He deserves.

HONOR GOD'S LEADERS

"'The staff belonging to the man I choose will sprout,
and I will rid myself of this constant grumbling
against you by the Israelites.'"

Numbers 17:5

$\mathcal{P}$laces of leadership are not always places of honor. Arnold Glasow said, "A good leader takes a little more than his share of the blame, a little less than his share of the credit." Thousands of years before Glasow, however, Moses and Aaron experienced a huge share of blame and very little credit for the leadership and responsibilities God entrusted to them. The rebellious Israelites, led by Korah, rose up against Moses and Aaron, insolently claiming their entire community was holy and Moses and Aaron had no right to exclusive leadership. Korah wanted more power and authority. This angered God!

As a way of proving He had honored Moses and Aaron with their leadership positions, God opened the earth and swallowed Korah and his men. Even so, the next day, the entire Israelite community grumbled against Moses and Aaron. This time God's wrathful response resulted in a plague killing nearly fifteen thousand people before Aaron intervened and offered atonement for their rebellion.

God decided to prove who was in charge once and for all by causing Aaron's staff to sprout, bud, blossom, AND produce almonds—all overnight! Surely Aaron and Moses smiled with relief as this creative display of God's power restored them to their rightful places of honor.

Let's honor those whom God has set over us—and be faithful leaders if we are in charge.

PREPARE

Some people enjoy living life as a wild ride, not knowing what might come next. But most people want to be prepared for whatever lies ahead. The best way to prepare is to stay close to God. If your heart is focused on Him, trusting in His plan will help you be prepared for anything that may happen.

BUILD, PRAY, KEEP, AND WAIT

*"But you, dear friends, build yourselves up in your most
holy faith and pray in the Holy Spirit.
Keep yourselves in God's love as you wait for the mercy
of our Lord Jesus Christ to bring you to eternal life."*

Jude 20–21

*N*one of us like feeling unprepared. Sometimes it can be helped, and sometimes it can't. Circumstances, situations, time, and resources typically dictate our state of preparedness. But Jude offers four solid steps for preparing for any obligation, opportunity, or crisis regardless of human limitations.

First, BUILD. Build your confidence, build your reputation, and build your experience while exercising your faith. Memorize scripture.

Next, PRAY in the Holy Spirit. Ask the Holy Spirit to prompt you, intercede for you, and guide you to whatever steps you must take toward accomplishing God's perfect will.

KEEP follows PRAY. Jude does not suggest his readers keep extra money, bread, water, gasoline, or emergency supplies. Instead, he tells us to keep ourselves in God's love. Surround yourself with reminders of how precious you are to God. Spend time with encouraging friends, and feed your mind and heart with godly wisdom or influence.

Finally, WAIT for His mercy. He is watching over you and longs to bless you, especially when you obey Him in hard situations. Remember to praise Him while you wait. That builds trust, demonstrates faith, and offers a pleasing aroma to God.

It is comforting to know that God is always prepared and because of that, we can be too. Nothing takes Him by surprise.

PREPARE WITH GOD'S PLAYBOOK

"'No eye has seen, no ear has heard, no mind has conceived what God has prepared for those who love him.'"

1 Corinthians 2:9

Seems like most football games on television are played on perfectly groomed green fields under blue skies with fluffy white clouds in the warm sunshine. But recently a game was played between Notre Dame and Clemson University in the middle of the worst flooding South Carolina had seen in a thousand years. Both teams knew it would be a messy game, won by the team who could overcome the adverse field conditions.

In a pregame interview, the Notre Dame coach, who brought his team from the sunny Midwest into the flood-ravaged South, was asked the question, "Coach, how did your team prepare for this game?"

Without hesitation the coach said with a smile, "We practiced with wet footballs all week."

It was, as promised, a very messy game. Torrential rains came down most of the time. But the Notre Dame coach had the assurance that he and his team had done everything they could to prepare for the adverse conditions.

Are you prepared for the most important game of all—life? You can't know what is ahead, but you know you will encounter some "wet" spots. The best preparation for that game is to study God's Word and deepen your relationship with Him. He is the One who knows the big picture and created us for a purpose. Using His "play-book" will make you a winner every time!

HE WILL PREPARE FOR YOU

"In my Father's house are many rooms; if it were not so,
I would have told you. I am going there to prepare a place for you.
And if I go and prepare a place for you, I will come back
and take you to be with me that you also may be where I am."

John 14:2–3

The entire community was still in shock and mourning over the tragic deaths of several college students in a tragic car crash.

"Can you imagine holding your child in your arms one week and the very next, planning and attending his funeral?" Leslie shook her head as tears formed in her eyes. "That would be so hard."

Her circle of friends nodded in agreement, each thinking of her own children and how incredibly difficult it was to conceive of such a loss.

"There's just no way to prepare for something like that. Here one minute, and gone the next. It happened so fast," Ellie said.

"But it's the same for Todd and his family. He's just been diagnosed with cancer, and that's almost like receiving a death sentence too," Ellie continued. "I'm just asking the Lord to show me how to comfort Todd's mother and to give her all the support and encouragement I can."

Though we cannot ever be prepared, especially not for the death of a child, we can prepare our hearts by staying close to the Source of all comfort. We can also claim the promise that God has prepared a place for us to be with Him for all of eternity.

BE PREPARED

"Be on the alert, stand firm in the faith, act like men, be strong."
1 Corinthians 16:13 *NASB*

*M*aggie spent the afternoon at the mall. She loved her purchases and quickly put them in the trunk. Getting into her car, she carefully locked the door behind her.

Glancing in the mirror, Maggie's eye caught sight of movement in the backseat. A strong arm came around her neck and she felt the cold, hard edge of a knife.

"Don't say a word. Just drive."

Maggie knew if she left the parking lot she was in more danger. So she drove slowly.

"What's your name?" she asked her captor.

"It doesn't matter. Drive."

"It matters to God. Do you know He loves you?"

"Ha! I doubt it. Drive."

Maggie looked in the mirror. "God loved you enough to send His Son to die for you."

"Hush, I don't need to hear this."

"If you are going to kill me, I am going to talk about Jesus with my last breath."

"I don't want to talk about it. Stop this car."

Before the car came to a complete stop, her assailant jumped out and disappeared into the woods.

Maggie remained calm and even shared her faith in an intense situation because she was prepared. She spent daily time with God, deepening her faith and trust in Him. Though she didn't think about it much, she was preparing for days such as this one.

How are you preparing for life? Don't forget your prep time today!

THE PLACES HE PREPARES

*"See, I am sending an angel ahead of you to guard you along
the way and to bring you to the place I have prepared."*
Exodus 23:20

*M*ama Jane handed each of her graduating high school senior girls a parchment scroll rolled up and tied with a bright blue ribbon. The words inside read: "Everything you are given to do, do as best as ever you can, for this is the best possible preparation for what you are called to do next." Nearly forty years later, I still have that saying prominently displayed on my kitchen windowsill. Mama Jane, our wise and gracious mentor, was absolutely right.

As a girl, working in my parents' drugstore taught me people skills and the importance of integrity and courtesy.

As a teen, a part-time stint after school in a dry cleaner's taught me how challenging it was to make money AND good grades.

As a college student, working summers caring for an elderly lady helped me learn compassion and responsibility. Later, a tedious factory job taught me the value of an education, which provides more choices and opportunities.

As an adult, each job or responsibility has opened my eyes and my heart to the realization that God truly does go before us, guard us, and prepare a place for us—a place of service, a place of humility, a place of learning, and a place of rest.

Today let's thank Him for the angels who go ahead of us and the places He prepares.

OBEY

Some adults may think this word only applies to children and their obedience to their parents. But as God's children, aren't each of us responsible for obeying God's laws and directives? He loves us more than anything else. We can be secure that obedience to Him is the key to a happy life.

CAREFUL TO OBEY

*"Be strong and very courageous. Be careful to obey all the law
my servant Moses gave you; do not turn from it to the right
or to the left, that you may be successful wherever you go."*

Joshua 1:7

The word *obey* typically refers to children's actions related to authority figures. However, in the book of Joshua, God directs the new leader of the Israelites to obey all the laws given by his predecessor, Moses. The Lord commands Joshua to demonstrate strength and courage, qualities available to him as long as he obeys.

Of course, the assurance he will be successful wherever he goes activates his courage to move forward, for God delivers on His promises. Yet the prosperity God promises depends on complete obedience. Therefore humility and a willingness to listen are required.

It is wonderful to know that no matter how overwhelming the task before us may seem, God intends to stay very involved in the leadership role He provides. Better than a GPS voice saying, "Your path is clear," God commands Joshua not to turn to the right or to the left. Sounds like a straight path, always a relief when trying to lead a group of people anywhere.

Today trust God to show you the straight path. Determine to stay so closely aligned to Him and His Word that you can be strong and courageous, certain of prosperity and success in the endeavors with which He has entrusted you for leadership.

So, what are you waiting for? Let's go forth and conquer!

STAY INSIDE THE FENCE

"Jesus replied, 'Anyone who loves me will obey my teaching.
My Father will love them, and we will come to them
and make our home with them.'"
John 14:23 NIV (2011)

arian's horses loved the freedom of the pasture. All except Midnight. While the other horses roamed free and content within in the confines of the fences, Midnight thought the grass outside the fence tasted better than what was in the pasture.

Midnight figured if she could put her foot in the wire square of the fence and push down, she could create a large opening, large enough for her head to go through. Then she could graze outside the fence.

Most of the time that worked for Midnight and went off without a hitch. However, once or twice her foot slipped as she pushed down on the thin wire, resulting in a gash on her leg or foot. But the injury never squelched her desire to be on the other side of her boundaries.

Have you ever been like Midnight? Rather than being satisfied within the boundaries your Master has set for you, you see things just out of your reach and desire those things more than anything. You might even get hurt trying to get to it, but you think it is worth the risk.

Doesn't the Master know best? Hasn't He placed us where we are because He knows it is for our greatest good? Can't we just be obedient to the boundaries set for us and not desire things out of our reach?

INSTANT OBEDIENCE

"It is the LORD your God you must follow,
and him you must revere.
Keep his commands and obey him;
serve him and hold fast to him."

Deuteronomy 13:4

"Sissy, please close the door. It is cold outside and we don't want the house to get cold too."

Two-year-old Sissy closed her eyes and turned her head away from her mother. She had reached the point of thinking that if she couldn't see her mom, obedience was not required.

"Sissy, I'm talking to you. I want you to obey Mommy. Please go close the door."

Sissy was already halfway across the room. "Do it 'ater," she replied. "Not now." Sissy sat down on the couch.

Mommy walked over to Sissy and took her hand. "I'll help you this time, but next time you have to do it yourself when Mommy asks you, okay?"

Sissy grabbed Mommy's hand and walked over to close the door.

How many times has God asked me to do something and I respond just like Sissy? I either close my eyes to ignore His voice or I respond with "'ater, God. I'll do it later."

When we are given a command whether at work, at home, or from God, we are expected to obey the instructions immediately. If we don't, the lack of instant obedience becomes disobedience.

Is there something God has told you to do and you have put it off? Don't put it off any longer. Today is a great day for obedience.

SACRIFICE AND CELEBRATE

*"Despite their fear of the peoples around them,
they built the altar on its foundation and sacrificed
burnt offerings on it to the LORD,
both the morning and evening sacrifices.
Then in accordance with what is written, they celebrated."*

Ezra 3:3–4

*E*zra begins with an account of how the Lord moved the Persian king Cyrus to give the Jews freedom to return from their Babylonian exile to build His temple in Jerusalem. Temple treasures were restored, and families gave freewill offerings. They built an altar and made sacrifices to the Lord. Then they laid the foundation of the temple.

As the Israelites shouted God's praise at this enormous accomplishment, they unintentionally alerted their adversaries. Soon their enemies showed up and "set out to discourage the people of Judah and make them afraid to go on building" (Ezra 4:4). In spite of their newfound freedom and clear directives from God, the Israelites experienced opposition in the form of threats, false reports, weariness, and intimidation—all enemy tactics. Still they persevered. Remarkably, King Artaxerxes supported the Israelites by ordering all the Trans-Euphrates treasurers to "provide with diligence" whatever Ezra asked (7:21). Their holy reputation restored, the people of God rejoiced and took courage. Finally, they celebrated the triumphant completion and dedication of the Temple.

How does this ancient account apply to us? Bottom line: Obey. Expect opposition, but proceed anyway. Whatever God commands you to do, do with diligence. Persevere. Leave the consequences to Him. Then remember to celebrate His goodness and His faithfulness!

OBEY HIS COMMANDS

"This is love for God: to obey his commands.
And his commands are not burdensome."
1 John 5:3

At least once a semester, I feel compelled to share with my students the lesson I learned on obedience. My principal at a previous school asked me to do something I thought was a little silly. It did not make sense to me and I didn't think it would work. In fact, I was pretty sure we were headed toward a calamity! However, because he was my boss and I respected him, I followed his directions without arguing or complaining. To my great surprise, things worked out precisely as he had intended. It was at that point in my adult life that I understood something important about obedience: I do not have to like, agree with, or even understand what those in authority over me ask me to do—as long as it is not illegal or immoral, I should obey in order to show my respect and submission to authority.

My students sometimes respond to my directives with a groan or a muttered "I don't want to. . . Do I have to?" I tell them they don't HAVE to WANT to—and then I share the lesson I learned about obeying authority.

Is there some act of obedience you've been complaining about? The Bible says obeying God is showing Him we love Him. And it also says His commands are not burdensome. So, even if we don't like, agree with, or understand, let's obey anyway—and bask in His approval.

WORK

Our work should be a gift to the Lord. Everything we do, whether our jobs that support our families or something that just bring us or someone else pleasure, is a gift to God. Offer Him your best every day.

PICK UP YOUR PEN

*"Whatever you do, work at it with all your heart, as working
for the Lord, not for human masters, since you know that
you will receive an inheritance from the Lord as a reward.
It is the Lord Christ you are serving."*

Colossians 3:23–24 NIV (2011)

"If you want to change the world, pick up a pen." Martin Luther's words seem to be targeted at writers. And, for sure, writing is an important vocation. Words are important and can change lives.

But isn't that true for every task we undertake? In order to accomplish something, you must first get started. In a writer's case, it is to "pick up a pen" or in today's world, get in front of your computer.

What job has God given you to do? Has He called you to be a writer, a teacher, or a plumber? Once you discover what God has called you to do, you must take the first step, get the correct training. Then pick up the tools necessary for the job and pour yourself into it.

You may feel inadequate for your job. Moses felt inadequate when God called him to lead the Israelites out of Egypt in Exodus 3. He said, "Who am I that I should go to Pharaoh and bring the Israelites out of Egypt?" (NIV, 2011).

God said, "I will be with you."

If you feel inadequate for a job, pick up your tools and take the first step. God will say to you, "I will be with you."

NOT IF, BUT WHEN

"When you pass through the waters, I will be with you;
and when you pass through the rivers, they will not sweep over you.
When you walk through the fire, you will not be burned;
the flames will not set you ablaze. For I am the LORD,
your God, the Holy One of Israel, your Savior."
Isaiah 43:2–3

The power of this scripture holds special meaning for the work teachers do and the overwhelming feelings that accompany that work, especially at the beginning of the school year: too many meetings, too much paperwork, too many new technologies, too many preps, too many students, and too little time! Yet we are blessed to have had the summer to recover and renew. We are privileged to be trusted with this awesome responsibility. More than that, we are blessed to know, no matter what floods or flames we face, we have the Holy One to hold our hands, steady our hearts, and carry us safely through.

Is your work overwhelming you today? May I challenge you to reread the promises from Isaiah 43 at least twice more? The first time, notice the three dependent "when" clauses. Dependent clauses, by nature, cannot stand alone and make sense or be complete. Neither can we! Now pay attention to the independent clauses, which are actually declarative statements: "I will be with you; you will not be burned; the flames will not set you ablaze. For I am the LORD, your God." These are complete and can stand alone.

Those declarations make me feel a lot better about the high waters and hot spots I'm facing in my work. How about you?

DO YOUR BEST

"Whatever your hand finds to do, do it with all your might."
Ecclesiastes 9:10

*T*his morning when I woke up and walked into the kitchen, it was the same scenario as most other days. The breakfast dishes were rinsed and neatly set on the counter right above the dishwasher.

For sure I appreciated the fact that others had rinsed the dishes. And it was nice they were near the dishwasher instead of across the room. But they were so close to where they needed to be, just not quite on the mark. Whoever ate cereal for breakfast had decided it was acceptable to place the bowl as near the dishwasher as possible without actually putting it in. How much longer would it take to open the door and deposit the dishes?

Definitely made me think. How many times has God asked me to do something, and I came really close to completing the task? Seems like my mindset became, *That should be close enough*, instead of, *God, I want to do the best job I can because You deserve the best.*

Sometimes I stop three feet short of the closet to take off my shoes, or just around the corner from the hamper with my dirty clothes, or maybe a few words short of saying what I think a friend really needs to hear. These things may seem like small tasks. But all things, no matter how small or seemingly insignificant, should be done in a way that honors God. No matter what I am doing, I hope I stop and thank God that His Son, Jesus, didn't stop short of the cross, where He died for me.

BEAUTIFUL GARDENS

"A planting of the LORD for the display of his splendor."
Isaiah 61:3

$\mathcal{B}$ill is a farmer. One of his biggest jobs is to plant the garden in the spring. Plowing is important in the winter and early spring. Then it comes time to put the seed in the ground.

There are a lot of new gizmos and gadgets to make a farmer's life easier. Bill has never found a substitute for good old-fashioned planting his garden by hand.

Bill carefully cultivates and makes a furrow just the right depth. (He uses a tool for that!) Then he patiently walks down each row placing every seed just the right distance from the last one. When the seeds are just where they need to be, he carefully covers the seeds and gently packs the dirt over each row.

Tedious? Yes. But Bill's garden is one of the most beautiful and prolific gardens you will ever see.

God's garden of people is a lot like Bill's garden of fruits and vegetables. God places each one of us exactly where He wants us to be.

Have you ever wondered why you live in the town that you do? Sitting in church, do you wonder how you chose that place to worship? When you arrive at work each day, do you ask God to bless the job He has given you to do? Do you look around at your family and think what a miracle it is that you are related to these wonderful people?

Well, that's where God planted you. Make the most of the environment you are growing in. Do everything you can to make it beautiful.

HUMMINGBIRD LESSON

"A sluggard's appetite is never filled,
but the desires of the diligent are fully satisfied."
Proverbs 13:4 NIV (2011)

*H*ummingbirds must consume more than their body weight in food every day. They do that in very small increments, usually between five and fourteen meals an hour. They work very hard to maintain the energy they need to fly with an average of fifty-three wingbeats a second.

In other words, hummingbirds have to work very hard just to maintain their lifestyles. They must constantly feed in order to stay alive.

So it is with our spiritual lives. They must be constantly fed in order to stay alive. The Bible includes stories of characters who strayed away from God and found themselves in hard places. Peter walked on the water successfully. But the moment he neglected to keep his eyes on Jesus, he began to sink.

The hummingbird works hard to keep himself alive. And just one meal a day won't accomplish that. He must feed constantly and never get too far away from the source of food.

Are you feeling like you have neglected your spiritual life? Don't get into a similar predicament as Jonah. Start today to read your Bible. There are lots of good studies out there. Spend time building your relationship with God. Obey Him. Keep your spiritual life in good shape so you can share the Gospel with those you see every day.

PLAY

$\mathcal{P}$lay is often forgotten as an important part of life. Yes, life is a serious matter, but play helps you lighten up and enjoy those you play with. This week why not think of someone you haven't seen in a long time and invite them to do something fun?

MURKY LURKIES

"Perfect love drives out fear."

1 John 4:18

"Are you getting in the ocean, Mom?" my daughter asked.

"Mmmm, not sure. I don't care much for murky water," I replied.

"Murky?"

"Yes, murky. Can't see what's swimming around you or headed toward you."

"You're going to let that stop you?"

"Might."

As it turned out, it didn't. In fact, I was the first one to crash over the first wave and fling myself unabashedly into the sea. This, of course, after a petition to heaven that the Lord of the universe, who created all living things, would kindly keep the stinging, biting, flesh-eating, blood-seeking ones away from us!

Hearing this prayer, my daughter asked if I would please include the crabs.

"Lord, please help us not to step on or get pinched by any crabs, either."

Feeling a little silly and a wee bit giddy, I cast my cares about murky water onto the Lord and fully enjoyed splashing into the surf, jumping giant waves, then lying on my back floating like a rag doll, letting the waves toss me forward and rock me back. Now and then I scanned the water surface for triangular black fins, but mostly, I felt perfectly safe and wondrously loved. God was watching His adult child play and smiling down upon me even as He lifted me up time and again in the waves.

Choose to trust the Lord with your murky lurkies today!

PARK IT IN THE PARK

"The city streets will be filled with boys and girls playing there."
Zechariah 8:5

$\mathcal{T}$wo blocks from our vacation rental, the recreation park beckoned. With everything from tennis courts to soccer fields, seesaws to zip lines, picnic tables to a Bark Park, rocking chairs and swing sets, who couldn't find an excuse to play? Not I!

However, I can't say I fared well on the zip line. Too heavy and too little arm strength.

The seesaw wasn't much better. I stayed on the ground while my husband stayed up in the air. Not exactly the balance I was hoping for. He really needs to eat more.

But the swings? On those I can soar and pump my troubles far away. Wind flipping my hair back, breeze singing in my ears, up and away I go. I know it's time to slow down when the posts in the ground start marching up and down to my rhythm. I begin to wonder what would happen if I flipped all the way over the top bar, but I really don't want to know.

Back to earth and the real world, I'm much better off for those moments of play. Then I'm ready for the rocking chairs, another wonderful invention meant for relaxation and refreshment for the soul. Admittedly, they are also much more manageable for the times I really should act my age.

No matter your age, make sure you look for moments of play in your day.

GOD IN THE CLOUDS

"The eyes of the LORD are everywhere,
keeping watch on the wicked and the good."
Proverbs 15:3

"Hey, guys, come here."

"What is it, Thom? Are you okay?" I knew it must be something out of the ordinary for Thom to give away his location. Hide and seek was his favorite game.

"Yes, I'm okay. But everybody come here. Hurry!"

I jumped up from my hiding place and ran around the house to see what the excitement was about. Fearing a snake might have invaded his space, I looked to see where Thom was.

Lying flat on his back in the driveway, he heard me coming and said, "Look." He pointed to the sky. "See, there's God's face in the clouds."

All the game players got as near to Thom as possible and flattened themselves on the ground beside him.

"Oh, yeah."

"I see His eyes."

Thom said, "Yep, He's watching us."

Someone else said, "I see His mouth."

"Oh, look how fat His cheeks are."

"He's smiling."

Thom smiled. "I just wanted you to see Him. I've never seen Him in the clouds before. But I know He is watching over us."

"Yes, Thom, He is," I said. "We are so glad you called us to come see Him even if we were in the middle of the game. What a great picture in the sky."

Indeed, it is always good to be reminded that God is watching us and smiling at us all the time.

KEEP THE FAITH

"I have fought the good fight, I have finished the race,
I have kept the faith."

2 Timothy 4:7

"Mom," yelled Bruce, "You never play video games with me."

"Oh, Bruce, I am not very good at those."

"But, Mom, I always have to play alone," Bruce replied. "Just one game?"

"Okay."

Mom worked at figuring the game out, and as the game progressed, her skills improved.

However, Bruce was an expert and after a few minutes, the electronic game board began to shake violently.

"What's that?" Mom asked.

"Time's almost up. Make as many points as you can."

Mom and Bruce frantically tried to score.

"Why didn't you tell me this would happen?"

"I thought you knew the game would end," Bruce answered with a grin.

"Yes, but . . ."

Sometimes life's circumstances treat us that way, don't they? Things seem to be going along fine and then everything starts to shake and we are out of control and panic sets in.

"Oh, if I had just known Dad was going to lose his job. If I had only known Blake was going to flunk out of school. If I had only known the washing machine hose was going to break . . ." The list could go on and on.

But we can't know everything that is going to happen. We must live in a way that no matter what happens, we know God is in control and everything is in His hands. That is the only way to have peace—keep the faith!

SNOW FUN—INSIDE AND OUTSIDE

"Let us therefore make every effort to do what leads to peace and to mutual edification."

Romans 14:19

*T*hree-year-old Kristi pressed her nose against the window. "Mommy, I want to play in the snow."

"I know. But you have the chicken pox. And fever," I said, feeling her forehead.

"But everybody else is having fun."

"I know. Not a good time to be sick, is it?"

I turned to see my husband coming through the kitchen carrying a big bucket. His fingers came quickly to his mouth, requesting I remain silent. He went upstairs, quietly came back, and went out the door. Kristi was so absorbed in the fun outside she didn't notice. Dad made several other trips. What was he doing?

On his next trip he was empty-handed. He stopped by the window.

"Kristi," he said, "I have a surprise for you."

"What is it?"

"It will be a better surprise if you close your eyes." Dad picked Kristi up and started up the stairs. She put her hands over her eyes. He motioned for me to follow.

Dad went into the bathroom, and I heard Kristi squeal. Dad had filled the bathtub with snow and plopped our little chicken-pox girl right down in the middle of it, clothes and all!

How many times has your heavenly Father done that for you? It seems nothing is going your way and then He scoops you up into something totally unexpected and fun. Thank Him for those sweet surprises.

PRAISE

A heart full of praise is one that acknowledges that God is our Creator and Maker and everything we enjoy comes from Him. Find something this week that you have forgotten to praise Him for and offer a prayer or song of praise.

MAKING A DIFFERENCE

*"Accept one another, then, just as Christ accepted you,
in order to bring praise to God."*

Romans 15:7

Not too long after I had children, a friend gave me a framed cross-stitched saying. "Praise Is a Child's Best Vitamin." I hung this by my back door and read those six words many times each day.

As I practiced the meaning of those words, I realized how true that saying is. How much better to say to my three-year-old, "You did a good job cleaning the bathtub. Thank you for helping Mama," than to say in a much-too-loud voice, "Why did you make a mess in the bathroom?"

Either way I was going to have to clean the bathroom again. But I had to choose how to respond to my little helper's efforts. If I responded negatively, both our days were ruined. If I responded positively, we could continue our happy day and I would remember next time I cleaned the bathroom to let her "help" while I supervised.

What is your response to praise? Is there someone at work who is quick to criticize but slow to praise? How do you react?

Our heavenly Father wants us to know how much He loves us and shows us in so many ways each day. He encourages us and praises us when He knows we have done our best as we serve Him. And many times He allows us to speak words of encouragement to our family and friends so they can know Him better.

HARMONIOUS DISCORD

"Speak to one another with psalms, hymns and spiritual songs.
Sing and make music in your heart to the Lord."

Ephesians 5:19

Cousins Orchestra practice was in full swing. Even though the musicians, ranging from age three to nineteen, had received music months in advance, it didn't sound like many had practiced. Parents didn't seem to notice as they videoed and sang along.

One thing that wasn't planned was the amount of love and encouragement that was part of the orchestra.

"C'mon, you can do it."

"Don't rest now, we need your trumpet notes."

"That triangle sounds really good."

On and on the praise and encouragement went. Many musicians were first-year students of their instruments and lacked confidence. But as practice continued and one cousin after another spoke compliments and encouragement, bodies relaxed and faces began to hint at smiles.

The song was recognizable as practice continued. Rather than lacking harmony and unity, those moments became full of love and praise for each other and God.

As we sang "O Come, All Ye Faithful," we couldn't help but reflect on the faithfulness of God in our lives.

How about you? Have you taken time lately to reflect on the goodness of God in your life and family? Maybe there are situations that feel out of harmony. Could you speak a word of encouragement to the family members involved and love them back into harmony with each other? It may not take a whole "orchestra," just a word or two.

PRAISE HIM

*"Praise be to the God and Father of our Lord Jesus Christ!
In his great mercy he has given us new birth into a living hope
through the resurrection of Jesus Christ from the dead."*

1 Peter 1:3

We stood in a circle. Our supper club had met since before we had children, over forty-two years ago. Today we watched as one of our precious friends rang the bell at the cancer center signaling the end of her chemotherapy. She could now start enjoying life again.

The eight of us moved from the hall where the bell hung to the waiting room where other patients waited their turns. We gathered around our friend. "Let's pray and thank God," one said.

"Let's praise Him that her treatments are over."

In the small waiting room of the local cancer center, we had a sweet time of thanks and praise. Hearts were full and eyes dripped as we acknowledged what a great God we serve.

The variety of people in the waiting room acknowledged that cancer was not selective, no age or gender or economic level exempt. For those who are believers, the same is true. God's love and grace is for everyone.

When Jesus died on the cross, He didn't look across the crowd with a pointed finger and say to every third person, "This is for you."

No, He loves every one of us so much that each one of us can respond to His invitation of "Come!"

Praise Him today for that!

SACRIFICE OF PRAISE

*"Through Jesus, therefore, let us continually offer to God
a sacrifice of praise—the fruit of lips that openly profess his name."*
Hebrews 13:15 NIV (2011)

*C*arol is one of the best secretaries around. She is efficient, organized, and runs the office for her boss with ease and a constant smile. When you meet her, there is no other word to describe her but *sunshine.*

Most people don't know, but Carol is a busy lady when she leaves work. She takes care of her mother and mother-in-law. She doesn't go home, but she goes to one nursing home for an hour, then another. She serves the mothers with love and patience. Once she gets home, she prepares a healthy meal for her husband. Then chores and housework, that is, unless her ailing brother needs something. Then she runs out again. Her days are long and her workload is heavy.

But if ever you run into Carol, she will be smiling. And you will never know of the heavy load she carries. Carol loves Jesus, and her life is a constant sacrifice of praise to Him. No matter what her outward circumstances, inwardly she knows she is in the hands of a God who loves her.

What about you? Do you constantly live with sacrificial praise in your heart? When life's circumstances don't go your way, do you praise God anyway, knowing His way is best? Try Carol's way of filling every day with sacrificial praise.

WORTHY OF PRAISE

"For great is the LORD and most worthy of praise. . . .
Splendor and majesty are before him;
strength and joy in his dwelling place."
1 Chronicles 16:25, 27

*W*hen I arise, one of the first things I do is open the front door to let our dog, General, out. While he conducts his business, I look up at the sky, still inky black and sparkling with splendor. It's the perfect time to say, "Good morning, Lord. Thank You for a restful night and for the privilege of living another day. Help me live it in a way that brings You glory." Then we make our way back inside for breakfast.

Somehow just starting the day that way helps me tap in to the strength and joy I need for going about my myriad duties as wife, mother, teacher, daughter, sister, and friend. Of course, to truly be ready for what follows, I know I must spend time with my Father in His Word. Nestled in His lap, I wrap His counsel, encouragement, and love around me like blankets to ward off the chill of despair or the heaviness of fatigue.

Splendor. Majesty. His attributes.

Strength. Joy. His dwelling place.

How marvelous. How glorious. How worthy of our praise.

Today let's pause to ponder the multitude of ways God proves His love and His power. Make a point of praising Him from early morning to end of day. Even in the dark of night, when we focus on the Father, we will also see the Son.

PRAY

The Bible tells us to pray nonstop. That means constantly being in fellowship with Him. He knows what is going on, but He loves it when we remember to include Him in our thoughts and conversations.

PRAYER WALK

"Be joyful always; pray continually; give thanks in all circumstances,
for this is God's will for you in Christ Jesus."
1 Thessalonians 5:16–18

Every year a small contingent of prayer warriors arrives at 6:45 a.m. the day before students arrive to walk and pray the halls of their school. Alone or in pairs, they take a section of the school and stop at each doorway, praying for the needs of each teacher, administrator, custodian, office worker, guidance counselor, and student. An hour later, they circle up to close in prayer.

This year's themes came from the Old and New Testaments: like Nehemiah, rebuilding and restoring the broken walls, and having the mind of Christ about every child and every decision.

What power. What compassion. What unity. What joy. What hope.

What if each of us walked and prayed the halls of our workplace fervently and faithfully, not just once a year, but weekly, or even daily, when we arrive in the parking lot?

It is interesting to note how the command to pray continually is right in the middle of two independent clauses: "Be joyful always" and "give thanks in all circumstances." Evidently our prayers should not only be petitions for heaven's help, but include joy and thanksgiving regardless of circumstances.

Today, like Nehemiah, let's set out to rebuild some broken walls. Let's pray to have the mind of Christ as we work and interact with others and determine to be joyful and give thanks. Sounds like a recipe for a splendid day!

INSIDE THE FISH

"From inside the fish Jonah prayed to the LORD his God.
He said: 'In my distress I called to the LORD, and he answered me.'"
Jonah 2:1–2

Just out of college, Brandi acquired a new job and leased an apartment, both scheduled to start in ten days. She drove twelve hours home to visit her parents, bought some secondhand furniture, and began to paint and re-upholster. Everything was falling into place . . . until the phone call that turned everything inside out. Through a change of circumstances beyond her control, Brandi learned her services would not be needed and she would have to find another means of income.

Mr. Nolan discovered his wife of forty-seven years required dialysis daily. On his custodian's salary, he could barely afford the gas to get to work, much less what it took to get to and from the hospital several times a week. Though his wife was on the kidney wait list, there was no way of knowing how long it would take to acquire the organ she needed to give her real hope.

Like Brandi, Mr. Nolan, and Jonah inside the fish, all of us face situations that cause distress and make us feel trapped. And yet, the Bible assures us that when we call for help, the Lord listens and He answers. Through prayer and diligence, Brandi eventually found employment. Through prayer and a generous love offering from his coworkers, Mr. Nolan's financial distress was eased.

Take heart. Have hope. As He did for Jonah, God will make a way for you to emerge from your distress and be back on dry land once again.

IS IT ENOUGH TO CURTSEY?

"Devote yourselves to prayer, being watchful and thankful."
Colossians 4:2

*A*rriving at the prayer room, I hurriedly signed in, turned briefly toward the prayer bench, and went to the prayer request boxes.

At my hour's end, I felt like I had only half-completed my job.

An image came to mind from childhood movies. When subordinates came into the presence of royalty, they crossed one leg behind the other and lowered their bodies into a curtsey. The process took only a few seconds. The subject then moved into the room to go about his business.

That was me in the prayer room. Just a brief acknowledgment of the fact that I was in the presence of the King. A curtsey. Was that enough?

I don't think so.

Here are a few suggestions to make your time with God more meaningful.

1. Praise Him. Let Him draw you into His presence.
2. Meditate on the scriptures. God loves to hear us honor Him by praying through His Word.
3. Focus only on Him.
4. Thank Him. Tell Him that you treasure the precious gift of His Son.
5. Be still and listen to Him. Have you ever tried to hear what someone else is saying when you are both talking at the same time?

Maybe in the movies a curtsey will do. But for the King of kings, a pause and a little body language are definitely not adequate preparation for the fellowship He longs for with us, His children.

HE ALREADY KNOWS

"Your Father knows what you need before you ask him."
Matthew 6:8

Every morning when I start my errands, one of my first stops is at Ricky's. As I pull up to the speaker to order, one of the girls comes to the window, smiles, waves, and says, "Large diet soda!" I never have to say a word. I just drive through the parking lot and up to the building.

At the window, I usually pause for a few minutes to chat as I pay for my drink. The conversation always ends with, "Bye, you have a nice day now, sweetie!"

I really like a diet drink in the morning. But even more important than that is the good feeling I have when I realize somebody knows exactly what I need before I ask. And as an additional bonus, they are glad to see me every time I come, even though I come often. In fact, if I miss a day or two, they want to know where I've been.

Coming to God at prayer time is kind of like ordering at Ricky's. He always knows what I need before I even open my mouth.

And He is always glad I came. No matter how or when I come, He is happy to see me. How thankful I am for my loving heavenly Father, who knows my every need!

Have you had your special time today with the One who knows what you need even before you get there?

FILLING THE GAP

"Brothers and sisters, pray for us."
1 Thessalonians 5:25 NIV (2011)

In Peter Lord's sermon about gap fillers, he noted that all of us have people in our lives whose "gaps" are oh-so-obvious to us, even though they seem to be oblivious to the problem. We know where they are, we know where they should be, and we're pretty sure what it would take to fill the gap. Our natural inclination is to fill that "gap" with advice, criticism, hints, how-tos, or even guilt. But that's not the most effective way to fill a gap.

"You have two choices," Pastor Lord said. "You can stand with Satan as the Accuser, or you can stand with Christ as the Intercessor. When you stand with Christ and pray for Him to fill the gap in the person you love and care about, He will." He knows exactly what it takes. Of course, the timing and the method He uses for gap filling may not match our ideas or preferences. Most likely, it will be better! It's not our job to fill the gap, but rather to release our need to control or contrive and let God Almighty exercise His perfect power His perfect way in His perfect timing.

Prayer unlocks this power and pulls the wayward one closer to the One who reveals and heals. Accusations, or fault-finding, on the other hand, push further away.

Is there someone in your life whose gap is goading you? Why not partner with Christ in intercessory prayer? Trust Him to be the Ultimate Gap Filler!

RELATE

Good relationships are key to getting along well with others. It takes time to build strong relationships but is well worth it. Think of a relationship that you haven't put much time into lately. Rekindle that relationship and learn a new way of relating to that person.

A NOTE IS ALL IT TAKES

"But encourage one another daily, as long as it is called "Today,"
so that none of you may be hardened by sin's deceitfulness."
Hebrews 3:13 NIV (2011)

"You are special—have a great day!"

"You're a cool dude!"

"You are my favorite peanut!"

"I am so proud of you and all your accomplishments."

"It's great to have a friend like you."

You might find one of these notes around our house. We have always been note writers—a note in the lunch box, a note on the bathroom mirror, a note on the shelf in the closet, a note taped to the steering wheel of a car.

Or if you're one of our friends, you might find one of these under your windshield wiper or stuck down in your purse or book bag.

Often we find notes left in unusual places. They aren't long and usually don't use a lot of words. But the message is always the same no matter what the words: *You are special and I'm glad we have each other.* Building relationships with each other helps us deepen our relationship with God, and notes are useful tools for doing that.

Encouraging one another is important. In fact, God told us to do that for each other. He even showed us how. He gave us His Word that is just full of notes written especially for us.

Why don't you read one of God's notes today and share it with a friend.

WHAT IS YOUR HALLMARK?

"Therefore, if anyone is in Christ, the new creation has come:
The old has gone, the new is here!"
2 Corinthians 5:17 NIV (2011)

Children often recognize a Hardee's or McDonald's long before they can say the words. "Dees, Dada!" or "Donald's, Mama!"

Not so in our family. Mother was an antique buff. She taught us to recognize an antiques sign hidden by overgrown brush. We could spell "antiques" long before we could read. Rarely did we pass an antique shop. We stopped.

Mother taught us to recognize the difference between a reproduction and an authentic antique. She showed us how to make sure things we looked at were genuine and could relate to the time in which they were made.

I remember one shop owner gawking at my five-year-old brother running his finger around the rim of honeycomb crystal to see if it was real or a reproduction. Many adult shoppers don't know how to tell the difference!

Mother was never interested in collecting old silver, but she loved thimbles. She taught us how to tell the old from the new and how to identify the hallmarks.

Hallmarks attest to the genuineness and purity of the metal. From the hallmark on a piece of gold or silver, you can know who created the piece, where it was created, and its quality. The hallmark is there to relate the piece to the creator.

We may not have a hallmark stamped visibly on our person, but those around us can tell by the way we act who created us and the quality of our character. It becomes obvious in just a few moments with us who we are related to and who created us.

What is the hallmark on your life?

THUNDERSTORMS OR FUNDERSTORMS?

"Can any one of you by worrying add a single hour to your life?"
Matthew 6:27 NIV (2011)

Growing up, a thunderstorm meant only one thing—go get the pots and spoons! With the first distant rumble, we headed to the kitchen.

Mama hated thunderstorms. It really wasn't her fault, though. When she was a little girl, her grandmother lived with them. Grandma was terrified of lightning and thunder. At the first dark cloud, Grandma began to shake . . . and get in the closet. Mama always went with her. I'm not sure if Mama went because of her relationship with Grandma or because she was afraid too. But after years of this weather-triggered ritual, Mama feared thunderstorms as much as Grandma.

Motherhood didn't take away Mama's fear of thunderstorms, but it changed her method of dealing with them. There were few thunderstorms in my childhood that were not downright fun!

When the clouds darkened and we heard thunder, we'd also hear, "Okay, everyone. It's time to play our game."

My sister and I went to the kitchen to get pots and spoons and my brother pulled down the shades.

We sat in a circle on the floor. Flash! With each lightning bolt we beat our pots and sang at the top of our lungs. The object was to sing louder than the thunder.

Often the game continued long after the sky had cleared.

Every day we make choices. Our reaction to situations greatly affects not only us but our relationships. How blessed I am that Mama knew that.

LOVE AND JUSTICE

"But you must return to your God; maintain love and justice, and wait for your God always."

Hosea 12:6

*T*eachers have incredible opportunity for building relationships. Through observation and conversation, they get to know their students' personalities, preferences, family situations, siblings, hobbies, beliefs, and work habits. Rarely ever do I remember a student's grade and sometimes not even his name, but I can easily recall whether we had a positive or negative relationship. By the same token, it's unlikely that a student will remember the specific content she learned in a classroom, but she will remember whether or not a teacher made her feel important and saw value in her work. Teachers also have an opportunity to model and teach compassion and justice. These qualities lead to strong relationships.

Not surprisingly, sometimes it's the students who provide the best teaching. Just today, Charley gave a presentation about her "hero": not a person, but an organization that provides crisis hotlines and counseling for students being bullied, especially those who are contemplating suicide. These hotline staff members not only relate to the callers but show them someone cares and values them. By reminding us that students who are bullied are eight times more likely to attempt suicide, Charley increased our awareness of the importance of relating to others with kindness.

Let's make a point of maintaining love and justice toward those in our realm of influence. Of course, the best way to ensure we do that is to return to God and maintain our relationship with Him. Then His love spills over into our conversations and our actions toward those around us.

YOU ARE UNIQUE

"If it is possible, as far as it depends on you,
live at peace with everyone."
Romans 12:18

God made each of us unique. We do not look alike, we do not like the same things, and we also have very different personalities.

Some of us consider ourselves introverts. Some extroverts. Others use terms such as *sanguine, melancholy, choleric,* or *phlegmatic,* or *otter, beaver, lion,* or *golden retriever.* No matter what terms you use, our temperaments, or personalities, are different, and if we recognize that, we will find ways to communicate with each other that promote clearer understanding.

For instance, if I want to give my powerful choleric friend some information, I know that she will get the point more quickly if I send her the information in short concise sentences or maybe even a bulleted list. This is because my friend loves lists and wants to-the-point information. However, my playful sanguine friend would receive the same information best if I embellish it with a really good story. Her personality type loves stories, the bigger the better! It takes effort to relate to our friends in ways they understand.

Relationships are important, but the most important relationship is our relationship with God. Understanding our personalities helps us deepen our relationship with God. Knowing how we communicate best enlightens us as to how we can grow closer to Him.

Spend some time today with the One who created you and understands you like no one else.

DREAM

*D*reams are fragile. Whether a dream occurs when we are asleep or at an awake moment when our thoughts drift, we must hold them lightly. Sometimes God takes our dreams and makes them a reality and other times dreams are enjoyed for the time they are in our thoughts. Whatever you are dreaming about now, ask God how that dream fits into your life and the plan He has for it.

NEVER TOO LATE TO DREAM

"Delight yourself in the LORD
and he will give you the desires of your heart."
Psalm 37:4

*T*wo strangers, destined to meet, were dining in the same restaurant that evening. The well-dressed woman at the next table commented on my menu choices and thus, our conversation—and our friendship—began. Vanessa was attending the same conference I was. That gave us another talking point. I invited her to join me, and our conversation turned to more personal things. Vanessa dreamed of acquiring her doctoral degree in education. Yet life circumstances, age, and responsibilities had created unexpected detours. I encouraged her to keep pursuing her dream. We exchanged contact information and once back home, I mailed her one of my books.

Weeks later, Vanessa e-mailed me about another dream God had placed on her heart:

> *After perusing your book, I was inspired to create GemStones, a faith-based support group for young women. I researched our system's policy and found that students may freely practice their religion at any time. I am the facilitator/leader of the group, but the participants provide input and plan what we do. I am excited about this new venture and rest quietly knowing that God's hand covers its purpose. God has changed my view. . . . No longer are they hard, loud, crass, young women, but unpolished gemstones with the potential of greatness. . .*

Sometimes our dreams are detoured or delayed for a reason. Keep delighting yourself in the Lord, and He will either change your dream or help you fulfill it.

HE IS NOT SLOW

"With the Lord a day is like a thousand years,
and a thousand years are like a day. The Lord is not slow
in keeping his promise, as some understand slowness."
2 Peter 3:8–9

*N*early two years ago my brother Richard left for the Philippines with the intention of returning in six months. He planned to marry Janeth, a wonderful Filipino woman he got to know on previous visits, and help fulfill her dream of coming to the United States. Yet Richard's heart gave out. He nearly died and had to undergo surgery in a foreign hospital and have a pacemaker installed. The doctors have done their best to restore his health, but his precarious blood pressure and heart condition still make it inadvisable for him to fly. His visa, long expired, has been revoked by the U.S. Embassy. Consequently, he is stuck.

Nothing happens fast in the Philippines, Richard has learned. Marriage laws require a couple to prove they have known each other for at least five years and have never been married. Janeth, who already possessed superior business acumen and people skills, had never attained her dream of attending college. While nursing Richard back to health, she enrolled in the equivalent of a CNA program and has consistently performed as one of the top five students in her class. When she arrives in the United States, she will have marketable skills.

Lord, when it seems You are slow, help us to trust You and wait patiently on Your perfect timing.

NOT A DREAM?

"A word was secretly brought to me, my ears caught a whisper of it.
Amid disquieting dreams in the night."
Job 4:12–13

"I'm moving soon. Just wanted you to know. I've got to get away." Her arms tightened around my waist and a muffled sob escaped from where her head pressed against my shoulder.

"What's wrong, Marlie?" I asked.

"Can't take it anymore. My doctor is worried because I'm starting to eat nonfood items."

"What do you mean?"

"Like glass, razors, anything with sharp edges."

"Well, I can see why. Precious, why are you trying to hurt yourself?"

"Because I'm not precious. Not to anyone. My boyfriend uses me all the time, and when I refuse he says, 'Remember, Marlie, you owe me.'"

"Owe him?" I repeated, not wanting to believe I had heard correctly.

She nodded. I held her tighter.

"Marlie, we're going to get you help."

Jarred from restless sleep, I realized this conversation was a dream, not real time! Yet, I could not shake Marlie's words or the image of Marlie's devastated face. She reminded me so much of another sick student. Was it possible God was revealing to me in a dream the actual nightmare some of my students face when confronted by something or someone too evil or too powerful to resist?

Today, Lord, open my sleepy eyes to see, hear, and help those whose dreams are being derailed or whose nightmares are all too real. Show me how to share Your dream for them.

IMPORTANT DREAMS

"I have no greater joy than to hear that my children
are walking in the truth."

3 John 4

"*I* have a dream!"

No matter where you hear those words, you probably think of Martin Luther King Jr. and his famous speech on the steps of the Lincoln Memorial. His dream was to end racism in the United States, and he was passionate about it. And even though his speech was over five decades ago, it is still identifiable by many in this country.

Everyone has dreams of things they would like to see happen one day. Some people dream to be Olympians. Others want to be movie stars. Many have simpler dreams—to own a home, to go to college, to see their children marry and have children.

Dreams in this sense are good because they give you goals to strive for and the determination to make them happen.

Every Christian mother and father share the same dream—to see their children come to faith in Jesus and have eternal life. Even while the child is still in the womb, mothers and fathers are praying for their salvation.

When was the last time you prayed one of your dreams for your children? If you pray daily for them, you are to be commended. If you don't, today is not too late to start. Ask God to bring your children to know Him and love Him. Ask Him to let your life be a vehicle of His love to your children.

GOD SPEAKS TO US IN OUR SLEEP

*"For God does speak—now one way, now another—though man
may not perceive it. In a dream, in a vision of the night,
when deep sleep falls on men as they slumber in their beds."*
Job 33:14–15

"Let not your heart be troubled." I heard the words of Christ clearly in my mind as I slept. But the voice I "heard" was of a former pastor who had given me excellent counsel regarding some relational challenges. In my dream, God had spoken through this pastor to comfort and reassure me.

A few times in my life God used dreams to get my attention or help me understand something. Although occasionally dreams can be troubling or mysterious (especially when I eat ice cream too close to bedtime!), I try to make sure to heed any warning they might offer, even if it is just the ice cream talking. Prayer is always a proper response.

In the Bible, we read about Jesus' earthly father's dreams, which God used to tell Joseph of impending danger. Yet more often, when I'm certain my dreams come from God, I feel honored and awed, comforted and challenged, inspired and refreshed. For example, dreams of my precious daddy after his "promotion" to heaven felt like a gift God sent me to help heal my heart.

Next time you have a dream you believe God sent to tell you something, simply ask Him to help you understand its meaning and know what you need to do in response.

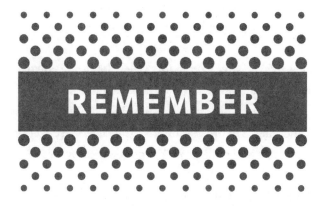

REMEMBER

*M*emories are important. But so are the things that should be remembered from day to day. What is the fondest memory in your childhood memory bank? What things bless you as you remember them from day to day? All are important. Treasure every memory. And never forget the One who gave you those memories.

YOU ARE NOT DEFINED BY . . .

"Your beauty should not come from outward adornment. . . .
Rather, it should be that of your inner self, the unfading beauty
of a gentle and quiet spirit, which is of great worth in God's sight."
1 Peter 3:3–4 NIV (2011)

*M*egan watched Miss Colorado, Kelley Johnson, emerge on the Miss America stage in her nurse's scrubs, telling the story of Joe, an Alzheimer's patient who suffered from night terrors. One night she found Joe crying. His frustration and fear led Nurse Kelley to say, "Joe, I know this is hard. But you are not defined by this disease. You are still Joe."

Although Nurse Kelley did not win the Miss America pageant, her speech took first place in many hearts and minds. One of those was Megan's.

Megan decided to write her own speech about what defines a person. She had signed up for Public Speaking because she wanted to overcome her fear of talking in front of others. Now was her chance.

"Have you ever felt judged by what you wear?" Megan began. "As you walk around this school, you may notice some people wear designer shirts, some carry Coach bags, and some sport Gucci shoes. Remember: You are not defined by what you wear, but who you are on the inside. God made each of us different for a reason." With her classmates' applause ringing in her ears, Megan sat down smiling. She would no longer be defined by nervousness!

Is there some limiting label you need to let go of in defining yourself or others?

A SCROLL OF REMEMBRANCE

"Then those who feared the LORD talked with each other,
and the LORD listened and heard. A scroll of remembrance
was written in his presence concerning those
who feared the LORD and honored his name."
Malachi 3:16

Calendars, alarms, texts, and e-mails remind of us important scheduled events. Bank statements and credit card or debit alerts inform us of our financial status. Of course, these tools assist in organization and budgeting, but even so, our in-boxes become flooded with a constant barrage of overwhelming information. It is not possible to process or act on it all, even when your primary goal and desire is to serve the Lord responsibly with your time and resources. Soon we find ourselves grumbling we simply do not have enough. We think others have it easier and wonder why. Yet as we know, complaining and comparing rarely resolve anything.

So, how do we regain the right perspective?

Malachi 3 offers a solution. First, of course, God requires our tithes and offerings, not because He needs them, but because He wants us to acknowledge Him as the Source of our ability to earn income and to trust Him to provide. If every time we made out our check to the church, we also updated our "scroll of remembrance" (or prayer journal) for the blessings since our last tithe, no doubt our awe of God's miraculous provision would increase exponentially. Even better is knowing that our names are written on His scroll of remembrance as those who fear and honor Him.

SWEET MEMORIES

"I will remember the deeds of the LORD;
yes, I will remember your miracles of long ago."
Psalm 77:11

Pauline sat in the closet floor packing her grandmother's things. It had been almost a year since Grandmother died, but she and her sister just now felt they were ready to pack up things she would never need again.

Pauline pulled a light blue bed jacket out of the bottom drawer. She lifted it toward the box and then brought it back to her nose. "Ah, smell that," she said to her sister, Lou.

She sniffed a few times and then handed the jacket to Pauline.

"Ummm, I smell it too. Funny how just a whiff of something brings back so many memories."

"Yeah, I'll never forget this powder smell. Grandmother smothered us with that powder puff and powder went all over the bathroom."

"And I sneezed half the night after one of those sessions. Remember that?"

"How could I forget? You kept me up."

The sisters' banter lifted their spirits as they continued cleaning and reminiscing about their grandmother. Almost everything they pulled out of the drawer brought on another story.

The girls traveled down memory lane because they had spent time with their grandmother and with each other. Thoughts of time together were special treasures.

Time with God can be that way as well. What triggers a memory of special times with God? Think about those memories and enjoy them today. Or better yet, make a new one!

PERFECT SUNSET

"For the Spirit God gave us does not make us timid,
but gives us power, love and self-discipline."
2 Timothy 1:7 NIV (2011)

Rob and his son, Clark, hiked to see the sunset. They were going through the woods to a hilly clearing. They found an old fallen tree. They climbed over it. A little farther they encountered a tree fallen against another tree. They went under it. Rob went ahead through the thick brush and pulled the briars back.

They settled on a big rock in the clearing. The sunset was the most brilliant either had seen. They sat in silence until it was gone.

Starting home, it was almost dark. Little by little they made their way. First the tree against the tree. Rob remembered the direction from whence they had come. Holding Clark's hand, Rob led him through the briars without getting scratched. They stopped.

"Dad, which way now?"

"Shouldn't be too far to the fallen tree. I remember it was that way."

Soon the distant lights of home shone and they quickened their steps. Before long they were telling the family of their adventures.

"And Dad walked through the dark woods and remembered every turn and every downed tree."

Life's obstacles are that way. The first time you encounter them, you have to figure out how to overcome them. Then if you encounter the same problems again, you overcome them and move on.

If you pay attention to God's lessons, you will learn how to face similar situations with confidence.

HIDING HIS WORD

"I have hidden your word in my heart
that I might not sin against you."
Psalm 119:11

*W*orship was sweet. Preparing to sit down after the last song, I noticed the quarterly on the pew in front of me. Across the back in big block letters it read: "You remember 30 percent of what you hear and 70 percent of what you see and write."

Whoa! There's a big difference there. And it's true! If I want to really remember something, either a story or a name or a fact, I will do best if I write it down. On our annual mission trip, I kept a pad and pen around my neck to write down specific needs of the missionaries. If I want to remember a passage of Scripture the best thing to do is to get a piece of paper and sit down and copy it. So the statistic on the quarterly made sense.

Our Creator knew that important things needed to be written down for us so we could remember them. He gave us an entire book of unchangeable truth to read over and over again. And if we continue to read His Word, those truths will become entrenched in our hearts.

If we read passages of the Bible over and over again, we will memorize them with very little effort. Hiding God's Word in our hearts not only blesses us upon remembrance but fortifies us for difficult days.

Start today and memorize a verse each week!

RESPECT

Respect is not demonstrated as openly or often as in decades past. But it is more important than ever to respect our parents, our elders, our friends, each other, and our Lord. One who respects others will respect himself or herself as the treasure God created.

RESPECT REDEEMED

"Boaz replied, 'I've been told all about what you have done for
your mother-in-law since the death of your husband—how you left
your father and mother and your homeland and came to live with
a people you did not know before. May the LORD repay you for what
you have done. May you be richly rewarded by the LORD.'"

Ruth 2:11–12

The book of Ruth resonates with respect. Ruth respected her mother-in-law and because of her noble actions, earned the respect of Boaz as well as her new neighbors. It didn't matter that she was a foreigner. What mattered was how she conducted herself and what choices she made.

When Ruth followed Naomi's instructions to lie at Boaz's feet and uncover them as a way of requesting him to enact his role as kinsman-redeemer, Boaz considered that an honor rather than an obligation: "This kindness is greater than that which you showed earlier: You have not run after the younger men, whether rich or poor. And now, my daughter, don't be afraid. I will do for you all you ask. All my fellow townsmen know that you are a woman of noble character" (Ruth 3:10–11). Their love story ends with a family tree with branches reaching to King David. And of course, our precious Savior was of that lineage too.

No matter who you are or who you're with, respecting others will always have redeeming value, perhaps further down the line than you will ever see.

NOW YOU CAN FINISH, GRANNY-MA

*"Stand up in the presence of the aged, show respect
for the elderly and revere your God. I am the LORD."*
Leviticus 19:32 NIV (2011)

Zan knelt by the little table where she and Granny-Ma had saved a 500-piece puzzle they had been working on together for the last several weeks. The scene depicted a deep blue Mediterranean sea, part of a sandy beach, a line of mountains in the distance, and several different hues of blue for the sky.

"This is a hard puzzle," Granny-Ma stated, rolling her wheelchair up a little closer. "Not sure I have ever taken this long to complete one."

"Yes, but you're one smart cookie," Zan replied. "You've made great progress since last time."

"I'm ready for some more help, though."

Zan pulled up a chair. "Okay. Let's see what we can do."

A short while later, the gaps in the puzzle had closed considerably. Both grandmother and granddaughter smiled with satisfaction.

"Now you can finish it, Granny-Ma."

"I'll do my best, but no promises. There's still a lot of sky left. All those blues look so much alike. I'll need your help again, I'm sure."

"Good. I like working puzzles with you."

"And I love being with my sweet granddaughter."

"Me, too. I can't wait to show you the puzzle we're going to do next!"

Today find a way to spend time with an elderly person who values your relationship. It will be time well spent for both of you.

WHAT RETURN
ARE YOU GETTING?

"The day of the LORD is near for all nations.
As you have done, it will be done to you;
your deeds will return upon your own head."
Obadiah 15

"You actually value our work, don't you?" Jay asked incredulously.

"Why wouldn't I?" I answered just as incredulously. You are fantastic writers with lots of wisdom to share."

"It's just that I've never had anyone think highly of what I say," he answered.

"You have a lot to offer."

One of my most reflective students reminded me that in a classroom, the teacher sets the tone for whether or not her students will feel acknowledged and respected as individuals with worthwhile contributions. Parents have the same responsibility in the home. Employers have the same opportunity in the workplace. Obviously, this concept is important, but I don't always get it right. Sometimes I set a negative tone by expressing dissatisfaction and frustration with my students' seeming lack of effort and interest. Either way, Obadiah is correct. My deeds and words and attitude return upon my own head. As the saying goes, you have to give respect to get respect.

Tomorrow I am going to look for the positive within each student and promote good deeds instead of berating the bad. I'm quite sure my head will be happier with the return.

Is there someone you find it difficult to respect? Ask God to help you do this in an authentic way. See the difference it makes in what comes back to you!

DADDY, DADDY!

*"The Spirit himself testifies with our spirit that
we are God's children."*

Romans 8:16

*A*lthough moms may try to encourage their babies to say "Ma-ma," most babies seem to find "Da-da" easier to say. What a thrill it is for a father to hear his baby call him "Da-da"!

One dad says, "I'll never forget the day I walked in the door and my child left his toys, jumping up and down, yelling 'Da-da!' Brent clapped his hands, and then reached out for me to pick him up! After a big hug, I set him back down, and he danced around the living room for another five minutes, still saying 'Da-da, Da-da'! I loved it."

As children grow, they may change the names they call their dads. Beginning with "Da-da," most children change to "Daddy" soon. After several years, they may shorten to "Dad," and then later change to "Dads," "Daddy-O," "Pops," or another popular epithet like "the Dad-ster!" In adolescence they may choose other nicknames, experimenting with their dad's given name or another adult name. However, most adult children revert to "Daddy" to show their respect for a good dad.

We don't always think of calling God our "Daddy." But He is our heavenly Father and wants us to love and respect Him just as we would our earthly fathers. He loves it when we recognize His presence and acknowledge that we love Him by our outward cries of "Daddy, Abba, Father!"

Spend some time with your heavenly Daddy today!

RENEWED RESPECT

"LORD, I have heard of your fame; I stand in awe of your deeds,
O LORD. Renew them in our day."

Habakkuk 3:2

The introduction to the book of Habakkuk states that the prophet wrote during a bewildering time of religious and moral crisis. Accordingly, Habakkuk offers prayers sounding more like distress signals. Then God's replies depict the coming justice of the wicked, dire warnings to evildoers, and the worthlessness of man-made idols. God assures Habakkuk that all His revelations will prove true at the appointed time and reminds him, "the righteous will live by his faith" (Habakkuk 2:4). Though the Bible defines faith as the evidence of things not seen, a time will come when the evidence is so clear and so pervasive, no one can miss it: "For the earth will be filled with the knowledge of the glory of the LORD, as the waters cover the sea," God promises in Habakkuk 2:14.

Although these proclamations don't change anything right away, they bring comfort to Habakkuk and remind him God is still sovereign, and one day all will be well. At that point, Habakkuk begins to rehearse an entire catalog of God's awe-inspiring deeds he has either heard of or witnessed for himself. Then he asks for an encore.

Next time you get discouraged, distressed, or bewildered by bad things happening around, remind God of your respect for His awesome past deeds and ask Him for an encore. Then get ready to applaud! He is still on the throne.

LAUGH

*N*othing is better for you than a good laugh. It not only helps your body physically but also is mentally refreshing. God even states in His Word that a merry heart is good medicine. Why not take a dose this week?

WHAT'S SO FUNNY?

"A happy heart makes the face cheerful,
but heartache crushes the spirit."
Proverbs 15:13

Three-year-old Kallie Rae and eighteen-month-old Brinn sat in the backseat of the car. Their dad was driving them to their grandmother's house to spend the night. Both girls screamed at the top of their lungs, seemingly unhappy about everything. They were well-fed, clean, dry, and safely buckled in their car seats with no apparent reason for their distress.

"I'm glad they are spending the night out," Dad said to Mom as they got closer to their destination.

"Me, too. Not sure I would want to listen to that all night."

About that time one of the girls stopped screaming and made a loud, new noise. Both began to laugh and laughed continuously until they got to Grandma's house.

What started out to be a hard trip to Grandma's changed to an exciting event once everyone in the car focused on the merriment instead of the screaming.

Even though these little girls had no idea what they were doing, they were practicing a scriptural principle above. The face cannot be truly cheerful unless the heart is happy. In a spontaneous switch from a negative spirit to a happy heart, Kallie Rae and Brinn had changed the entire atmosphere in the car and family.

Are there times when you have to remind yourself that what shows on your face comes from inside? Truly, a cheerful face is the result of a happy heart, a heart that overflows with God's love.

GREAT NEW RECIPE

"A cheerful heart is good medicine,
but a crushed spirit dries up the bones."
Proverbs 17:22

"Mom, this is really, really good."

"Yeah, Mom, you've never made this recipe before. What's it called?"

Paulette's family gathered around the table with spoons in hand. Some had already dipped into the pan in front of them. Some even used their fingers to dish up the new concoction.

"What is this creamy stuff in the middle? It's amazing! I've never tasted anything so good."

Paulette had been silent as long as she could stand it. She began to laugh.

"What's so funny?"

"It's a new recipe. Obviously I haven't perfected it yet! This is my second attempt. My first chocolate pound cake flopped terribly. Number three is in the oven. "

"Oh, good. We get more."

"No, you don't," Paulette said. "The first one went in the trash can."

"You threw one of these away?"

"Yes. The third will surely be better."

"Mom, this is the best thing you've ever cooked. If the third one turns out like this, you'll be the hit of the Sunday school class social. Just give it a fancy name and spoon it out into cute glasses with a little garnish. Everyone will love it!"

The family enjoyed a good laugh together as they devoured Chocolate Pound Cake Number Two.

Paulette was a perfectionist even in her baking endeavors and didn't like do-overs. However, from the reaction of her family, perfection was not a prerequisite for acceptance of this new recipe.

TURKEY TROUBLE

"Watch out that you do not lose what you have worked for,
but that you may be rewarded fully."

2 John 8

For weeks, my family and I dreamed and drooled about the fresh young turkey we ordered for Thanksgiving. The online reviews and description made our mouths water: raised in Pennsylvania's Amish country; fed a vegetarian diet; guaranteed unmatched taste and tenderness. This turkey sounded foolproof! And it was, until I did something foolish.

But first, I followed the baking directions precisely, and the beautiful Amish turkey emerged from our oven golden brown and incredibly tender and tasty. We carved enough for our first Thanksgiving feast and then afterward, I shooed everyone out of the kitchen so I could put away leftovers and pick the rest of the meat off the bone. After painstaking plucking, I wrapped tinfoil around the platter, set the bones aside to boil for broth, and stuffed the platter into the refrigerator in what seemed a secure spot. Yet seconds after closing the refrigerator door, it popped open again and the platter clattered to the floor. Our beautiful Amish turkey from Pennsylvania spread his wings a final time.

Fiasco? Disaster?

No, sympathy and laughter!

My family found me sprawled in the floor, looking and feeling ridiculous, trying to rake up the turkey. No one fussed or blamed me for the accident. They just expressed their regrets, then laughed along with me.

Next time something you worked hard for has an epic fail, don't get gobbled up by shame or regret; try responding with laughter.

LAUGHTER IN THE LATRINE

*"They demolished the sacred stone of Baal
and tore down the temple of Baal,
and people have used it for a latrine to this day."*
2 Kings 10:27

$\mathcal{T}$ypically, bathroom humor is off-limits in polite conversation, but for some reason, a bit of latrine levity is included in the account of the destruction of the Baal temple and all its ministers. Of course, Jehu, son of Jehoshaphat and newly appointed king of Israel, probably did not find it funny when informed of his job description by the prophet who anointed him: "You are to destroy the house of Ahab your master, and I will avenge the blood of my servants the prophets and the blood of all the LORD's servants shed by Jezebel" (2 Kings 9:7).

Instead, he took his new responsibility seriously and took care of God's business with military cunning and precision. Once Baal worship was destroyed in Israel, the structure once used for worshiping Baal turned into a bathroom. I don't know about you, but I find that somewhat humorous. Perhaps it is just the unexpected mention of a latrine in the same sentence as that of a temple. Perhaps it's the kind of nervous laughter that comes after you have been holding your breath to see what was going to happen in a very tense situation. Or just maybe the writer, traditionally held by the Jews to be the prophet Jeremiah, was putting a "So, there!" kind of pronouncement on the former site of Baal worship to show how detestable this practice was to God. Looks like this kind of bathroom humor just might be okay after all.

HUSH WHEN YOU'VE SAID ENOUGH

*"Do not be quick with your mouth, do not be hasty in your heart
to utter anything before God. God is in heaven
and you are on earth, so let your words be few."*
Ecclesiastes 5:2

Scheduled to speak in two short hours, I found it laughable that I was still unsure of my presentation. When I accepted the engagement months prior, I thought I would have ample time. I had my PowerPoint and my notes, but I had not practiced. Nervously, I made my way to the breakfast area. There I heard an elderly gentleman laughing out loud and blessing the Lord for his wife's birthday and for what she meant to him. When he got up for coffee, I made my way to her table.

"Ma'am, I overheard your husband's laughter and his blessing. I realized you must be Christians, so I wanted to ask for your prayers. I'm speaking to a group of future educators and want to say only what God wants me to say—no more, no less."

"Oh, honey, I got you covered. I will pray. Here's a quote to help you: 'Lord, fill my mouth with worthwhile stuff and nudge me when I've said enough.'"

I smiled, realizing I could trust God to fill my mouth and to help me hush! The event went beautifully in spite of noisy construction work going on beneath. In fact, I laughed when my remarks were punctuated by the sounds of hammers and drills. Thanks to my breakfast buddy, they were also punctuated by God's grace!

Lord, teach me to trust You enough to laugh at myself and my circumstances.

The first thing that comes to mind when you see the word *stop* is a red octagon. But when applied to our lives, the word *stop* can create good boundaries and foster freedom. Ponder the stop signs in your life, or the lack of them.

IT'S OKAY TO REST

"Be still, and know that I am God."
Psalm 46:10

We live in a world where DOING trumps BEING. Insufficient rest results in ravaged relationships. Health heads downhill when the pace is too fast too long. God does not mean us to be rushed and frazzled. He promises His yoke is easy and His burden light. Yet some never seem to receive or act on that promise.

Jimmy worked the same job thirty-five years, never taking an entire week off since his honeymoon three decades earlier. His work phone was a permanent appendage, requiring him to respond to emergency maintenance requests 24/7. In addition, he was primary caretaker for his elderly uncle. What little "free" time he had, Jimmy used to maintain Uncle James's yards and home as well as his own.

On his sixtieth birthday, Jimmy's wife informed him that instead of presents or a party, she had reserved a week at the beach.

"I can't take a whole week," he protested.

"Why not?"

"Can't stay away from work that long. Something would blow up. Can't stay away from Uncle James that long, either. He'd go crazy."

"Then we'll take two cars, just in case. But we're still planning for a week. A man ought to be able to take a week's vacation every thirty years."

As it turned out, Jimmy and his family drove one car and stayed all week. Clearing the calendar created some much-needed calm and quality family time. They learned that it's really okay to rest. After all, it was God's idea!

GIVE THANKS FOR
THE STOP SIGNS

"For my thoughts are not your thoughts,
neither are your ways my ways, declares the LORD."
Isaiah 55:8

Why do we get stuck with jobs, obligations, or relationships that are NOT good for us? How do we get unstuck? Sometimes it seems we have no choice. Yet if we don't choose to change unhealthy habits, reestablish our priorities, or say good-bye when advisable, God may just do it for us. He really does know what's best, even if it does not make sense to us.

Caleb had difficulty understanding why his girlfriend all of a sudden was pushing to get married. Things had been going pretty well until he said he wasn't ready for a more permanent commitment. Consequently, Ellen broke up with him. Not long after, he was terminated from his job and had no choice but to leave the area and head back home. How had things become so unstable so fast?

Was this just a streak of bad luck, or was God intervening in his life to work His perfect will? Time would tell.

Sooner or later, everyone encounters uncertain times or unforeseen circumstances that make it seem like life is spinning out of control. But since nothing takes God by surprise, we can rest assured He has a plan even when our own plans are thwarted. So, even though it's hard, give thanks for the stop signs. And while you are "stopped," look and listen for what you might need to learn.

REVERSE THE CURSE

"If anything is excellent or praiseworthy—think about such things."
Philippians 4:8

*O*ur natural tendency, when hurt by someone's words or actions, is to replay the ugly scene over and over again in our minds. Often, seeking sympathy or reassurance, we share with someone we trust what has transpired. We probably pray about the matter as well. Then what?

STOP! That's what.

Stop nursing it. Stop cursing it. Stop rehearsing it. START reversing it.

How?

Luke 6:27–28 points the way: "Love your enemies, do good to those who hate you, bless those who curse you, pray for those who mistreat you."

When we choose to love, bless, and pray for those who have done us wrong, we reverse the damaging effects of their unkind words or actions. Love builds up what hatred destroys. Blessings overpower curses. These are supernatural remedies that require humility and dependence on the Holy Spirit to empower and enable.

Try it. Refuse to mull over someone else's mistakes, misdeeds, or misspoken words. Stop trying to fix that person. It's not your job.

Instead, choose to bless. Choose to pray for those who hurt you. We can activate good deeds. And we can STOP thinking about negative things by replacing them with positives.

Controlling our thoughts and actions demands discipline, but the payoff brings priceless peace that cannot be purchased. It is far too valuable.

Try this today: "Don't nurse it; don't curse it; and don't rehearse it. Just reverse it."

START SOONER; GO SLOWER

"Those who hope in the LORD will renew their strength. . . .
they will run and not grow weary, they will walk and not be faint."
Isaiah 40:31

Some of my mom's best advice was to "Start sooner and go slower." I need to follow it more often. Thankfully, I have gotten better at starting sooner. Now I need to go slower too. Family members comment about how out-of-breath I sound and how fatigued I look.

Some of my students phrase it more euphemistically. Brittany said she knew "important people" were busy. Courtney said I looked like a hummingbird, flitting back and forth. These are not compliments, but warning signs.

Late for a conference meeting, I careened down a two-lane road and saw a construction worker frantically waving a "SLOW" sign. The look in his eyes as I skidded to a stop jolted me to my senses. I vowed to pay more attention and start sooner so I could go slower. After all, I could have endangered his life by my haste.

Even if I do not actually hurt someone physically, I might wound them with thoughtless words or actions because of my hurrying. Recently, my husband injured his knee and as a result, hobbled along for several weeks. One Sunday, late for church, I called to Pat: "Hurry up! Limp faster." Hardly the way to set the stage for worship, right?

Starting today, I want to make a deliberate decision to stop hurrying by starting sooner and going slower. How about you?

TIME TO STOP

"This is what the Sovereign LORD, the Holy One of Israel, says:
'In repentance and rest is your salvation,
in quietness and trust is your strength.'"
Isaiah 30:15

When someone asks you to do one more thing, STOP! Evaluate its cost in time away from the people you love or things you find restorative.

When your conversation is getting nowhere and the person you are talking to remains unreasonable, STOP! Think about who is the unreasonable one if you keep talking in circles and rehashing what you cannot agree on. Stop arguing, quietly intercede in prayer, and ask God to confirm the truth.

When you have overextended yourself, STOP! Rest. Instead of reaching for a sugary snack, reach for your pillow and take a nap. Or reach for your tennis shoes to walk off some stress.

When you've done the best you can with what you have to work with, STOP! You can plan to make it better next time, but there's no need to fret about what went wrong. My friend Naomi offers this reminder of how to resist regret: "All I can do is all I can do and all I can do is enough!"

Thinking you have to do more or have to prove yourself right all the time is not healthy. STOP!

Today ask the Lord to help you stop whatever thoughts or habits are keeping you from sound sleep, sound reasoning, or sound judgment. Rest in Him and then leave the rest to Him.

SING

*M*usic is one of the greatest connecting points we have to God. When we sing as an expression of the love we have in our hearts for Him, He is blessed. Why not see how many ways you can bless God and others with a few notes of praise this week?

SINGING A BLESSING

"The LORD your God is with you, the Mighty Warrior who saves.
He will take great delight in you; in his love he will no longer
rebuke you, but will rejoice over you with singing."
Zephaniah 3:17 NIV (2011)

The Bible doesn't specifically state that Mary sang and rocked Jesus to sleep. But my guess is that she did! No mother can forget the joy she experiences when she rocks her baby to sleep.

There are probably plenty of mothers who, long after their babies are asleep, continue to rock and sing. Singing praise songs and choruses that include the baby's name are another form of blessing your child as you pour out your love to him or her. The motion of rocking is calming and not only lulls the baby to sleep but also puts Mommy in a state of relaxation and joy because she is in a state of such closeness and peace.

Have you ever thought about God singing blessings over you? Can you imagine yourself sitting in His lap and just resting in the peace and joy of being near to Him?

You may think you are too old to be rocked. And you may also think that your problems are too big to be sung away. Have you tried spending some time in His lap lately? He delights in you and would love to sing you back into a peaceful state. There is an empty spot ready just for you.

SWEET HARMONY

"How good and pleasant it is when
God's people live together in unity!"
Psalm 133:1 NIV (2011)

Ginny had enjoyed a fun afternoon with her four grandchildren. Now they were all buckled safely in the car for the ride home. As Ginny pulled out of the driveway, they all began to sing, loudly enough for Ginny to discern what each was singing. All had sweet voices and she loved to hear them sing. But the sounds of four voices singing four different songs in four different keys made it hard to enjoy any one of them.

The youngest child was three and sounds of "Twinkle, twinkle, little star" were easily recognized. Always in her own world, she was pretty oblivious to the other three songs. As Ginny drove on, she realized that her ten-year-old granddaughter had changed songs and was singing along with her three-year-old cousin. In just a few more blocks, Ginny heard her nine-year-old grandson change his song to "Twinkle," and in a few more blocks, the six-year old had joined in. Now there was a harmonious chorus in the backseat enjoying singing together.

The three-year-old beamed as she realized she was the leader. Ginny beamed as she had observed a tremendous act of kindness from her oldest grandchildren to the youngest. And I'm sure God was beaming seeing some of the youngest of His family combining to make harmony.

Is there somewhere in your life that you are holding on to your song when you should join in with someone else's?

WHO DO YOU HEAR?

"But if we walk in the light, as he is in the light,
we have fellowship with one another, and the blood of Jesus,
his Son, purifies us from all sin."

1 John 1:7

The older I get, the more I sound like my mother when I sing.

Mother has been in heaven for almost twenty years, and I have missed her beautiful voice beside me. I thought I would never again hear her gorgeous soprano finding just the right notes for each hymn.

But I realized last Sunday what I was hearing as I sang "Great Is Thy Faithfulness" was not my own voice but one very much like my mother's. I looked over to see if my dad noticed, but he was caught up in his own private worship.

People say when you live with someone for many years, you begin to look alike. Wonder if that's true of singing as well. Do you begin to sound like your loved one?

Perhaps that is true. But whether or not you begin to look or sing like someone, if you spend time with someone, you are bound to take on some of their characteristics.

God created man for fellowship with Him. He wants to be our best friend. But as we spend time with God, we become more like Him. As we talk with others we become His voice on earth and the love of Jesus just oozes out of us.

What do people see or hear when they are around you?

ORDERED TO SING

*"So they sang praises with gladness
and bowed their heads and worshiped."*

2 Chronicles 29:30

Often when someone in authority gives an order, the response varies from muttering, groaning, complaining, or even rolling of the eyes. But singing? How often does that happen?

King Hezekiah gave lots of orders when he began his reign in Jerusalem. He ordered the temple to be cleansed and repaired; he ordered the Levites and priests to consecrate themselves and reassume their duties; and he ordered sacrifices to be burnt. He ordered his people to gather. He ordered the Levites to gather their musical instruments and stationed them in the temple. Then he ordered singing.

Nothing exists regarding 2 Chronicles 29 that records any muttering, groaning, complaining, or rolling of the eyes in spite of the precision and diligence of the work required. Because Hezekiah confidently claimed the word of the Lord as his leadership guide, his orders were carried out quickly and precisely. Even at age twenty-five, he knew the five steps a confident leader must execute: Communication. Consecration. Congregation. Conflagration. Celebration.

Today, whether we are giving orders or taking them, let's respond like Hezekiah and his people did. Communicate clearly the priorities and steps God directs through His Word. Consecrate your body, your temple, to His service. Congregate with like-minded believers to worship. Conflagrate, or be willing to sacrifice. Celebrate! Start singing praises to your King, the Master of everything, and thank Him for the privilege of serving Him and following His orders.

MUSICAL COMFORT

"O sing to the LORD a new song,
For He has done wonderful things, His right hand
and His holy arm have gained the victory for Him."

Psalm 98:1 NASB

My granddaughters sat in the backseat. Two-year-old Mae had been babbling along happily for a while but then stopped and began to cry. At first softly but it grew into an all-out wail. The trip just became too much. Five-year-old Ellie gave her toys and her pacifier and tried to distract her in every way she could find. As the driver, I was not much help.

Then I heard Ellie begin to sing "Mama Loves You with the Love of the Lord." This was part of their bedtime ritual after prayers. Suddenly Mae's crying stopped. I glanced into the mirror to see Ellie rubbing Mae's foot, holding her hand, and singing softly into her ear. Mae responded to the soothing notes of the song and the sweet love of her sister. It wasn't long before she was asleep.

Where do you go for comfort when you are tired, upset, or feel alone? Do you ever think about just finding a quiet spot and singing praises to God? Or maybe you just need some quiet conversation, a time to pour out your feelings and thoughts to God. Whatever your method of self-comfort, I would recommend you do as Mae did. Let the sweet melodies and praise in song take you to a serene place of rest.

CELEBRATE

*H*ow do you celebrate? Do you celebrate enough? Life gives us so much to celebrate, especially when we look at all of God's beauty around us. Find something right now to celebrate and invite someone else to celebrate with you!

SOMETHING TO BRAG ABOUT

*"Therefore, as it is written:
'Let him who boasts boast in the Lord.'"*
1 Corinthians 1:31

The first faculty meeting of the year started in a positive way. Mr. Graves, our new principal, asked anyone with good news or a recent accomplishment to "brag" about it so others could know and celebrate with them. He promised every meeting would start this way.

It was fun to hear about new babies and grandchildren on the way, job promotions for adult children, recent or upcoming marriages, and of course, since it was school, improvement in test scores! Smiles and applause circled the room.

Later, the celebration continued at a larger level as our new superintendent, Mr. Blackwood, lauded the dedication and accomplishments of all district personnel and challenged them to be "all in" as they sought to reach and serve "every child, every day, whatever it takes." His assistants passed out sunglasses to each participant in the audience because, as he said, "With this kind of commitment, we'll be shining so bright, we're going to need shades."

Wouldn't it be wonderful to carry this school mandate into the spiritual realm as well? This week, as we seek to serve those in our sphere of influence, make sure to celebrate the good we find in each person. Let's go all out to be all in for what we are called to do, remembering that anything we accomplish or can brag about is because of Him. Let's shine so brightly for Jesus that those around us need shades!

CELEBRATE HIS GLORIOUS CREATION

"Ah, Sovereign LORD, you have made the heavens and the earth
by your great power and outstretched arm.
Nothing is too hard for you."
Jeremiah 32:17

Photographer Sharon Warner Brisken knows how to celebrate! Every picture she publishes reveals a masterpiece of creation and always gives glory to the Creator. In a recent post on her Facebook page, Sharon wrote: "We are so grateful! We have seen glorious sunrises and stunning sunsets, night skies filled with stars, the Milky Way, and the moon shining brightly. We have seen incredible mountains, clouds, the sea, water lilies, sunflowers, birds, creepy crawlers. . . . I am so thankful I am able to share God's glorious creation with my friends through the images I capture with my camera."

Sharon is quickly becoming a master photographer. However, she is also quick to attribute the credit for her subject matter to the One who created it. In addition, she thanks those who have helped teach her all aspects of the creative art of landscape photography.

Today, make a conscious effort to celebrate the glories of heaven and earth by venturing out into nature, perhaps pretending to be photographers who pay close attention to the lighting, the shadows, the contrasts, the contours, the textures of what we see. Give thanks to the One who provided these wonders. We can also take with us the calm and confidence that comes from observing God's creation, a constant reminder that nothing is too hard for Him! That's cause for celebration!

WE ALL NEED APPLAUSE

"Therefore encourage one another and build each other up,
just as in fact you are doing."
1 Thessalonians 5:11

*Y*esterday I pulled up to a four-way stop. As usual, I looked over to the other cars waiting at the intersection.

A minivan stopped at the corner. A lady at the wheel clapped excitedly and nodded her head, smiling into the mirror.

Once I got closer, I saw the toddler in the backseat, also smiling and laughing.

There was no clue as to exactly what the accomplishment was but it was obviously cause for celebration.

My thoughts went back to my days of having toddlers in the backseat everywhere I went. Many times I looked into the rearview mirror just to see a child point to her nose on demand, retrieve his own pacifier, play pat-a-cake, or correctly identify a dog or cat or light.

All definitely appropriate occasions for applause.

I don't remember being applauded for discovering my nose. Or learning to sit up by myself. But from the time my memory bank begins, I remember having my own personal cheering section. Whether learning to share a toy, ride a bike, climb a tree, or drive a car, Mom and Dad were there applauding. And their applause encouraged me to set my goals a little higher each time.

No matter what our age, we need a little applause every now and then. Sometimes we can even hear it from heaven.

CELEBRATE DELIVERANCE

"These days should be remembered and observed in every generation by every family, and in every province and in every city. And these days of Purim should never fail to be celebrated by the Jews—nor should the memory of these days die out among their descendants."

Esther 9:28 NIV (2011)

*P*urim celebrates the deliverance of the Jews from Haman's evil plot to exterminate them, all because one devout Jew, Mordecai, refused to bow down and pay him homage. In his egotistical rage at being ignored, Haman underhandedly sought to annihilate all Jews from the 127 provinces under King Ahasuerus's rule. Unfortunately, the king trusted Haman and failed to read the fine print before approving his decrees. In God's perfect plan and provision, Mordecai's cousin Esther was in the right "palace" at the right time. As the new queen, she had access to King Ahasuerus, but still ran the risk of losing her life if she approached him without his approval. Days of fasting and prayer preceded her bold request.

When the king held out his golden scepter to Esther and promised to grant her petition, Esther won for her people the right to protect and defend themselves against Haman's onslaught. The Jews still had to fight for their freedom, but they had the king's approval, and so were victorious. Meanwhile, Haman hung from the very gallows he had constructed with the intention of shaming Mordecai.

All of us have something from which we have been delivered by the authority of our King. Celebrate and give thanks.

CELEBRATE HIS FAITHFULNESS

"O LORD, God of Israel, there is no God like you in heaven above or on earth below—you who keep your covenant of love with your servants who continue wholeheartedly in your way."

1 Kings 8:23

After seven years, the Temple was complete. King Solomon stood before the altar and the Israelites in Jerusalem and dedicated this magnificent structure to the Lord. His prayer included supplications for God's continued mercy, care, judgment, forgiveness, rain, and assistance for those besieged by disaster or disease. Sounds like he covered everything!

Solomon not only knew how to pray, but also to whom he should give the credit. As he celebrated the completion of the Temple and the fulfillment of God's purpose and plan, Solomon did not direct attention or praise toward himself or the laborers and craftsmen who built the Temple. He celebrated God's faithfulness: "Praise be to the LORD, who has given rest to his people Israel just as he promised. Not one word has failed of all the good promises he gave through his servant Moses. May the LORD our God be with us as he was with our fathers; may he never leave us nor forsake us" (1 Kings 8:56–57).

Celebrate how God watches over those committed to Him. Praise Him for His purposes and provisions, for keeping His promises, and for allowing us the satisfaction of completing the projects He assigns us, both great and small. And don't forget to celebrate getting to rest once the job is done!

SACRIFICE

*M*any people today don't even think about the word *sacrifice*. But the things that are true sacrifices bring great joy. Think about something you could do this week that would be a sacrifice for you but that would bless someone else.

A SACRIFICE TO BE SURE

*"Gideon replied, 'If now I have found favor in your eyes, give me
a sign that it is really you talking to me. Please do not go away
until I come back and bring my offering and set it before you.'
And the LORD said, "I will wait until you return."'*

Judges 6:17–18

*I*sn't it just like God to anoint and appoint one who feels so hopeless
he's having to hide just to survive? Gideon was just such a man.

Because of the Israelites' unfaithfulness to Him, God allowed
them to be oppressed by the Midianites for seven years. Most found
shelter in mountain clefts and caves. They could not sow or reap a
crop without the Midianites invading. But when the Israelites cried
out to God, He sent a prophet to answer them and an angel to talk
to Gideon.

The angel called Gideon a "mighty warrior" and assigned him
the mission of saving Israel from the Midianites. Belonging to the
weakest clan in Israel, Gideon needed confirmation of this dialogue.
He prepared a sacrifice to make sure—meat and bread, which were
scarce during this time. When the angel's staff touched the sacrifice,
"fire flared from the rock, consuming the meat and the bread" (Judges
6:21). That's when Gideon knew he was hearing from God. He built
an altar there "and called it The LORD is Peace" (v. 24). This initial
sacrifice prepared his heart to listen.

What might we might need to sacrifice in order to be sure we are
hearing from God?

WORTHWHILE SACRIFICE

*"And walk in the way of love, just as Christ loved us and
gave himself up for us as a fragrant offering and sacrifice to God."*
Ephesians 5:2 NIV (2011)

Gladys is a big-city lawyer. If you met her, she would be the picture of success. But it wasn't always that way.

Gladys grew up in a housing project. As a little girl she was exposed to drugs, gangs, and much more. She wanted out of that life but didn't know how to get there.

One day, while Gladys was begging, a wealthy lady stopped to talk to her. The woman took an interest in the little girl and later even paid for her college tuition. When Gladys decided to go to law school, the lady again provided her tuition.

To take advantage of such a great opportunity, Gladys let her children live with relatives. Gladys slept every night in the school's conference room and ran across the street every morning to freshen up in the restroom of a restaurant.

Not exactly the way you want to attend law school. It involved tremendous sacrifice for Gladys and her children. It was also a sacrifice for the woman who believed in a little girl whom she met on the side of the street. They both knew the sacrifice would be worth it in the end, and Gladys persevered. She graduated from law school with honors.

Today Gladys, her husband, and children enjoy a wonderful life because of her sacrifice. She has a special ministry to girls who are growing up as she did, carrying forward the work of the one who chose to bless her own life.

Jesus made a tremendous sacrifice so that we could enjoy our eternal life. Thank Him.

SOMEONE ELSE'S BULL

"Then build a proper kind of altar to the LORD. . . .
Using the wood of the Asherah pole that you cut down,
offer the second bull as a burnt offering."
Judges 6:26

God commissioned Gideon to fight the fierce, merciless Midianites. Then He directed him to sacrifice something that was not even his: his father's seven-year-old bull. The Midianites had destroyed nearly all livestock, but somehow this bull had been spared. It was a valuable hunk of meat! Yet God told Gideon to take it from his father's herd, remove the Asherah pole, which was in honor of the goddess of motherhood and fertility, beside his father's altar, and build a proper altar using that wood and sacrifice that bull.

Talk about risky business! Gideon obeyed under the cover of darkness; he feared his father's wrath and that of the men in town. Rightly so. When they discovered his deed, they demanded Gideon's death. Fortunately, Dad defended Gideon. It was then "the Spirit of the LORD came upon Gideon, and he blew a trumpet, summoning the Abiezrites to follow him" (Judges 6:34). After gathering his troops, Gideon needed more reassurance that God planned to keep His promises about delivering Israel. This time he sacrificed his pride and requested the fleece test: The first night's fleece was wet with dew while all the ground was dry; the second night the fleece was dry and all the ground was wet. Now he was ready to do what God commanded.

Father, thank You for the reassurance You give when You ask us to sacrifice, even when it's someone else's bull!

UNDER HIS WINGS

"He will cover you with his feathers, and under his wings
you will find refuge; his faithfulness
will be your shield and rampart."

Psalm 91:4

Cleaning up after a large forest fire, firefighters found very few signs of life. However, when they came to the top of the hill, they sighted a large evergreen tree toppled on its side. In the top was a big nest so they walked over to the site, hoping to find signs of life.

Just a few feet from the tree they spotted a large eagle with wings spread wide. Even though the air was still, the feathers on her wings seemed to be moving. The firefighter walked over to the charred bird, stooped down, and gently lifted the feathers. There, all safe and sound, were four little eagle babies. The mother had sacrificed herself in order to save her babies. Her body protected them from being burned to death.

Sound familiar? Jesus stretched out His arms and covered you with His blood so that you might be saved from a different fire. If you are a believer, you know that the sacrifice has been made for you. You don't have to worry about what may come. You are protected by the blood of Jesus.

The sacrifice of Jesus Christ must not be taken for granted. Thank Jesus for providing eternal life for you. If you don't know Him, don't let another day go by without accepting His amazing sacrifice.

JUST NEED A FEW

"But the LORD said to Gideon, 'There are still too many men.
Take them down to the water, and I will sift them for you there.'"

Judges 7:4

*G*ideon's assigned job involved ousting Midianites who had invaded the Israelites' land "like swarms of locusts." Most likely Gideon was feeling pretty confident when he rallied 32,000 men to defeat their enemy. Yet God did not allow Israel to boast that "her own strength had saved her" (Judges 7:2). He made Gideon send away huge numbers of men until his forces dwindled from 32,000 to 300, sacrificing any advantage of manpower.

At that point, God arranged an eavesdropping session for Gideon and his servant that they might be encouraged. Sure enough, even though "the Midianites, the Amalekites and all the other eastern peoples had settled in the valley, thick as locusts" and "their camels could no more be counted than the sand on the seashore" (v. 12), God sent a dream to a Midianite. It frightened him but gave Gideon reason to worship God and call his men confidently into battle. Only he did not arm them with swords—only trumpets and jars with torches inside. Because it was God's plan and for God's glory, that's all it took. At the sound of the trumpets and the noise of the smashing jars, the Midianites killed each other with their swords.

Can we sacrifice our own "sensible" strategies when God asks us to trust Him and do things His way? May we obey and give Him all the glory.

PUSH

$\mathcal{P}$ushing often requires hard work, especially if the pushing is uphill. Is there something in your life this week that feels like an uphill battle? Keep on pushing!

DON'T GET CAUGHT
BY THE LATE BELL

"Can any one of you by worrying add a single hour to your life?"
Matthew 6:27 NIV (2011)

"*B*ye, have a great day!"

Each morning after waving good-bye to my son, I linger a moment to watch him walk down the hill to his classroom.

Most days he ambles a few feet at a time—calling to a friend, kicking a rock, watching a bug. He knows he will eventually get to his class on time. With the curb as his balance beam, he sways precariously as he tries to see how fast he can run before toppling off.

Running late one day, I reminded Jeff to go straight to his class and not dawdle along the way. I knew he needed a little extra push to make it before the door closed to his classroom. After our usual good-bye, he hurried down the hill. No stopping to kick rocks, collect leaves, balance on the curb, or chat.

Many days I, too, amble along. Distractions in my path are welcomed since I feel no urgency in my schedule. But if I am "late" or have unexpected stress—illness, unplanned emergency, concern about one of my children—I hurry to my heavenly Father.

I want to push through the door before the late bell rings.

SIN IS SIN

"For all have sinned and fall short of the glory of God."

Romans 3:23

"*I* better run," Mary said. "I've got to pick up the kids across town."

"Be careful," Gretchen said. "And don't go more than five miles an hour over the speed limit. You are usually safe there."

"Go over the speed limit?" Mary asked. "You actually drive that way?"

"It's only five miles an hour. No cop would bother with you for that!"

"Well, I never thought my pastor's wife would encourage me to step on the gas just because I was in a hurry!"

"Ha, ha," said Gretchen. "I'm a law-abiding citizen. Just a little over the limit is okay!"

With a wave Mary was out the door and in the car. She thought about the conversation with her pastor's wife. *Isn't breaking the law a sin? Even five miles an hour above the limit? In what other ways have I pushed the limit on sin?*

Have I gossiped about a friend and just told a little of the bad stuff? It's okay as long as I didn't tell all the really bad things, isn't it? And I asked the person I told to pray for her.

When my husband asked if we could have his boss over for dinner and I said, "Yes, honey, that will be wonderful," my inner attitude was not pleasing to God. Was that okay?

Have you pushed the limit of sin recently? Ask God to wipe the slate clean so you can start over.

ARE YOU READY TO FLY?

"To equip his people for works of service,
so that the body of Christ may be built up."
Ephesians 4:12 NIV (2011)

Most people have watched a bird build its nest on their porches or in a tree near a window. The mama bird works hard, back and forth, back and forth, with materials to build her nest.

Once she is satisfied, she sits on her nest and lays her eggs. And waits and waits. In fact, the entire (human) family waits anxiously for the moment they will hear the little "Cheep, cheep, cheep!"

As the baby birds grow, the next milestone, the maiden flight from the nest, is anticipated. But there is one problem. The baby birds don't know how to fly, so it is up to the mama bird to teach them.

When the day arrives, the mama bird feeds the babies their breakfast, then one by one gently pushes them from the nest. Even though they don't know how to fly, their instinct is to open their wings when they are pushed from the nest. So very quickly and with little instruction they learn they can fly.

Often God calls us to do something that we don't even know we can do. But as we are "pushed from the nest" into a new area of service, we find we are equipped with what we need to get the job done.

Do you feel inadequate for something today? Ask God to help you "fly."

PUSH ON

"As for you, brothers, never tire of doing what is right."
2 Thessalonians 3:13

Marlene, her husband, Brant, and their children were on the way to the store. With only a few things on their list, they planned a picnic at the park after the errand.

As Brant turned to cross the railroad track, the car stalled. He tried to restart it but couldn't.

"Marlene," he said, "you steer and I'll push. We can't leave the car on the tracks."

The kids cheered Brant on, but even their encouragement was not enough to budge the car. "I am not strong enough," he said.

"Maybe you could flag someone down to help," she suggested.

Another car passed by and Brant flagged him down. The driver got out to help, but even with both men pushing they were not able to move the car.

Ding ding ding! The warning train signal began to sound, and red lights flashed.

Another passerby stopped and hopped out to help. The three men pushed the car off the tracks just minutes before the locomotive whizzed by.

Brant checked on his family then turned to thank the men. But they had already gotten back in their cars and driven off. "Thank you, God, for those men who helped me push!"

Sometimes we need a friend to help us. We think we are equal to the tasks before us, but find once we get started we need a little help.

Is there someone in your life who could use a little extra push today?

PUSHED AWAY

"Forget the former things; do not dwell on the past.
See, I am doing a new thing! Now it springs up; do you not perceive it?
I am making a way in the desert and streams in the wasteland."
Isaiah 43:18–19

Sundays are special days for our family. Not long after our granddaughter Katrina was born, the family gathered for lunch. Everyone wanted a turn to hold and love on the sweet baby, including Mazie, who had just been replaced as the youngest grandchild. Mazie's little three-year-old arms wrapped around the precious baby and she smiled at Katrina sitting in her lap.

When it was Grandpa Bud's turn to hold Katrina, he sat on the couch and cradled the baby in his arms. When Mazie saw this, she climbed up on Grandpa's other knee. It looked like she just wanted to stay as close to Katrina as she could. However, she reached out and pushed Katrina and said, "Give him back." Mazie didn't want to share "her" grandfather with anyone. She felt he belonged to only her!

Have you ever had a relationship with someone and you really did not want anyone else intruding in that relationship? Did you try to push the intruder away? Perhaps even in your relationship with God you have felt possessive.

We can be secure knowing that God loves us so much and there is enough love to go around for everyone. You may find that by letting God love someone through you, your relationship with Him is strengthened.

HOPE

$\mathcal{W}$e are the most blessed of all people because whatever happens in our lives, we have hope. If you have forgotten about that, stop today and ask God to restore your hope.

THE BEST HOPE OF ALL

*"Now faith is confidence in what we hope for
and assurance about what we do not see."*
Hebrews 11:1 NIV (2011)

Joy sat on the porch with her head down. She tried to pray but couldn't seem to conjure up any words. She clung to her Bible, knowing that the answer to her despair was in those pages.

"Joy, you have a kidney condition. It could stay as is for years or not. My best prognosis is that you will need a transplant within five years." At the doctor's words, Joy felt her life was over despite the doctor's assurance that kidney transplants were highly successful.

Lord, she prayed, *I know You know what is best. But what about my family? What about my precious grandchildren? I want to see them grow up, get married, and have children. Is that too much to ask?*

Ever so gently God began to speak to Joy's heart. She heard Him almost audibly. "Joy, don't you trust Me? Don't you know if I take you to heaven with Me, it will be even better than being with your grandchildren? That is the hope I gave you when you accepted Me into your life."

"Oh, God, I'm sorry," Joy said, tears flowing. "I know that. It is really hard to believe there is anything better than grandchildren. But I do trust You. And I know that without You I would have no hope at all. Help me to rest in the hope that You know best."

Do you need to cling to the hope of heaven? Or do you know someone who does? Jesus is our hope in every situation.

HOPE FOR SUFFICIENT COURAGE

"I eagerly expect and hope that I will in no way be ashamed,
but will have sufficient courage so that now as always
Christ will be exalted in my body, whether by life or by death.
For to me, to live is Christ and to die is gain."
Philippians 1:20–21

The e-mail pleaded for prayer. Terrorist groups targeted another town, terrorizing Christian families and killing children in their parents' presence. Missionaries serving in this area asked not that they be spared, but for the courage and ability to comfort those parents and when necessary, to be martyred themselves. What a prayer request! It makes my own concerns seem so silly.

Paul must have experienced some of those feelings when writing to the Philippians from his Roman prison. Yet he determined that good would come from his situation, regardless of whether he lived or died. Because of his chains, he believed "most of the brothers in the Lord have been encouraged to speak the word of God more courageously and fearlessly" (Philippians 1:14). Sounds unnatural that watching someone suffer for his faith could increase another's courage, doesn't it?

How do we keep hope alive in dire situations? Paul provides the answer in Philippians 1:19: "For I know that through your prayers and the help given by the Spirit of Jesus Christ, what has happened to me will turn out for my deliverance." Today let's pray for the courage and deliverance of those trapped in scary situations because of their faith and the ability to hope and trust in God's plan whatever we might face.

THE RICHEST HOPE OF ALL

"Command those who are rich in this present world not to be
arrogant nor to put their hope in wealth, which is so uncertain,
but to put their hope in God, who richly provides us
with everything for our enjoyment."

1 Timothy 6:17

"I don't know what I'm going to do," Gwen confided. "I can't pay bills or my car payment. Looks like I'll have to borrow more money on my son's student loans."

"That's scary," Sally responded. "But we know God doesn't want you in more debt. Let's pray and brainstorm about cutting expenses or increasing your income."

"I hope you've got some ideas. I'm out. I've filled out so many applications in the last few months, I could do them in my sleep."

Gwen was in a tough place financially. Consequently, her faith was being tested. As a single parent, she struggled to keep her family clothed and fed, but she knew God could and would "richly provide." It just seemed He was holding out!

With a humble, obedient spirit, Gwen determined she would keep the job she had while waiting and hoping for something more lucrative. "I Surrender All" became her theme song. All day long, she claimed God's promises: "Evening, morning and noon I cry out in distress, and he hears my voice. . . . Cast your cares on the LORD and he will sustain you; he will never let the righteous fall" (Psalm 55:17, 22).

Though not yet rich in money, she could still be rich in hope!

HOPE OVERFLOWING

"May the God of hope fill you with all joy and peace
as you trust in him, so that you may overflow
with hope by the power of the Holy Spirit."
Romans 15:13

Debbie is an ordinary woman whose life radiates Christ in extraordinary ways. Though she and husband, Mickey, released their precious Hannah to the Host of Heaven many years ago, they still minister to others who are hurting in order to give them hope. On the Hannah's Hope Ministries website, Deb shares an entry from her prayer journal: *Oh, Jesus, before I went to bed last night I walked outside and looked up at the night sky and the splendor of the moonlight. And from that moonlight You reminded me once again—as You do every night when the moon is shining brightly—of the night You drew me outside, showed me the full moon encircled perfectly by a rainbow, and spoke so clearly to me that Hannah was in the center of Your will for her life—so weak—so frail!*

The entire Sobeski family has committed to asking God to bring beauty from the ashes of their earthly loss in order to give Him glory and help others find heavenly hope. Oh, that we, too, would invite God to fill us with joy and peace so that in spite of our circumstances, we may overflow with hope by the power of the Holy Spirit.

AN OPEN DOOR

"These are the words of him who is holy and true, who holds
the key of David. What he opens no one can shut,
and what he shuts no one can open. I know your deeds.
See, I have placed before you an open door that no one can shut."
Revelation 3:7–8

When a skydiver steps to the open door of the airborne plane, he may wish, momentarily, for the safety of a shut door. Yet, in order to experience the rush of adrenaline and thrill of freefalling through the atmosphere, he has to emerge through that door. Of course, for the first-timer, an experienced skydiver jumping in tandem with the beginner offers a significant sense of security. That person serves as living proof that the jump is likely to end safely. Naturally, prayers to that effect certainly can't hurt, either.

Most Christians realize how significant prayer is for opening closed doors or shutting open doors. Consistent, faith-filled, fortified prayer works in tandem with the One who is holy and true, the One who has the power to open and shut whatever is necessary to accomplish His perfect will, the One who serves as a guide and assurance that because He lives, there is always love, faith, and hope.

So what are you waiting for? Take the faith leap and hold on tight to your tandem partner!

FIGHT

There are times when this word has a negative connotation. But it doesn't have to be that way. There are many things in the world that are worth fighting, for so stand your ground. Put on the armor of God and stand firm for what is right.

RETURN TO THE WALL

"'Don't be afraid of them. Remember the LORD, who is great
and awesome, and fight for your brothers, your sons
and your daughters, your wives and your homes.'
When our enemies heard that we were aware of their plot
and that God had frustrated it,
we all returned to the wall, each to his own work."
Nehemiah 4:14–15

Sometimes the enemy singles out a family, school, or community on which to concentrate his assaults. This becomes evident through a dark sense of oppression or depression, or a series of mishaps or evil deeds takes place. Frank Peretti's bestseller, *Piercing the Darkness,* made this kind of spiritual warfare real to me. Along that time, a friend named Charlene taught me how to pray against the unseen adversary. She reminded me Satan has no authority over my home, my yard, my family, or any other person or place dedicated to the service of Christ. Praying in the powerful name of Jesus becomes even more essential when fighting against the powers of darkness.

Just as in Nehemiah's day, as soon as the enemy knows we are aware of his plot, and that we have called on our mighty and awesome God to deliver us, he will usually turn and run, knowing his plan has been thwarted.

God is aware of the conflict and committed to fighting for you and your family; you can "return to the wall," get back to work, secure in His love and protection. What a mighty God we serve!

MINDING HIS OWN BUSINESS

"Be strong and courageous. Do not be afraid or discouraged
because of the king of Assyria and the vast army with him. . . .
With him is only the arm of flesh, but with us is the LORD our God."
2 Chronicles 32:7–8

"*He's* just asking for trouble" is commonly used to describe someone who seemingly creates strife or conflict. But there are times when trouble comes with no provocation. The person being attacked may be minding his own business.

This was the case for King Hezekiah, who was not only minding his own business, but "doing what was good and right and faithful before the LORD his God." (2 Chronicles 31:20). Yet immediately after this report, the king of Assyria invaded. With his threats, intimidation tactics, boasts, and insults, Sennacherib apparently expected to unnerve Hezekiah and the people of Judah before he attacked.

Hezekiah's response? He consulted his officials, blocked the enemy's water supply, rebuilt broken sections of the wall surrounding Jerusalem, and appointed military officers to protect the city. And he prayed, right alongside the prophet Isaiah. Though physically prepared, Hezekiah realized he was fighting a spiritual battle as well.

The end result? Not only did God save Hezekiah and his people from the Assyrian king, but also "from the hand of all others. He took care of them on every side" (32:22). They didn't even have to swing a sword.

When facing a battle you did not initiate, take heart. Prepare all you can, but trust God to do the fighting.

LINE UP, SHEEP!

*"He is my loving God and my fortress,
my stronghold and my deliverer, my shield,
in whom I take refuge, who subdues peoples under me."*

Psalm 144:2

"How did it go today in fourth block?" Carolyn asked.

"Much better. They paid attention, followed directions, and actually tried."

"I knew it. That spirit is broken. Those sheep are going to line up!"

Carolyn had been praying for a difficult class where several students were more interested in each other's attention than in paying attention to their frustrated, beleaguered teacher—me! Carolyn shared a radio mini-sermon where the pastor had once been a shepherd.

She recalled the pastor's words: "You can have a thousand sheep to care for, but if you can get just one of them to line up properly, the others will follow." My precious friend told me she was praying for my unruly "sheep" daily at two o'clock: "I pray and say, 'Line up, sheep. It's time to line up!'"

Sure enough, after a couple of weeks of Carolyn's prayer, along with my claiming the battle song of Psalm 144:2 for "subduing my people under me," things were better. Jeremy stopped clowning around; Eddie actually tried to complete his work; Billy spoke kindly instead of condescendingly. Some days we even laughed together. I even dared to take my "sheep" outside for some fresh air and a quick break from their studies.

Perhaps you could try this fight strategy for whatever seems out of control for you: "Line up, sheep! Sheep, line up!"

FORTIFIED FOR FIGHTING

"Praise be to the LORD my Rock,
who trains my hands for war, my fingers for battle.

Psalm 144:1

*H*ave you ever really pictured yourself as a soldier? Not necessarily one participating in a physical battle, but how about a spiritual one? In her book *Prayer and Spiritual Warfare*, Dr. Amilliah Kenya instructs Christians how to develop and implement the trained soldier's qualities of endurance, efficiency, and effectiveness in order to gain victory over the unseen, but very real, enemy. She parallels the intense physical training required of a soldier with that of those doing daily battle for Christ. With powerful examples of irresistible Christian love and fervent prayer, Amilliah encourages us to utilize God's Word as our chief weapon of warfare. Dr. Kenya writes: "The Word of God is the most powerful weapon ever known to change man . . . that formidable artillery so efficacious that no giant in the name of Satan can withstand it."

In preparation for spiritual warfare, the first scripture passage Amilliah challenges her readers to memorize is Psalm 144:1–2. Those verses remind us that Christ, our Army General, not only trains us, but promises never to leave us alone in battle.

Fortify yourself against enemy attacks by reading, claiming, and memorizing these verses today. Ask God to open your spiritual eyes to see the enemy's schemes of oppression, unrest, and discouragement. Thank Him for equipping you for battle and for being your fortress in the fight.

BE READY

*"Fight the good fight of the faith. Take hold of the eternal life
to which you were called when you made your good confession
in the presence of many witnesses."*

1 Timothy 6:12

During World War II, our soldiers knew D-day was coming. And they wanted to do everything they could to be ready.

In anticipation of the enemy fire, our soldiers created dummies with parachutes that they dropped out of planes. The dummies had firecrackers attached to them so they would explode on the way to the ground. The enemy, the Germans, saw the dummies, heard the bangs, and fired at them, thereby expending ammunition. Our troops knew if the enemy fired on the dummies, they would not have as much ammunition to use against them.

We may not be involved in a physical war. But we are constantly involved in a spiritual battle. Satan knows if he can distract us and get us to use all our energy to fight battles against him, we will not have as much energy to use for the things God asks us to do.

Dummies out of an airplane are not modern-day distractions. But what about overcommitment, social events, social media, and work? Even church commitments that seem like good things can become distractions. God wants us to be ready for the things that are coming that He asks us to do. He wants us to have our priorities in order. He sees the big picture and knows the very best for us.

TRANSLATE

$\mathcal{T}$ranslation is needed in so many areas of life—language, feelings, technology, and more. Perhaps you could help someone understand those things today. Translators are the difference between knowing what something means and remaining clueless.

WE ARE INTERPRETERS

"My mouth is filled with your praise,
declaring your splendor all day long."
Psalm 71:8

The guest pastor from China preached enthusiastically with his translator at his side. The Chinese pastor paused every few sentences and waited patiently for the interpreter to enlighten the English-speaking congregation.

Watching Mr. Wu, the interpreter, you could really get excited right along with him. His enthusiasm was evident. In fact, there were times he was so excited about what the pastor had said, he almost didn't let him finish before starting his interpretation. His contagious smile and gyrating arms punctuated his words. He translated and spoke every sentence as if its message was the best news he had ever heard. And it was!

The Chinese pastor was bringing the Gospel from his perspective, having been a believer in another country for many years. He wanted to share the most wonderful news he had ever heard—God loves him.

In a way, we are all translators. God has given us a message, a gift of love, His Son. There are many people around us who don't know Him. We must share that message with such enthusiasm that those around us want to know more. We must find the words that nonbelievers will understand so they can internalize what we are saying. We must be the spokespeople for God.

Do you know of someone you could translate for today? Maybe all they have needed is someone who could make the Gospel clear enough to understand!

HEARTFELT WORSHIP

*"LORD, you are my God; I will exalt you and praise your name,
for in perfect faithfulness you have done
wonderful things, things planned long ago."*
Isaiah 25:1 NIV (2011)

The beautiful young lady moved her hands gracefully signing music as the choir sang. She smiled, and her body kept the rhythm of the song. You would never guess that she, too, could not hear but was interpreting using the words on a screen.

My hearing is very good. I don't need anyone to sign the words for me. But each Sunday as Bethani signs the beautiful music, I find it equally as beautiful to watch Bethani as she translates for our deaf congregation. She beams at the message she interprets; her whole body is a picture of her love for Jesus; every movement is an act of worship.

Growing up in a very large, conservative church, we worshiped with our voices. Rarely did we use our hands or sway to the music. But now I enjoy not only singing but also occasionally clapping, swaying, or raising my hands to participate more fully in the act of worship to God. Many in the church agree and feel free to worship God in whatever manner they choose.

How fortunate for our deaf congregation that someone makes sure they "hear" the messages in song. How fortunate for our entire church family that we can watch pure, sweet worship right before our eyes every Sunday.

So what is your favorite form of worship? Practice it throughout your day, every day.

THE TRANSLATING SPIRIT

*"Utterly amazed, they asked: 'Aren't all these who
are speaking Galileans? Then how is it that each of us
hears them in our native language?'"*
Acts 2:7–8 NIV (2011)

𝒻or several years my husband and I lived in Portugal. We attended a small church whose membership included Americans and Portuguese. Our church had a close-knit fellowship even though few Americans spoke Portuguese and vice versa.

The first Sunday we attended church after our arrival, I wasn't sure exactly what to expect. There was no interpreter, and I expected to feel left out of the service. After the welcome we stood for the first hymn.

Half of the congregation began to sing "Showers of Blessings" while the other half sang "*Chuvas de Bencaos.*" One hymn—two languages. As the group sang, there was an incredible spirit of unity in that church family. Faces beamed, and I didn't hear a jumble of words I didn't understand. I heard musical praise to Jesus like I had never heard before.

As the pastor preached in Portuguese, there was no sense of feeling left out or unengaged. The Holy Spirit translated the message into our hearts regardless of the language of the messenger.

Just as the Holy Spirit came at Pentecost to be the Interpreter among nations, we can rely on the Holy Spirit today to help us interpret the words and the needs of others. Whether our differences are cultural, age, or language, God's Holy Spirit can bridge the gap and open the way for holy communication.

TRAIN BEWILDERMENT

"My mouth will speak words of wisdom;
the meditation of my heart will give you understanding."
Psalm 49:3 NIV (2011)

"*Meine Damen und Herren, bitteaussteigen.*" The train came to an abrupt halt and the announcement was repeated. "*Meine Damen und Herren, bitteaussteigen.*" The passengers around us stood and moved toward the exit.

Not speaking German, we sat still. This was not our destination, and we had no idea where we were or how many more stops until we arrived.

"What do you think that announcement was?" I asked my husband.

"Not sure, but either we are the only ones traveling farther or something else is wrong."

A young couple stopped on their way to the exit. The young man was dressed in military garb. "You are Americans, right? Do you need help?"

"Yes, we do. We are not sure what all the announcements are about. Can you tell us what is going on?"

The kind twentysomething lady said, "There is a problem with the train. Everyone has to get off and change trains. Why don't you follow us?"

Relieved to know what to do, we stood and followed the couple. Just a few minutes ago we had felt stranded because of the language barrier and now we were completely at ease since we understood the situation.

Language is important. But even more important is the understanding. Without it the words have little value.

Perhaps you could translate for someone who crosses your path today. It could help them get to their ultimate destination—heaven.

LOVE IN ANY LANGUAGE

"Then make my joy complete by being like-minded,
having the same love, being one in spirit and purpose."
Philippians 2:2

Thomas, a young man my daughter met at a church on the island of Corsica, accepted our invitation to visit us in America for three weeks. Because of his zest for life, his delightful sense of humor, and his love of Jesus, Thomas's time with us seemed far too short. The French Bible he gave me as a hostess gift and his recordings of my favorite scripture passages in his native tongue are treasures I will keep forever. Thomas brought us great joy and much laughter, along with a rich understanding that love in any language can be understood without translation. I am so grateful Thomas came into our lives, our home, and our country. We hope our paths will cross again.

Wherever we travel in life, near or far, we have the opportunity to "translate" Christ by the way we love Him, serve people, demonstrate respect, and take care of what God has entrusted to us in terms of physical and financial resources. When we find others along our journey who are like-minded and "one in spirit and purpose," it is as though God has personally orchestrated the resulting delight and joy. It is yet another way He provides for our every need.

Today, purpose that all you say and all you do will be in love—translated easily any place, any time, and in any language.

REACH

$\mathcal{R}$each is often associated with goals. But your reach extends beyond just personal goals. Our reach can also be our influence, and many times we don't even know the scope of that reach. Be mindful this week that your reach may extend far beyond your sight range.

REACH OUT TO GOD

"God did this so that they would seek him
and perhaps reach out for him and find him,
though he is not far from any one of us."
Acts 17:27 NIV (2011)

Almost two-year-old Elizabeth burst through the front door. Always a bundle of energy, she ran straight to her grandpa. "G'pa, G'pa!"

G'pa turned around to see Elizabeth, who stood at his feet with her little chubby arms stretched upward. "There's my girl," G'pa said. "C'mon up here and let G'pa see how you are today."

Elizabeth beamed as G'pa lifted her up into his arms. She stopped squirming and settled in for a few minutes of loving.

What a perfect picture of how God wants us to reach out to Him every time we are in His presence. Elizabeth demonstrates unadulterated joy every time she sees G'pa and gets as close to him as possible.

Are you that close to God? Do you want to have Him pick you up and hold you?

Sometimes the busy pace of today's world has us going in so many directions that days may go by without us spending time just holding on to God and loving on Him.

But that's not what He wants. If you feel like you need some time in God's arms today so you can get closer to Him, spend time in prayer and reading His Word. Then reach up as high as you can to feel His arms around you. Praise Him for the amazing God that He is.

REACHING OUT

"But eagerly desire the greater gifts."
1 Corinthians 12:31

𝒲aiting to be seated at the American Girl restaurant, I observed this make-believe world. Every little girl had her doll seated beside her in a special doll high chair. In front of the doll was a little saucer and cup just for her.

My eye was drawn to a table with three generations seated together. (Well, if you count the doll, I guess it was four generations!) The mom and grandmother were talking, and the little girl was fiddling with her doll. They had been served their food, and the doll's little saucer had a small cookie and some other morsel sitting on it.

The little girl, uninterested in the adult conversation, looked around to make sure the adults weren't paying her any attention. Then she reached out her hand and quickly snitched the cookie from her doll's plate. In a matter of seconds it was in her mouth and she was smiling as she discreetly chewed her secret prize.

Have you ever been that little girl? Wanting something that was obviously meant for someone else? And then when you thought no one was looking, you reached out and snatched it for yourself?

There's good news and bad news here. The bad news for you is that Someone was looking. The good news is that God has many wonderful things for you and wants to give them to you. All you have to do is ask!

RECOGNIZED BY A TOUCH

"I write to you, dear children, because you know the Father."
1 John 2:14 NIV (2011)

*F*ive moms lined up in the middle of the room. Their children were on the other side of the room. One of the children stepped forward and was blindfolded.

Once the child couldn't see, the moms exchanged places in line. The child was led to the line. Approaching the first mom, the child reached out her hands. Running them over the mom's face, the child shook her head after a few seconds. Then she moved to the next mom and repeated the action. When she stood in front of the fourth mom, just a touch or two and she was smiling. She nodded and lunged into her mother's arms.

This was repeated five times and five different times all it took was a few seconds for each blindfolded child to reach out and touch the hair or face of the mother and determine if that mother belonged to him or her.

Though one or two of the mothers were actually surprised their children recognized them so quickly, they shouldn't have been. After all, mother and child spend a lot of time together.

That same aspect of the mother-child relationship works for our relationships with God. If we have spent lots of time reaching out for Him and getting to know Him, we will recognize Him in an instant. When He hovers close to us or blesses us in some unexpected way, we recognize it immediately.

Reach out to Him today.

REACHING FOR A FRIEND

"This is My commandment, that you
love one another as I have loved you."
John 15:12 NKJV

First day of first grade was great. Grant's dad was with him. But from the next day on, Grant struggled with separation anxiety, so much so that several times he ran away.

Grant's dad talked to his teachers. They tried several plans with no success. Finally, Grant's dad found something that worked.

"Grant, come here please, I want to talk to you," Dad said.

"What is it, Daddy?"

"I notice when I drop you off at school every day, there is a little boy always by himself. Do you know him?"

"Yes, Daddy, that's Teddy."

"Well, seems like he could use a friend. Do you think maybe tomorrow you could talk to him?"

"Yeah. I can do that. Some of the kids make fun of him. He never says much."

"Grant, sometimes we need to reach out to kids who look like they need a friend. I think you would be a great friend for Teddy. Could you do that?"

"I think I can. I won't let those other kids make fun of him."

"Awesome, Grant. I know you can do it."

After that conversation, Grant didn't have any problem staying at school. He became Teddy's protector.

Has God ever prompted you to reach out to someone who needed a friend? You can be His hands here on earth. Think about your life. There may be someone who needs a phone call or visit from you.

REACHING THE UNREACHABLE

"'Lord,' Ananias answered, 'I have heard many reports about this man
and all the harm he has done to your saints in Jerusalem.'...
Then Ananias went to the house and entered it. Placing his hands
on Saul, he said, 'Brother Saul, the Lord—Jesus, who appeared
to you on the road as you were coming here—has sent me so that
you may see again and be filled with the Holy Spirit.'"

Acts 9:13, 17

No doubt reports of Saul's journey toward Damascus preceded him. Because of Saul's reputation, the disciples rightfully feared for their lives. At the very least, they expected to be arrested once he arrived. That was his mission. But after Jesus appeared to Saul on the road to Damascus, convicted him, humbled him, and instructed him, Saul had a new mission. However, no one in Damascus knew that yet.

When God appeared to Ananias in a vision and told him to find Saul and restore his sight, Ananias first had to reach a different conclusion about Saul. In his mind, Saul was the least likely person on earth to follow Christ and the most likely to persecute those who did.

In a recent sermon about Ananias needing his own "conversion," not of salvation, but of thinking, Dr. Greg Wilton challenged listeners to learn from Ananias not to decide whom God could reach. Instead, when confronted with the "unreachable," acknowledge your doubts and fears, then obey God and speak Jesus into their lives.

Remember, nothing is too hard for God.

RELAX

$\mathscr{I}$n today's busy world, there is way too little relaxation. The best solution may be to schedule it. That's right, put it on your calendar. This week try to find a few moments each day to spend with your family, a friend, or God.

IT MAKES ME NERVOUS
TO RELAX

"Anyone who enters God's rest also rests from his own work,
just as God did from his."
Hebrews 4:10

*M*y parents lived only half a mile away, so I stopped often for what I intended to be a brief visit. Only my dad had other ideas, even if we'd just had a lengthy phone conversation or visit.

Regardless, he greeted me with a kiss and a hug and then boomed out a hearty welcome: "Come in. Sit down. Relax. Make yourself at home. Stay awhile."

Unfortunately, I had much to learn about the fine art of relaxing. My typical reply was, "Sorry, I can't stay long. Besides, it makes me nervous to relax."

Daddy worked hard, but he knew how to relax. He loved to take time eating, sometimes stretching a meal into a several-hour marathon that included several courses and cups of coffee. That was his way of extending the conversation as well.

When I lived at home, Daddy stretched out on his bed with his feet hanging over the edge while I knelt on the carpet to give him a foot massage. After several appreciative "Ahhhhhs," he began snoring. When he was sound asleep, I crept quietly into my room. Next morning, I found a sweet note of appreciation and a five-dollar bill.

Daddy is gone, and I'll have to wait until he greets me at heaven's gate to hear his hearty welcome again. Meanwhile, I'm going to practice what he taught me about relaxing. Won't you try it, too?

FLIP AND RELAX

"But the Counselor, the Holy Spirit, whom the Father will
send in my name, will teach you all things, and will remind you
of everything I have said to you. Peace I leave with you;
my peace I give you. I do not give to you as the world gives.
Do not let your hearts be troubled and do not be afraid."

John 14:26–27

The flipped classroom is becoming more and more the norm at many schools. During their planning periods or from home, teachers record their lectures or their responses to student work, and students can access them online. In some cases, students watch these videos online at home, thus "flipping" instructional time to where they receive the content outside of class and practice skills inside the class. In this way, instruction is individualized and the student has more control over his learning pace. The teacher's class time may then be devoted to offering extra help sessions or materials for struggling students. With time pressures removed, teachers and students can afford to relax a little without sacrificing content.

In a way, God flipped His classroom when He offered the Holy Spirit as a Counselor in place of Jesus remaining physically on earth. He promises to teach us all things and to remind of us all that Jesus said. One bonus no technology can ever offer is the peace that comforts and gives courage in every situation. Best of all, because of Christ, we still have access to God "live" at any time, day or night, through prayer.

Now, that's a reason for relaxing!

GO FLY A KITE

"Do not conform any longer to the pattern of this world,
but be transformed by the renewing of your mind.
Then you will be able to test and approve what
God's will is—his good, pleasing and perfect will."

Romans 12:2

In the theatrical version of *Mary Poppins*, Bert the chimney sweep reminds the Banks children: "Troubles you have never seem so bad when you look at them from higher up." From the rooftops of London, Jane and Michael view the stars and their troubles. The children encounter nanny problems; their mother, an identity crisis; and their father, financial woes. Yet Bert and Mary Poppins help the entire family learn to relax and renew their minds with a view from "higher up." Compared to the vastness of the starry sky, their troubles shrink to proper size.

Mary Poppins demonstrates family values, along with kindness, courtesy, flexibility, humor, and confidence. By the time "the wind changes," the Banks family has a higher view of what life should be like and Mr. Banks even learned it's okay to relax long enough to go fly a kite!

Though we may not spend much time on the rooftop, we can ask God to fix our thoughts on a higher plane and to help us relax and enjoy the simple pleasures of life. Now and then let's step outside on a starry night and renew our minds by asking God to reveal His heavenly perspective. Even Mary Poppins, "practically perfect in every way," would approve!

PUT YOUR HAND IN HIS

"You open your hand and satisfy the desires of every living thing."
Psalm 145:16

*M*ardie woke up from knee surgery. Still groggy, she looked around the room. Her husband and adult daughter were there, watching for signs of her waking up. What she didn't expect to see was her three-year-old granddaughter sitting patiently in the armchair in the corner.

Shaking her head to clear the cobwebs and focus, she realized her granddaughter Autumn was holding a Styrofoam cup, waiting to give Mardie a drink. When Autumn saw Mardie looking at her, she slid out of the armchair, brought the cup over to the bed, and offered Mardie a drink.

"Thank you," Mardie said. "That tastes great."

Autumn smiled and climbed back in her chair.

Mardie reached out her hand to Autumn, thinking nothing could make her feel better than to hold that sweet little hand. Autumn scooted down from the chair and headed around the bed. Everyone watched as she walked around to the other side, took her grandfather by the hand, and led him back to the other side and Mardie's extended hand. Gently she placed her grandfather's hand in her grandmother's. Then she climbed back up into her chair.

Holding hands with someone you love can calm fears, diminish pain, and rekindle love. Holding hands with your heavenly Father can keep you grounded and ready to face whatever each day brings.

Whose hand are you holding today? Can you just relax with your hand in His, knowing everything will be taken care of?

HE'S GOT THIS

"God is not a man, that he should lie, nor a son of man,
that he should change his mind. Does he speak and then not act?
Does he promise and not fulfill?"

Numbers 23:19

People in charge naturally have more decisions to make, directions to give, and resources to allocate. Consequently, they also receive more credit—or blame. Leaders take on extra responsibility and are accountable when their directives are not carried out by unreliable people who promised but do not deliver. Whether the head of a household or the head of a corporation, seldom do leaders get a day off. Eventually, this constant state of stress can cause problems.

However, God does not intend for us to carry a burden too heavy or too long. In 1 Peter 5:7, He reminds us to "cast all your anxiety on him because he cares for you." As long as we have asked the Lord for wisdom, acted on what we know at the time, and done the best we can, there should be time to relax. In fact, refusing to relax could actually indicate a lack of faith. If you say you believe the promises of God and you know He has promised to supply all your needs, then aren't you failing to trust Him when you continue to fret and fidget and try to fix everything and everybody?

Look again at Numbers 23:19 and read it aloud. Then take a deep breath, blow it out, and relax. He's got this.

DANCE

Some readers may immediately respond, "I'm not a dancer!" But you don't have to be a dancer to dance a sincere, heartfelt dance of joy. Try it! You will be amazed at the freedom and delight you will experience.

DANCING DOWN THE AISLES

"Let them praise his name with dancing
and make music to him with timbrel and harp."
Psalm 149:3 NIV (2011)

*M*ost of my life I have worshiped in a large conservative church. Knowing no other form of worship, it sometimes feels a little awkward to experience different styles of worship.

On one occasion I was at a Florida conference. Folks from all denominations were present. Worship was sweet, and I didn't feel uncomfortable sitting next to someone who raised their hands or clapped during the praise and worship.

Once or twice, I walked into the sanctuary behind "Miss Irene." She was a beautiful older lady who exuded love. As she came through the door her demeanor changed. There was a lift in her step, and the minute she heard music she began to sing. She stopped briefly at the first pew and put her conference bag and purse on the bench.

Then she began to dance. Miss Irene changed her slow walk to a lilt, singing, praising, and clapping her hands all the way. I had never seen anything like this, but it was beautiful. The joy that was in her steps was amazing. And even though my conservative upbringing would staunchly frown upon dancing in the church, I found myself wanting to follow this sweet, petite lady with snow-white hair and dance all the way to the altar.

Your position on dancing in the church doesn't really matter. The important thing is that your heart sings and dances in praise to our God.

DANCING FOR JOY

"Again I will build you and you will be rebuilt,
O virgin of Israel! Again you will take up your tambourines,
And go forth to the dances of the merrymakers."

Jeremiah 31:4 *NASB*

In the summer, one of our favorite family activities is swimming. This year our three-year-old learned to swim. Grace quickly progressed from doggie-paddling a few feet between two adults to confidently navigating the whole pool. She was never afraid to jump in and join in whatever the older kids were doing.

So Grace followed her cousins onto the diving board. However, Grace didn't imitate the cannonballs, swan dives, and can openers. Once on the diving board Grace began to dance. All eyes were on this energetic three-year-old, standing at the end of the diving board, bouncing up and down and singing all the songs she learned in Vacation Bible School. This was her norm, not just a once-in-a-while trip to the board. When I looked around, several of her cousins were smiling, singing along, and mimicking her dance. This made Grace even happier.

Dancing is definitely a joyous activity. And quite often it is contagious.

How long has it been since you danced with so much joy that others wanted to join you? Affirmation and camaraderie in your joy makes it even sweeter.

Can't think of anything to dance about today? Knowing how much God loves us is dance-worthy every day.

GETTING CARRIED AWAY

"So that is what the Benjamites did. While the girls were dancing,
each man caught one and carried her off to be his wife.
Then they returned to their inheritance
and rebuilt the towns and settled in them."

Judges 21:23

Dancing is customary at wedding receptions. Songs for the bride and groom and family dances are carefully selected. Sometimes the dancing couple surprises the guests with a uniquely choreographed routine. Everyone is exhausted but satisfied the celebration is complete.

However, what if the courtship and celebration actually began with dancing? In Judges, "Israel had no king; everyone did as he saw fit" (Judges 21:25). The Benjamites and the Israelites suffered heavy losses. The Israelites grieved because of the huge gap in their tribes. They longed to restore the tribe of Benjamin. They needed wives to produce heirs and restore their tribe. But what a way to choose a wife!

Hiding in the vineyards at the festival in Shiloh, the Benjamite men watched the Shiloh girls dance, then rushed upon them, seized them, and took them as their wives. Talk about getting carried away while dancing! Yet the newlyweds must have made a go of it because "they returned to their inheritance and rebuilt the towns and settled in them" (v. 23).

Is something out of control? Or a surprising situation not anticipated? Ask God to help you make the best of it for His glory. Before long you may feel like dancing again. Just don't get carried away!

CLOSE THE BLINDS
AND DANCE

"Praise him with timbrel and dancing,
praise him with the strings and pipe."
Psalm 150:4 NIV (2011)

"*D*ance like no one is watching." That is the first phrase in a popular slogan you see on pillows, wall hangings, and art.

Have you ever asked yourself the question: *What would my dance be like if I thought no one was watching me?* It might be very different than if you were dancing in front of an audience.

I once heard a well-known, national Bible teacher say she often closed the blinds, put on her praise music, turned it up loud, and danced. I have done the same thing. But why do we feel the need to close the blinds? Are we afraid someone would see us and think we shouldn't dance that way? Or maybe that we shouldn't dance at all?

Dancing before the Lord is biblical. You may not see a lot of dancing in many churches today but some encourage dancing.

There is freedom in praising God through dancing. You can move to the strains of praise music. You can stand on your tiptoes and reach out to God so you are as close as possible. You twirl and slide with reckless abandon and then stop just to bask in God's love.

Dancing is a form of worship that always blesses the dancer. So today, why don't you try dancing like no one is watching? You can even close the blinds if you want to!

THE HAPPY DANCE

*"And David was dancing before the LORD with all his might,
and David was wearing a linen ephod."*

2 Samuel 6:14 NASB

What exactly is the "happy dance"? To put it simply, these are the times when you are so overjoyed there is nothing left to do but dance. The result—the happy dance.

David danced before the Lord with all his might as they brought the ark into Jerusalem (2 Samuel 6). Can't you just see that joyful procession?

On a beautiful fall day a three-year-old outfielder at a tee-ball game twirls with arms outstretched, doing the happy dance of fall.

A football player runs the length of the field, catches a pass for a touchdown, throws the ball to the referee, and begins to dance. The victory dance goes from player to player as they celebrate the score.

A mother sits with her daughter, who has said she has news. Mother is anxious to know what is going on with her married daughter who lives several states away. The daughter grins and says, "Well, how are you, Grandma?" The new grandma-to-be jumps up and immediately launches into her happy dance.

In Ecclesiastes 3 Solomon says there is a time to dance.

Have you experienced a time of dancing in your life lately? God wants you to be happy and to express your delight in whatever way feels appropriate. But if you are a dancer, follow the example of David and dance with all your might.

SHARE

"That's mine!"

"No, mine!"

Our first knowledge of any kind of sharing usually happens over a toy or "blankie." But as we get older we learn there is much more to share with others. Take a moment this week to share something good with someone else.

TASTER'S CHOICE

"And do not forget to do good and to share with others,
for with such sacrifices God is pleased."
Hebrews 13:16

"And when you come, please bring me some coffee. Taster's Choice, please. Regular, not decaf."

Ms. Syble's voice mail made me smile. She never asked for much, but she did ask often. More than the item she requested, she just wanted to see me and have some fellowship and a prayer together.

I regularly looked for her preferred coffee and bought some when I found it on sale. There was always a cup on her table when I dropped by, and sometimes I asked her to fix me one so I could see what she found so great about it. In addition to the taste, it must have been the warmth and ease of preparation, important qualities for the elderly.

We shared countless moments together around Ms. Syble's table. She told me about her life growing up, struggles she was going through, and then asked about my children, husband, and work. We prayed together, clasping hands tightly, and ending with a joint, "Thank You, Jesus!" After all, He shared this time with us.

My next voice message from Ms. Syble would be one of gratitude and inquiry about any prayer concerns I had told her. She didn't have much to give materially, but Ms. Syble was rich in spiritual gifts. She gave me a "taster's choice" of what it means to share and care. Thank you, Ms. Syble!

LEAVE SOME BEHIND

"When you reap the harvest of your land, do not reap
to the very edges of your field or gather the gleanings of your harvest.
Do not go over your vineyard a second time or
pick up the grapes that have fallen. Leave them for the poor
and the alien. I am the LORD your God."

Leviticus 19:9–10

Looking out for those who come behind seems to be a lost consideration. Notice the next time you go in a business or school how many people hold the door open for the person coming behind them. It doesn't cross their minds.

When God gave Moses the commands on Mount Sinai, He expected Moses to share them with the Israelites. Following these moral and civil laws would help create order out of the possible chaos from their time in the wilderness. They had been slaves in Egypt; living without taskmasters would be quite a transition. The Israelites needed standards and boundaries by which to conduct themselves.

God gave many laws that required discipline and sacrifice, but when obeyed they indicated reverence for Him. He wanted His people to show compassion and consideration for each other.

Next time you have an opportunity, consider whether God is nudging you to ease the burden of an overworked waitress or a homeless person. It won't be true for every case—and you have to be cautious—but with the discernment of the Holy Spirit, you can share with those in need and point them to the One who can provide their deepest needs.

A TREASURED MOMENT

"Not looking to your own interests
but each of you to the interests of the others."
Philippians 2:4 NIV (2011)

$\mathcal{I}$ had not missed a game. At least, not until today.

It was almost kickoff time, and I was in a hospital bed recuperating from surgery as my oldest daughter took the field with her college band.

The telephone rang. "Hello."

It was my friend Brenda. "Thought you might like to hear the band's pregame show. Hang on and listen."

The band began to play. The Clemson University Tiger Marching Band. The band with the most precious mellophone player in the world! My daughter.

I had lamented missing this first football game of the year. I am not a sports fan, but I hadn't missed a game. It was the band, however, that kept me buying season tickets!

I sat propped up in my bed, listening to the strains of "Tiger Rag." So I missed the game but not the band. The biggest bonus was a special dose of loving care from a precious friend!

The spirit with which that phone call was made touched my heart like little else. Because of the depth of my friendship with Brenda, the sweet spirit of her thoughtfulness filled my day. The love of Jesus spread around my hospital bed. That phone call changed my day from a really lonely, difficult time to a time of blessing.

Perhaps you could make a phone call today that would be the voice of Jesus to someone you know.

BREAD LABELS
AND BOTTLE CAPS

"Command them to do good, to be rich in good deeds,
and to be generous and willing to share."
1 Timothy 6:18

A bread company and a soft drink company joined forces and offered reduced admission to the Radio City Music Hall Christmas Show if the purchaser had a bread label and a bottle cap. Wayne's congregation collected for months so everyone could get a discount. One bread label and bottle cap were left over. Wayne stuck them in his pocket. Someone might be able to use this, he thought.

A lady with a little girl stood behind Wayne in line. He handed them the extra bread label and bottle cap. He said, "Here, these may help you with a little discount."

Once inside, the little girl scurried up to Wayne. "Mister," she said, "Mama wants to talk to you." Wayne walked over to find a tearful mother.

"I've been saving to take my daughter to this show," she said. "It was all she wanted for Christmas. When I saw the price, I didn't have enough. I couldn't afford even this one gift for her for Christmas. But you gave me this bottle cap and bread label. I doubted they were worth much, but mister! It was a good discount. Look here." She showed Wayne a handful of change, smiling broadly. "I can buy a snack for her. This will be our best Christmas ever!"

Is there something you could share with someone that would make a huge difference in their lives?

A HELPFUL HAND

*"Truly I tell you, whatever you did for one of the least
of these brothers and sisters of mine, you did for me."*
Matthew 25:40 NIV (2011)

There are only two other houses on our street. The lots are spacious considering they are in the city, but you can easily see the neighbors' yards.

One Saturday afternoon my husband was digging a hole in order to improve the drainage in the backyard. He was working very hard, and it was obviously going to take him a long time to finish the task. I was watching from the kitchen window as I worked there.

At one point I walked into another room for a minute. When I returned to the kitchen, I looked out the window and saw our neighbor, Tom, coming across the yard, shovel in hand. My husband looked up, smiled, and together they continued digging. Tom definitely gave my husband encouragement as well as help. They didn't finish the drain that day.

On Monday, I looked out the window and saw Tom adding a "postscript" to his encouragement. He was out there finishing the drain. Tom is retired and at home during the day. He was helping my husband while my husband was at work.

Because our neighbor shared the work, the job was easier, and my husband finished the job a lot sooner. And every time I looked at the new drain in the backyard, I thanked God for good neighbors.

Is there someone to whom you could lend a hand today?

CLEAN

$\mathcal{B}$eing clean and orderly brings freedom to your life. Is it hard for you to keep your desk tidy or the dishes all put away? Make an effort to put some organization into one area of your life that is in need of attention.

JUST DROP IT

"For God is not a God of disorder but of peace."
1 Corinthians 14:33

Currently, I am under long-term conviction to be leaner and cleaner in my life. Although these qualities may take a decade or more to develop, at least I have begun. Baby steps are turning into bigger steps. My cousin Sarah showed me a painless method of reducing clutter.

"Keep a box in a corner. When you find something you rarely use or don't like, drop it into that box. Once a week or so, donate the box to charity. You'll be surprised how easy this becomes and the difference it makes over time."

Sarah is right. The "drop box" method is painless and makes a difference. But sometimes, bigger things need to go.

This year, I determined to have less stuff and more room. I had accumulated so much I wasn't sure what I had. I emptied one large bookshelf and a storage closet from my classroom and donated them to a friend setting up hers. Another teacher seemed grateful for extra books I never used. And a colleague who had no place to safeguard her purse was happy to acquire a locking file cabinet.

I have not missed anything! And I'm loving having less mess. Maybe this will be the year I am healed of my hoarder disorder, or maybe it will take ten. At least I have begun. If you, too, desire a cleaner home or workspace, won't you start your drop box, too? You'll be glad you did!

TAKE INVENTORY

*"She watches over the affairs of her household
and does not eat the bread of idleness."*

Proverbs 31:27

For Bess, a registered dietician, planning and cooking meals comes naturally. In fact, she delights in meal preparation, starting weeks in advance making menus and studying her "Bess-i-pes." She purchases the right ingredients and executes her plan beautifully, with nutritious, tasty results. Best of all, Bess makes it seem easy and fun.

For Dee, however, meal planning rates as a chore and a bore. Nearly every dinner is a hodgepodge scavenged from the cabinets and thrown together. Though the cupboards might be full, there is no plan for using what's available, and therefore, it often seems there's nothing to eat. Of course, Dee has other talents; cooking is just not among them.

Consequently, Dee dreaded putting a meal together. Her family got by, but dinner was a duty, not a delight. Finally, one day things began to change.

"Mom, let's make a list of what we have and see what might go together before we buy anything else," her daughter suggested. They took inventory, organized the available food, and planned several tasty meals. Best of all, mom and daughter prepared the meal together, enjoying the camaraderie and the results. The green beans, carrots, broccoli, and salad were healthy and delicious.

Today, like Bess, let's watch over the affairs of our household, whether it's in the kitchen or somewhere else where we need to take stock of what's available and use it more resourcefully.

A HARD ACT TO FOLLOW

"Consecrate yourselves now and consecrate the temple. . . .
Remove all defilement."
2 Chronicles 29:5

"*That's* a hard act to follow." Usually, these words are spoken after someone's outstanding presentation makes anything after it hard to match. However, sometimes it is hard to follow someone who has made a mess of things!

Twenty-five-year-old King Hezekiah had a hard act to follow. His father, King Ahaz, "had promoted wickedness in Judah and had been most unfaithful to the Lord" (2 Chronicles 28:19). Yet Hezekiah wasted no time establishing different priorities. The first thing he did was to open the temple doors and repair them. He brought together the priests and Levites, charging them to consecrate themselves and the temple.

The Levites held a grand spring cleaning. Every unclean thing King Ahaz had brought into the temple had to be taken out. Everything he'd removed from the temple had to be restored to its rightful place. Yet under Hezekiah's direction, this process took only sixteen days. No doubt his positive leadership renewed passion and purpose. King Hezekiah gave clear directions as to what needed to be done to reverse the curse his father had brought onto the Israelites. Consequently, temple service was reestablished, and "Hezekiah and all the people rejoiced at what God had brought about for his people, because it was done so quickly" (29:36).

If you find yourself with a hard act to follow, take heart and take charge. Ask God to help you reestablish order so that His purposes becomes priorities again.

DIRTY DISH TOWELS

"By wisdom a house is built,
and through understanding it is established."

Proverbs 24:3

"You wash them every day?" I asked Carolynn after the subject of dirty dish towels popped.

"Of course. Didn't you know that wet dishrags are one of the best places for bacteria to grow?"

"Somehow I missed that memo. I just use mine until they smell sour. Oh my!"

Evidently, I've missed quite a few housekeeping memos. There's so much to keeping a home tidy and clean, and for some, it is more natural than for others. I am not one of the naturally neat or clean, but I admire those who are! Instead, this is the sign I like to put up in my kitchen: "The only reason I keep my house like this is to make you feel better about yours." Recently, my mother uncovered a plaque that hung in our home when I was a child. Since it fits my housekeeping habits, Mama donated it to me: "Although you'll find our house a mess, come in, sit down, converse. It doesn't always look this. Some days it's even worse."

Clearly there's a balance between too messy and too clean. And since I err on the side of too messy too often, I'm going to keep trying to follow my clean friend Carolynn's advice!

Lord, grant me the wisdom and understanding I need to keep our home clean enough to be sanitary and inviting enough to be sociable.

For starters, I'm going to wash the dish towels today!

CLEAN DRAWERS

"Your love has given me great joy and encouragement,
because you, brother, have refreshed the hearts of the saints."
Philemon 7

"*W*ant me to clean out your desk?" Mason asked Mrs. Malone. "I'm good at organizing."

"That would be wonderful," she answered, surprised at the offer. After all, Mason didn't get paid for his internship in her office. He was mainly there to observe. But this question showed some real initiative—and boy, did she need help!

"What should I do with the extra stuff?" Mason queried.

"How about I get you a box and anything you're not sure of, put it there."

"That works."

An hour later, Mrs. Malone checked on Mason's progress. He had completely organized the two worst desk drawers—and of course, filled up the box completely. But how wonderful to see what had been buried for so long and to find items she had been missing.

"This is so helpful, Mason. I really appreciate it, and I promise not to put anything in the box back in the drawers. Looks like most of it should be donated to charity anyway. And look! You found all those notepads I knew I had stashed somewhere! Bless you!"

"Not a problem," Mason replied with a smile. "I like cleaning up."

"That's good. It won't be hard to keep you busy in this office!"

Today, ask God for the help you need or thank Him for the help He sends when your "stuff" gets overwhelming. It's amazing how refreshing a clean drawer can be!

BARTER

$\mathcal{B}$*arter* is a somewhat old-fashioned word. But even today barter is practiced among merchants, businessmen, and friends. Never tried to barter something? This week would be a good week to try something new.

BARTER BARGAINS

*"Be very careful, then, how you live—not as unwise
but as wise, making the most of every opportunity."*
Ephesians 5:15–16

*M*ost people really like to get a bargain. But not everyone likes to barter. Before coins were minted and currency printed, people traded what they had for what they needed. That is still the case today for resourceful people who have learned to negotiate deals. Instead of money, they trade skills or services. In some cases, the exchange may just be for fun, convenience, or preference, for example: "I'll rub your back if you'll wash the dishes." But on other occasions, the stakes may be much higher and the value much greater. Like putting braces on children's teeth, for instance.

Tynette Petty, a licensed massage therapist, knew both of her teenagers needed braces. But she also knew she could not afford them. So, she bartered with the orthodontist: In exchange for braces for Alexander and Juliet, Tynette offered the orthodontist and her family members massages for as many years as would equal the payments. The braces went on and came off before Tynette completed her end of the bargain. Two years later, she's still giving massages. But she's okay with that. It was a great deal for both parties. Now, that's something to smile about!

Think of a skill or service you might offer in exchange for a skill or service you need. Ask the Lord to help you be wise and make the most of every opportunity.

SPIRITUAL BARTERING

*"For God so loved the world that he gave
his one and only Son, that whoever believes in him
shall not perish but have eternal life."*
John 3:16

Robert Porterfield, an enterprising young actor, lived during the Depression. But he saw that as no excuse for people not to enjoy good entertainment and theater. So on June 10, 1933, Barter Theatre opened its doors in Southwest Virginia. The price of admission? Forty cents or the equivalent amount of produce. During the early days 80 percent of theatergoers paid their admission with fruit, vegetables, dairy products, or livestock.

Barter Theatre was popular from the time it was opened. All of the seats were filled for the very first show. Still operational today, donation to an area food bank is the price of admission for one show a year.

Bartering is not a common practice in our culture today. But in some form, from very early times people have traded one thing or service for another.

The greatest exchange in history occurred when God sent His Son to die for our sins. He granted our freedom in return for our belief in the death and resurrection of His Son, Jesus Christ. Now that's a life-changing bartering process!

You may have a friend who is not aware of the sacrificial gift God gave us in His Son. Maybe you could barter for a little time to tell him or her about Jesus.

YARD SALE YIELDS

"She is like the merchant ships, bringing her food from afar."
Proverbs 31:14

Every summer Susan and Calvin load suitcases with stuffed animals, backpacks, and tennis shoes gleaned from yard sales. Susan makes a practice of looking in the newspaper ads, circling sales that interest her, and frequenting yard sales. She maps her routes for best use of time and gas. Although open to unexpected or unusual treasures, Susan is mainly looking for items to barter, so she tries very hard to ensure the items are in excellent condition. Often, they still have tags attached.

Why such an intentional shopping plan? This couple loves to travel, but they also love to save money and get a bargain. They have learned that the inhabitants of a small island off the coast of Mexico are eager to trade tourist necessities like taxi rides, restaurants, and hotel stays for items hard for them to access or afford.

After several years of this kind of exchange, the residents of the island have come to trust Susan and Calvin and eagerly await them each summer. Children from the community tag along on their excursions, hanging off their golf cart, knowing they will likely get treated to ice cream at the end of the ride.

Yet more than just the bargains that bartering brings are the relationships this couple has formed with island inhabitants. Susan is a modern-day Proverbs 31 woman, dealing more in relationships than with merchant ships! After all, those are the most valuable commodities of all!

TROPICAL PLANTS, CHICKENS, AND GOLDFISH

*"Whoever can be trusted with very little
can also be trusted with much."*
Luke 16:10

Doug and Sarah have to be the most adventurous couple ever. They just returned from a three-week house-sitting "job" in the Caribbean, where they were responsible for feeding chickens and goldfish and watering more than a hundred kinds of tropical plants. After a morning of chores like these, they were free to explore the private island, go snorkeling, or take the sailboat out for a ride on the aqua ocean waves. Fishing yielded the entrée for most of their meals, and fruit trees provided dessert. Sounds like a beautiful barter!

Yet, there has to be trust established for this kind of exchange to happen. With their laid-back personalities, sense of humor, and generous hearts, Doug and Sarah make friends easily and earn trust quickly. They have proven this trustworthiness on the home front as well by providing gentle, loving caregiving 'round the clock for aging parents for several years. Only recently have they regained some of the freedom and flexibility that allows them to say yes again to adventures.

Perhaps you are in a situation where your time and energy are consumed by the needs and expectations of others, and adventure seems to have taken off without you. Remember that your acts of service can still be a kind of barter for the valuable trust, experience, and understanding you receive in reciprocation. In God's perfect timing, you will be fully paid.

INFERNAL STATISTICS

*"Let us consider how we may spur one another on toward
love and good deeds. Let us not give up meeting together, as some
are in the habit of doing, but let us encourage one another."*
Hebrews 10:24–25

*I*nferential Statistics, dubbed "Infernal Statistics," was the most dreaded course in my doctoral program. Not being naturally mathematically inclined, I needed a lot of grace to get me through and God provided!

Though I attended class faithfully, studied diligently every evening, and showed up for each conference the professor offered, things still looked bleak. Finally, in desperation, I asked Grace, a Korean student, if she would be my study buddy. What that actually meant was that as we worked our assigned problems after class, I would interrupt her every minute or so to ask her to remind me of the next step. In return, I offered to coach her in her English speaking since she lacked confidence in projection and pronunciation.

This bartering turned out to be extremely beneficial—for both of us, I hope.

"How do you do it, Grace? You said you don't really understand our textbook. So, how do you know how to work these formulas?"

"Oh, it's easy. I just listen for important words."

It was God's grace that led me to Grace and a double dose of grace that got me through!

Today let's look for someone to encourage and thank God for those He has placed in our path to encourage us.

COUNT

$\mathcal{C}$ounting isn't always about numbers. Do you have a good friend in your life whom you can count on for anything? If not, make it a priority this week to work on deepening your relationships.

ALL THE FRUIT

"But the fruit of the Spirit is love, joy, peace, patience,
kindness, goodness, faithfulness, gentleness and self-control.
Against such things there is no law."
Galatians 5:22–23

Does anyone ever attain all nine spiritual fruits? Not me! Seems like when my faithfulness blossoms, my patience putrefies. When joy blooms, my self-control needs fertilizing. Rarely is all the fruit ripe at the same time!

Yet I have met two women whom I could count on to exhibit fruitfulness faithfully. My aunt Ruth was one of them. Though her young pastor husband was ravaged by multiple sclerosis and paralyzed from the waist down, Ruth never complained. She exuded love, joy, and peace while raising two young children and caring for Uncle Robert. Until their last breaths, they both yielded great spiritual fruit.

My neighbor Wanda is another who tirelessly helps others, her kindness and gentleness ever present. Recently, with her permission, I shared her number with my friend Sharon, who needed advice about her elderly mom. Wanda's administrative experience with assisted living makes her a valuable resource. She dropped her plans, went out in the rain, and advocated for Sharon's mother, having never met either of them! The next day Wanda visited the facility and sent Sharon a picture of her mom, along with a reassuring report. She continued to visit until Sharon's mom moved back home.

So, yes, it is possible to develop all the fruit of the Spirit. I'm going to count on the Holy Spirit to keep giving me role models and opportunities until I can count all nine fruits in my own life.

COMPLETE HONESTY

"They did not require an accounting from those to whom
they gave the money to pay the workers,
because they acted with complete honesty."

2 Kings 12:15

"*I* trust you."

Three simple words, but oh, the depth they imply. Yet how rarely they actually apply anymore. How many times have you had to follow up on business transactions or work-for-hire because of someone unreliable? When did you last allow someone you barely knew in your home without securing your valuables?

In most every situation involving work or money, records must be maintained, invoices filed, time clocks punched, or some form of accountability required. But not in King Joash's day. The temple repair he ordered proceeded in an orderly fashion, and all the carpenters, builders, masons, and stonecutters got paid. Interestingly enough, "the money brought into the temple was not spent for making silver basins, wick trimmers, sprinkling bowls, trumpets or any other articles of gold or silver for the temple of the Lord; it was paid to the workmen, who used it to repair the temple" (2 Kings 12:13–14). Evidently the supervisors had agreed on their priorities, and restoration took precedence over refinement.

Today, think about how trustworthy you are when it comes to keeping your word or choosing how to use your resources most wisely. It would also be a great time to give thanks for those God has brought into your life who have the rare quality of complete honesty.

CHILD NUMBER SIXTEEN

"May he give you the desire of your heart
and make all your plans succeed."
Psalm 20:4

"Mom, Mom, come look at the list. We know which one we want!"

"Girls, we are going to let Mama Jane pick which child is best. We have prayed about it. I'm sure God already has one for us."

Ever since the Berryfields decided to host a choir child from India for a year, the children could hardly contain their excitement. They studied the list of children and examined each one's likes and dislikes.

"Mom, look at the fifth one. She looks like fun," said Joy.

"The twelfth girl likes to play dolls," said Lulu.

"But the one we really want is number sixteen." Joy began to move her finger down the list. "She is perfect for us."

"Well, girls, we are going to wait. I'm sure we'll hear before long."

Just then the phone rang. "Hello." Mom covered the microphone. "It's Mama Jane," she whispered.

The girls got closer to their mother. "Tell us, tell us." They jumped up and down as they spoke.

Mom finished her conversation and hung up the telephone.

"Get the list, girls. Mama Jane said to count down on the list. Our child is child number sixteen."

"That's the one we wanted. Look, Mom, her name is Kim."

"You see, God knew the desires of our hearts and picked out the very best child for us. He always gives us what is best for us. You can always count on Him."

ARE YOU GROWING?

"The righteous will flourish like a palm tree,
they will grow like a cedar of Lebanon; planted in the house
of the LORD, they will flourish in the courts of our God."
Psalm 92:12–13

Our neighborhood has lots of big trees. Because of recent storms, some of those big trees have fallen.

Looking at the remaining stumps, I see many growth rings. Just by counting those rings, I can tell the age of a tree.

Most trees have knots and irregularities at several points and some rings are not perfectly round. But the growth rings have adjusted. They either go around the knot or incorporate it into that year's growth.

But the basic outside appearance of those trees has not changed for a long time. The growth occurs from the inside. And each layer of growth makes the tree stronger.

Those big trees are not a lot unlike our spiritual lives. We often grow slowly, and we encounter many bumps, knots, and detours along our paths. People who see us may not even know the growth is occurring. But every layer of growth contributes to who we are. Each "ring" builds character and strengthens us against the strong winds of life.

Our rings won't always be smooth, but Jesus will always be there to help us around the knots and hard places. And if we count on Him, as we continue to grow on the inside, it will make a difference on the outside.

Have you added a growth ring lately?

HEAD COUNT, PLEASE

"'Who can hide in secret places so that I cannot see them?'
declares the LORD. 'Do not I fill heaven
and earth?' declares the LORD."
Jeremiah 23:24 NIV (2011)

The Trail Life Troop was on its first campout of the year. They had a caravan of six cars and made a stop at the rest area. Troopmaster Bill had given them fifteen minutes to do what they needed to do and walk around a bit.

When it came time to go, the boys piled back into the cars and took off. Their policy was to count the boys when they returned to the vehicles. But somehow they got a few miles down the road and Tray asked, "Where's Joe?"

Each car thought Joe was in another car. In the end, it seemed Joe was not in any of the Trail Life cars.

The caravan turned around and headed back to the rest stop. When they turned in, there sat Joe on the cement wall, waiting for them to come back and get him. He smiled and waved.

This time they took a head count and once again pulled into traffic. They were on their way.

Have you ever felt left behind? There is one group you can always be part of—God's family. God always knows where you are. Once you are part of God's family, you don't have to worry about the "cars" pulling out and leaving you sitting on a wall. God will keep a watchful eye on you.

Thank Him for that today!

LEAN

*L*eaning on others gets us through hard times. But God is the most important Person to lean on. Is there a situation this week where you would benefit from doing a little heavier leaning on Him?

HUGS AND HANDOUTS

*"Carry each other's burdens, and in this way
you will fulfill the law of Christ."*

Galatians 6:2

*H*olli sidled up close to her teacher and looked at her with tear-filled eyes.

"I need a hug."

"Of course."

Holli's baby sister had died unexpectedly just a few days prior, and Holli's family was having a hard time coping. Holli's teacher gladly hugged her and offered to let her step outside the room anytime she needed to regain her composure.

Tina, Holli's classmate, was having a hard time too. When her teacher asked her to print her mailing address on the postcard she was sending home, Tina whispered: "We don't have a home right now. We're living in a hotel."

On her break, the teacher e-mailed the school social worker and the guidance counselor to make sure they were informed. Together, they secured a gas card to give Tina's dad to help and encourage him. Later, clothes were donated and Christmas gifts purchased to continue helping this family while they needed someone to lean on.

Mr. Nesbitt, beloved custodian at Holli's school, asked his teacher friends to pray for his wife , who was experiencing kidney failure and having to take dialysis treatments several times daily. He was struggling emotionally, physically, and financially to keep up with the demands of her medical needs. Before long, the teachers rallied around him and presented him with a $2,000 check to help with expenses.

Sometimes we are the ones who need a hug or a handout, and sometimes we are the ones who can give one. Either way, whether we are the leaned-on or the leaning-on, Christ is glorified.

BY HIS SPIRIT

"Not by might nor by power, but by my Spirit,
says the LORD Almighty."
Zechariah 4:6

*H*ave you ever felt under qualified for or overwhelmed with the task or responsibilities with which you are entrusted? That's great! Why? Because when we are forced to acknowledge our own inadequacies, it is then that we lean and depend on God, and thus, He receives the glory.

That seems to be Zechariah's message as well. Not might, not power, not brains, schemes, plans, investments, or the perfect body, spouse, or house, but "by my Spirit, says the LORD Almighty."

Through Christ, we already possess all we need to overcome situations, responsibilities, or concerns dominating our thoughts and time. We don't have to summon up the strength. We don't have to figure a way around it. We don't have to lift, push, struggle, or strain. Just lean on the everlasting arms and He will guide and steady your steps.

In the battle of Jericho, Joshua and the Israelites found themselves literally up against a wall. Archaeologists estimate the walls were six feet thick and up to twenty-six feet high, a seemingly impregnable fortress. And yet, in obedience to God's command, the Israelites didn't even have to lean on the walls for them to fall; they just had to lean on the One who called them to conquer this city. Not by might, nor by power did the walls fall, but by His Spirit.

Today may you experience the expectant joy of leaning on Almighty God as you abide in His Spirit and depend on His power.

JUST LEAN YOUR HEAD AGAINST THE WALL

"This is what he showed me: The Lord was standing
by a wall that had been built true to plumb,
with a plumb line in his hand."

Amos 7:7

"Sharon, can you spare five minutes? I have a paint question."

"A paint question?"

"Yes. Mother had painting done at her house, and I'm supposed to inspect it before paying the painter. I stopped by, but it just doesn't look right."

"Sure, I'll take a look."

At first glance, Sharon agreed. The molding looked gray against the khaki walls and dull compared to the bright white of the windowsills. Yet the painter assured me he'd used the same paint everywhere. He said the room was too dark to see well, and the molding was so flat it didn't reflect light.

"Lean your head against the wall, and you can see what I mean," he insisted.

I didn't buy it. I could tell by looking and touching it just wasn't the right color or finish.

Sharon leaned her head against the wall. "He's right. You can't see it from straight ahead, but if you lean your head here, you can see the gloss. And the color is the same. The light is throwing you off."

"Man, I feel terrible. I gave him such a hard time. What am I going to do?"

"Pay him and apologize," Sharon said matter-of-factly. "That's what you have to do."

She was right. He was right. I was wrong. Sometimes we are the ones who need to lean for things to be straight. *Thank You, Lord, for friends who act as my plumb lines!*

SHE KNEW WHERE TO LEAN

"The LORD is good, a refuge in times of trouble.
He cares for those who trust in him."

Nahum 1:7

"Don't leave until you pray with me," Ms. Syble said. In the tiny kitchen of her little mill house, we visited, talking over her concerns and needs. Sometimes we discussed the Sunday school lesson she read each day in preparation for the Sundays she could go to church. She taught me and my daughter to make biscuits from scratch. Ms. Syble worked hard into her eighties, rising at three o'clock in the morning to report to Hardee's by five to work the backline for breakfast. In the afternoons, she often ironed or cleaned at a different home each day. No one could outwork Ms. Syble.

Though our ages and lifestyles were eons apart, Ms. Syble and I had something extremely important in common: We both knew God is good and He cares for those who trust Him. We both needed Him as a refuge in times of trouble. I could count on her to pray for me, my family, my children, and my job, and I still have several of her voice mails letting me know she was doing so.

My favorite memory of Ms. Syble is when after our prayers she would look up at the picture of Jesus on her wall and say, "Thank You, Lord." Ms. Syble trusted God, knew He cared about her, and humbly leaned on Him all of her life. Oh, that we might leave that kind of legacy.

WHEN LIFE GETS MEAN, LEAN!

*"But as for me, I watch in hope for the LORD,
I wait for God my Savior; my God will hear me."*
Micah 7:7

When you're given a task beyond your capabilities or far from your comfort zone, what is your normal procedure? Do you procrastinate, dread building each day? Do you harbor resentment, thinking someone more qualified should have this job? Or do you chip away at the task little by little, hoping it will become easier?

What if you've made a huge mistake and wronged those you love or those who trusted you? How do you rebuild a damaged reputation and relationships?

In Micah, we see Israel judged for misusing the wealth and power God provided. Once again, God's people turned away from Him and embraced idols, violence, deception, and dishonor. Micah had the "mean" job of pronouncing God's judgment against Israel. Considering Micah's detailed description of his untrustworthy neighbors, friends, family members, and judges, this prophecy of doom likely did not win him a popularity contest. Yet, he was faithful.

At the same time, he reminded the Israelites what pleased God and would return His favor upon His people. He told them how they could right their mistakes and rebuild the trust of those they'd wronged.

Regardless of the reactions of his audience, Micah leaned on God for the strength to obey Him and for the patience to watch and wait for His perfect will to be done. When we have a "mean" job to perform, we can always lean on Him.

TASTE

*W*hat is the tastiest thing you have experienced this week? Perhaps it was food. Perhaps it was a new outdoor experience. Or perhaps you connected with God in a way that was totally new to you. Savor that "taste" this week.

GOD IS SO GOOD

"Taste and see that the LORD is good;
blessed is the one who takes refuge in him."
Psalm 34:8 NIV (2011)

"Mom, what is that smell?" Kim came through the front door after her school day. "I can smell it from the porch."

"It's chili, Kim." I beamed. Kim was our daughter from India. Just the other day Kim and I were talking. She asked me why we never ate chili in this country. I had never made chili before, but I was willing to learn. I looked up a recipe and secretly made a trip to the store for the ingredients so I could surprise Kim at dinner.

Kim walked over to the pot and lifted the lid. "Hmmmm. What do you call this?"

"Chili," I said putting my arm around her shoulder. "I wanted to surprise you."

"Oh, Mom. I have never seen this kind of chili before. I was talking about the little chilies you see in the store. You know, they are green and about this big." Kim held up two fingers to show me. "I like to carry them in my pocket to eat at school."

Kim and I had a good laugh at my misinterpretation of her request.

Have there been times when you and a friend misunderstood one another? The only Friend who is never misunderstood and never misunderstands us is God. He has made Himself clear in His Word. Have you had your taste of God's goodness today?

SHARED EXCITEMENT

"Now that you have tasted that the Lord is good."
1 Peter 2:3 NIV (2011)

The band was loud, and the parking lot was full. Lawn chairs of all shapes and sizes were filled with old, young, and somewhere-in-between people.

Across the parking lot, I noticed our friend Bob, ninety-four years old. He was alone. As the music played, Bob swayed in rhythm. After a few minutes, Bob got up and left.

I'm not surprised, I thought. *He really doesn't understand the culture of the younger generation. It was probably a little too lively for him. It is probably just not his taste.*

I focused on the band and enjoyed watching all the teens and young folks connect with the music.

A few minutes later, Bob came back with his wife. Sitting in the row where Bob had sat, they, too, began to enjoy the music and the energy of the crowd.

After the concert, I spoke to Bob. "When I saw you leave, I was afraid that you didn't like what was going on. I'm so glad you came back."

Bob answered, "This is fantastic. Virginia really didn't want to go out tonight so I came alone. But I didn't want her to miss this, so I went home and got her!"

Has there been an experience in your life that you couldn't wait to share? Perhaps it is something you thought you would not like, but when you "tasted" it, you found that it was good. Maybe you are afraid to share your faith journey because you don't think another will like it, but you can't know until you try. Don't hesitate. Go get your friend and share your story today.

THE FRAGRANCE OF CHRIST

"But thanks be to God, who always leads us as captives in
Christ's triumphal procession and uses us to spread the aroma
of the knowledge of him everywhere. For we are to God
the pleasing aroma of Christ among those who are
being saved and those who are perishing."
2 Corinthians 2:14–15

Close your eyes for a moment. Imagine walking into a room and taking a deep breath. Popcorn! Your favorite. Someone has popped a big bowl. No matter what time of day, you immediately think it is snack time. Maybe you just enjoy the smell. Perhaps you think back to the last family movie time. Or you may immediately look for the person who is responsible for the popcorn to ask if you can have some. Why would you have done any of that? Because of the aroma of the popcorn. The smell of popcorn stirs something up within you that is pleasant and desirable. So much so that you may have even asked for some for yourself.

Isn't that what Christians want to do? We want to live in such a way that the fragrance of our lives causes people to draw closer to God, to travel in their memory banks to a time when they felt a closeness with God, or to come to us, e-mail us, or call us and ask for some of what we have.

Shouldn't that be our ultimate goal? To exude Christ from our lives in everything we do, in a way that draws others to Him? Find someone you can share that fragrance with today.

SEASONED WITH SALT

"Let your conversation be always full of grace, seasoned with salt,
so that you may know how to answer everyone."

Colossians 4:6

When my mother nearly died from congestive heart failure, doctors ordered a salt-free diet as part of her protocol for the rest of her life. We had no idea how difficult it was to find a restaurant that would offer salt-free options, or a cook who could make food taste appetizing without adding the sodium. My sister Rebecca had to advocate strongly on Mother's behalf for unprocessed meat, fresh vegetables, and unsweetened fruit. The entire family began to experiment with other ways of seasoning food and found many were satisfying, but still none that tasted as good as salt.

When it comes to conversation, though, the more salt, the better. Not salty language, of course, but the kind of "seasoning" that comes from thought and reflection, experience and wisdom, kindness and empathy. Without those qualities, how quickly we can ruin relationships and reputations with thoughtless words that taste bitter and linger long after swallowing.

Before becoming a Christian, no doubt Paul tasted the consequences of his caustic comments, but now as a believer, he advocated for conversation full of grace. Synonyms for *grace* include *refinement, beauty, elegance, polish,* and *poise.* Those qualities speak clearly of one's upbringing or education and always demonstrate good taste.

Today, may our conversation be seasoned with the Savior's salt, bringing reminders of His love and grace to the ears of those with whom we speak.

SWEETER THAN HONEY

"How sweet are your words to my taste,
sweeter than honey to my mouth!"
Psalm 119:103

When Morgan and Matt got married, one of their most unusual gifts was a quart jar of honey. However, because of Morgan's masters in nutrition and her love of organic and natural foods, it actually was a perfect gift. In addition, the card that accompanied the present provided a sweet challenge for all married couples: "May all the words you speak to each other be sweeter than honey."

The benefits of honey to the diet are many: nutrition, variety in taste, antioxidant and antimicrobial properties, to name a few. How many more benefits there are to the sweetness of God's Word: refreshment for the weary, encouragement for the despondent, guidance for the confused, instruction for the seeking, correction for the wayward, and direction for life.

Many Christian weight-loss programs actually make good use of the "sweetness" and strength of God's Word to provide a necessary supplement to their calorie-counting, exercise, or accountability methods. Memorizing scripture is advised and expected in Christ-centered weight-loss programs. Regardless of one's health condition or dietary concerns, however, God's Holy Word provides a sweetness and satisfaction that can only be realized as it becomes a natural and regular part of daily spiritual nutrition.

Have you had your honey from the Word today? Why not pull up to the Father's feast table and enjoy some delightful deified decadence right now?

PERSEVERE

Don't give up! Keep going.
You're almost there. You can do it!

*A*ll of us need a cheerleader now and then to help us believe and achieve what we set out to accomplish. But the real motivation has to come from within, a commitment to carrying out and completing whatever task or dream God has placed on your heart. This week ask the Lord to help you prioritize your to-do list and make a decision to follow through to the finish line, knowing He will walk beside you every step of the way. Because He is faithful, you can be too.

HANG IN THERE!

"But as for you, be strong and do not give up,
for your work will be rewarded."
2 Chronicles 15:7

Vera loved watching the leaves fall. The colors were bright, and they floated gracefully through the air. But she didn't like seeing them pile up in her yard.

When her grandson came to visit, she said, "Jeremy, would you blow all the leaves off the yard for me? I would love for my yard to look nice."

"Sure, Grandma." Jeremy went out and started blowing leaves. They swirled around and around. When Jeremy got near the street, he blew the leaves into a pile by the curb. However, every passing car made the pile become a whirlwind of leaves that scattered all over the yard again. With each passing car, Jeremy patiently blew the leaves back into a pile.

Jeremy finally put the blower away and went inside. "Grandma, that was hard. I didn't realize how much mess the cars made!"

"Thank you, Jeremy. You improved my house tremendously and lifted my spirits."

Jeremy could have given up. Every time he got the leaves in a nice, neat pile, a car came along to rearrange them. Then his job started over again. But he got the job done and Grandma was happy!

Are there things in your life that seem to need a lot of hard work? Ask God to help you hang in there. You can do it!

A LITTLE MORE MOISTURIZER

"Be joyful in hope, patient in affliction, faithful in prayer."
Romans 12:12

Gigi took her granddaughter shopping. As she filled her buggy, Carmen checked out every purchase. Gigi selected a new bottle of moisturizer and put it in the buggy.

"What's that?" asked Carmen.

Handing her the blister-packed bottle, Gigi said, "Here. You can read about it."

Studying the bright package, Carmen looked up. "It says it will get rid of wrinkles in two weeks."

"Yes. I have been using it every day." Gigi smiled. "What do you think?"

Carmen looked up at Gigi's face. "Well, I think you can save your money. It doesn't work."

Gigi was a little taken aback. She always appreciated the honesty of her grandchildren, but this time it surprised her. She took the bottle from her granddaughter. "Maybe I haven't been using it long enough. I am going to buy it and use it a little longer. I'm sure we will see some results soon."

Some things do seem to take a long time for results. We have to do the same work over and over again. And seeing results is slow. But like Gigi's moisturizer, perhaps we just need to hang in there and not give up.

If you need a fresh start and a little encouragement, remember to be joyful as you wait to see results, patient even though the waiting is often not fun, and faithful to cling to God's promises for you.

NEVER GIVE UP

"Be strong and take heart, all you who hope in the LORD."
Psalm 31:24

Throughout history there have been many inspiring stories of successful people who had to struggle to get where they are today. But we rarely hear of the failures they had to overcome and the perseverance of their characters it took to achieve success.

Did you know:

- After more than 10,000 attempts, Thomas Edison was successful at inventing the incandescent light bulb.
- Dr. Seuss's first book, *To Think That I Saw It on Mulberry Street*, was rejected 27 different times before being published.
- Walt Disney's first animation company went bankrupt, and he was fired by a news editor because he lacked imagination.

What do the three people above and the many more who have overcome obstacles to be successful in their fields have in common? Perseverance.

Most of us will not achieve world acclaim as famous inventors, authors, or animators. But we can emulate those same qualities that led them to success: persistence, determination, tenacity, and holding fast to a course of action.

We also have the privilege to take our needs in prayer to God, to hope in the future He has planned for us, and to act in His supernatural strength. God wants us to be successful but not necessarily in the eyes of the world, and sometimes that takes more courage than otherwise.

Real success comes from never giving up on becoming the person God created you to be. That is something worth persevering for.

KEEP PRAYING

*"You need to persevere so that when you have done the will of God,
you will receive what he has promised."*

Hebrews 10:36

Shana was embarrassed to admit it, but her daughter had joined the ranks of the prodigals. As much as Shana had loved her, provided for her needs, and prayed for her, it just didn't seem enough for Alexis.

Shana asked God what she could do. *How can I show her that the lifestyle she has chosen is wrong? What can I do to help her?*

Many sleepless nights Shana sat in the recliner clutching her Bible and hoping for an answer. *God, bring her back to our family.*

The message Shana heard was to love Alexis and keep the relationship as open as possible. *Keep what relationship open?*

Shana began to try to live that out. She left messages on Alexis's phone. Alexis was obviously watching the caller ID and didn't answer her mom's calls. Occasionally Shana wrote notes and mailed them. And she prayed every day. But after a while she wanted to be closer to Alexis as she prayed. So she drove the forty miles over to Alexis's apartment to sit in the parking lot and pray.

It wasn't immediate, but God eventually answered Shana's prayers and brought Alexis back to her family. Now they have a wonderful relationship and enjoy every moment together.

Is there a prodigal in your family? Do you have a wayward friend? Be faithful in praying for him or her. God answers prayers, and His timing is best.

CONTINUED WORK PAYS OFF

"Being confident of this, that he who began a good work in you
will carry it on to completion until the day of Christ Jesus."

Philippians 1:6

"You have nice handwriting."

As a perfectionist, Verna knew her handwriting was neat and legible. But those were not the comments she had expected on her college essay.

Verna wrote about her journey through a blizzard and was convinced she had done such a good job that her professor was going to suggest she send it to a national publication. But that was not the case. Just above the comment about her handwriting was a C+.

Verna's dream of being a writer seemed to be dashed by one professor's comments. She muddled through the rest of the year, but her pursuit of a writer's life slowed considerably.

Verna continued to write letters and information for her church.

Years later her husband reminded her of her dream of being a writer. "You ought to try your hand at publication," her husband said. "You are a good writer."

"Okay, I'll try," she said.

From that point on Verna wrote constantly. During the middle of the night when she couldn't sleep, she was at the computer. She finally realized her dream of being a writer. She did it! Verna now has many books and hundreds of articles to her credit and she has no plans to stop!

Is there something in your life you are working to achieve? Persevere. Keep working at it and God will honor your efforts.

KNOW

To know something is to be certain or sure of it. To know someone is to understand him fully and completely. This week, thank God for the things He has made known to you and for the personal relationships you know you can count on.

SOMETHING TO CHIRP ABOUT

*"Because I know whom I have believed, and am convinced
that he is able to guard what I have entrusted to him."*
2 Timothy 1:12

Susanne's flight from Atlanta to Paris had an hour before landing. But the Flight Tracker showed no little blue plane and the green flight path indicator dipped into a deep V—toward the ocean and back up.

What does that mean? I wondered.

I checked the flight log. Bad idea. A rapid decrease in altitude from 36,000 feet to 600 feet—and then . . . Nothing.

Okay, Lord. I trust You. You know where she is, in the ocean, on land, or in heaven. There is nothing I can do, so I'm going to trust You.

I refused to worry, but I was definitely concerned. When negative thoughts surfaced, I prayed and pushed them down.

Midmorning, I went to my room and knelt by the bed. And I prayed.

Father, You love my child more than I do. You have ordained her days. If You have chosen to take her home with You, You know what is best. I trust You.

I looked at the computer again. No change. But there were two messages on my phone: "Chirp from Paris. Chirp from Corsica." Susanne's "Chirps" are her code to let Momma Bird know Baby Bird is okay.

Now my tears and fears felt foolish. I KNOW God is in control. Nothing can touch me or anyone I love without His permission. Now, that's something to chirp about!

ALL THE DETAILS OF THE PLAN

"'All this,' David said, 'I have in writing from the hand
of the LORD upon me, and he gave me understanding
in all the details of the plan.'"

1 Chronicles 28:19

First Chronicles 28 details David's plans for the temple he had hoped to build for the Lord but could not because of his warrior status. Instead, God selected Solomon from David's sons to carry out this sacred task. Yet God entrusted the precise details of the plan to David, and he, in turn, conveyed them to Solomon. And what details they were!

God revealed to David everything from the exact measurements of building supplies to the precise weights of each gold and silver article to be used. Nothing was left to chance. And even though David did not build the temple, God gave him the privilege of knowing the plans and requirements for this sacred responsibility.

Parents may not always get to fulfill all their own dreams in their lifetime, but they still rejoice in knowing their children show interest and aptitude in similar areas of accomplishment. Sometimes God just wants to know we are willing to follow His design for us, but we may not see the final stages of a completed project.

Regardless, we can know that whatever task or responsibility God assigns to us, He will also provide the knowledge, skills, and resources we need to carry it out. Let's rejoice in the One who provides the blueprint for all that He has planned for our lives.

WHAT YOU TAKE INTO THE TEMPLE

"Do you not know that your body is a temple of the Holy Spirit?"
1 Corinthians 6:19

$\mathcal{A}$ tray of pastries to choose from for breakfast. Cookies and coffee for break time. Pasta and bread for lunch. The conference was intended to enrich the mind, but the carb-rich food provided could kill a body! Myriam knew better than to eat what was offered. She dug into her tote, reaching for the protein bar that would give her energy and keep her blood sugar stable. At every opportunity, she refilled her water bottle with infused water available in the hotel fitness center. Those floating cucumbers and strawberries looked pretty and gave the water a light, refreshing taste. In the evenings, Myriam would walk a mile or two on the treadmills and then sleep soundly. She knew that choosing what is good over what tastes good feels great!

Paul's comparison of the body to the temple means we should consider it sacred, an actual place of worship where our Holy God resides. As was the temple carefully designed and designated for sacrifice, meeting, learning, and serving, so are our bodies. Trouble is, temptations tantalize and attempt to thwart the purpose of these temples. Let's purpose to fix our eyes on Jesus, invoke the power of the Holy Spirit, and choose wisely what we take into the temple as well as how we use it for His glory.

Today let's show we know and celebrate God's plan for our bodies, His temples.

HE KNOWS US BY NAME

"Moses said to the LORD . . . 'If you are pleased with me,
teach me your ways so I may know you and continue to find favor
with you. Remember that this nation is your people.' . . .
And the LORD said to Moses, 'I will do the very thing you have asked,
because I am pleased with you and I know you by name.'"
Exodus 33:12–13,17

For those who have a name difficult to pronounce or one that varies from a common spelling, getting that name right really matters. Yet for Moses, entrusted with the care of 600,000 men, plus women, children, and livestock, hearing the Lord say He was pleased with him and knew him by name had to be great comfort and encouragement.

Even though Moses knew God intimately, he needed constant reminders of His sovereignty and provision. After all, after living in Egypt for 430 years, the Israelites weren't prepared for freedom or travel. And Moses had never led anything before but sheep! No doubt he grew overwhelmed with the responsibility and weary of hearing complaints.

Fortunately, Moses remembered who to ask for directions and was willing to do as the Lord commanded him. The entire book of Exodus testifies to the beauty of this personal relationship and the comfort of knowing God sees, hears, and cares about every detail of His people's lives.

Today, let's thank the Lord for knowing our names and providing for our needs, especially in the wilderness times of our lives.

HIS SERVANT, HIS WORD, HIS WILL

"For you know your servant, O Sovereign LORD. For the sake of your word and according to your will, you have done this great thing and made it known to your servant."

2 Samuel 7:20–21

*I*n his prayer-changing powerhouse *The Circle Maker*, author Mark Batterson suggests that our prayers and God's Word are inextricably linked: "We often view prayer and Scripture reading as two distinct spiritual disciplines without much overlap, but what if they were meant to be hyperlinked? What if reading became a form of praying and praying became a form of reading?" (Batterson 96).

Batterson reminds us the Bible was meant to be prayed through, not just read through. We need never have meaningless prayers. God wants us to talk to Him about great things He has done and the big dreams we are trusting Him for. King David asked God to allow him to build the temple, and even though the answer was no, God reminded David of the great promises He had already fulfilled for him: promotion from shepherd boy to Israel's king, God's constant presence, protection and rest from enemies, a lasting legacy. God also gave David the future promise of allowing his offspring to complete the temple dream.

In 2 Samuel 7, we see a triple link or chain reaction: God knows His servant; His servant knows, prays, and believes God's Word; God's will is done. We can know we are praying God's will when we are praying God's Word.

Thank You, Lord, that You know us and You help us know You through Your Word.

WORSHIP

Worship is a verb, so it's meant to be active and engaged, not just a designated time or place one day of the week. We can worship anywhere and any time. This week, look for ways to worship the King—through praise, through service, through sacrifice, through silence. Offer back to Him that which He has given you, and feel His smile of approval.

ABC PRAYERS

"'You alone are the LORD. You made the heavens, even the highest heavens, and all their starry host, the earth and all that is on it, the seas and all that is in them. You give life to everything, and the multitudes of heaven worship you.'"

Nehemiah 9:6

Karen Seddon of Christian Educators Association International features a podcast called Around the Word in 180 Days. Intended to provide a brief way of connecting public school educators with Bible study and prayer, Karen begins her message with an ABC Prayer of Adoration. By listing God's praiseworthy attributes, Karen reminds listeners that worship is the starting point to every successful day.

Her prayers go something like this: *Our Father who art in heaven, Hallowed be Thy Name. You are the Almighty One, Bountiful in Blessing, Courage-giving, Dedicated to delighting your children, Excellent in everything, Faithful, Giver of life, Holy, Holy, Holy, above all we can Imagine, Just, Kind, Loving, Measureless in Your Mercy, Noble, Omnipresent, Powerful, Quest-fulfiller, Redeemer, Savior, Triumphant King, Understanding, Victorious and Valiant, Wonderful Counselor, eXtraordinary, Yahweh, and Zealous for Your children.*

Karen follows this prayer with a devotion, quotation, and a closing prayer. In less than fifteen minutes, she directs her listeners toward the One worthy of worship. (Her podcast can be found under Media on the CEAI app.)

Challenge: Next time you are on your way to work or any place where you want to magnify the Lord, try out your own ABC prayer of adoration. It's another way to worship our King.

IN THIS PLACE

"'The glory of this present house will be greater than the glory of the former house,' says the LORD Almighty. 'And in this place I will grant peace,' declares the LORD Almighty."

Haggai 2:9

$\mathcal{E}$die was none too thrilled about living in her grandmother's old country home while finishing her senior year in college. The mold, mildew, and mice were bad enough, but having no working shower really aggravated her. Drab walls and hideous green carpet didn't help, either. Depression hung in the air like stale smoke. Even when MeMaw used to live there, it was a place of little light or laughter. Yet Edie knew God had a plan for her, and she was grateful to have a place to live. He even sent her a thankfulness tutor—her roommate, Merri.

With Merri's help, the girls added bright, creative touches—colorful wall hangings and pillows. Next came a giant, slobbery chocolate Lab named Maximus to keep them safe. They invited friends from church to hold a weekly Bible study. Soon MeMaw's old home took on new life. Edie learned to be thankful and make the most of her surroundings. To her delight, Merri even met her future husband at the Bible studies the girls hosted. Laughter, light, and love became the norm, not the exception. Edie now looks back on that year with tremendous gratitude and fond memories.

After all, any place we worship God can bring peace. And any time we surrender to God our disappointments about a depressing situation, He redeems it and brings a greater glory than we could have asked or imagined.

THE SACREDNESS OF SILENCE

"But the LORD is in his holy temple;
let all the earth be silent before him."
Habakkuk 2:20

Silent sustained reading. Silent sustained writing. Silent sustained worship. The first two phrases are quite familiar to me as classroom practices. Naturally, we experience varying degrees of success regarding the silence or the sustaining. Yet, I believe that the opportunity to read, even for just fifteen minutes a day, is a gift built into the school day. Since a classroom can't provide true solitude, we simulate it with our silence. Amazing things happen when we respect each other's desire to read or need to write.

Amazing things may also happen when we participate in silent sustained worship. Quakers practice this discipline in their unprogrammed Friends meetings. They assemble in an unadorned room with no pulpit, just chairs or benches facing each other. No program, music, or message, just expectant waiting for the still, small voice of the Spirit to speak to individuals. These "leadings" or promptings of the Holy Spirit may or may not be shared. Perhaps this practice is one of the reasons Quakers are known for their simplicity and their serenity.

Create a cocoon of silence around you for the purpose of worship. Find a simple place where you can be still for fifteen minutes. Sustain the silence by turning off all technological gadgets. Breathe deeply. Concentrate only on God. Ask Him to quiet your mind so that you discern His voice clearly. What do you hear in the silence?

GOD'S PLEASURE

"Therefore, I urge you, brothers and sisters, in view of God's mercy,
to offer your bodies as a living sacrifice,
holy and pleasing to God—this is your true and proper worship."
Romans 12:1 NIV (2011)

Many people think if they go to church on Sunday they have worshiped for the week. But true worship should be a daily life lived in awe of our God and His greatness.

Benjamin is an artist. He paints from the time he gets up until after the sun goes down. Benjamin loves God and recognizes his artistic gift comes from God. He is conscious of that as he paints. Every stroke is an act of worship to God.

Selena is a writer. She writes almost every day. As she writes, she feels God's presence. Her books are an offering to God and as she writes, she feels His approval.

The movie *Chariots of Fire* is the story of Eric Liddell, athlete and missionary. In a conversation with his sister, she is afraid his sport ranks higher in his life than his devotion to God. In explaining his feelings he says, "When I run I feel God's pleasure!"

What do you do that allows you to feel God's pleasure? Ben paints. Selena writes. Eric Liddell ran.

Maybe you never thought about God expressing His pleasure over your activities. When you find what He has created you to do, you will feel it. Spend some time today thinking about that. How are you using your God-given gifts? Do you feel His pleasure?

CONSTANT WORSHIP

"My mouth is filled with your praise,
declaring your splendor all day long."
Psalm 71:8

𝒥 love being in our worship services. But today my husband was working in the church control room where the service was broadcast every Sunday to hundreds of thousands around the world. My husband asked me to come see the production crew in action.

I couldn't imagine what could be so great about watching a bunch of people run soundboards and manage cameras.

From the minute I walked in the door of the control room, however, I was overwhelmed by the presence of God. I looked to my left where the director was not just saying which camera to go live but his hands were moving as if pointing here and there. The assistant director sang along with the hymn as he directed the cameras to the choir and orchestra. The lady putting the words up on the screen moved her fingers across the keyboard with lightning speed and total precision. The cameramen spoke softly through the headsets as they communicated to get the best possible shots. Every person in that room was not just working to provide a worship experience for their viewers, but was worshiping as they worked. I was in awe of the ministry of that television production crew. I thought I was missing worship and instead walked into a unique worship experience.

Everything we do can become an act of worship to God. Give Him your best and lay it before Him as a praise offering.

MULTIPLY

$\mathcal{R}$egardless of your mathematical skills, you can participate in the Master's multiplication mission— that of bringing as many as possible into His Kingdom. This week, watch for ways God multiplies your resources, your time, your gifts, and His love.

MULTIPLY YOUR WORDS

"And he directed the people to sit down on the grass.
Taking the five loaves and the two fish and looking up to heaven,
he gave thanks and broke the loaves. Then he gave them
to the disciples, and the disciples gave them to the people.
They all ate and were satisfied, and the disciples picked up
twelve basketfuls of broken pieces that were left over."
Matthew 14:19–20

One of Jesus' most famous miracles is feeding 5,000 people on the bank of the Sea of Galilee. Today most of us don't go sit on the water's bank to hear speakers. We are in air-conditioned auditoriums. And rarely do we multiply bread and fish.

But what about our words? Can they be multiplied and enjoyed over and over in the lives of our family and friends? Can we make a "meal" of them that will nourish and encourage?

For years my husband and I packed lunch boxes for our children. We always enclosed a note of encouragement saying we were praying for them during the school day. Usually the notes were short, but occasionally longer ones expressed our pride at something they had done.

My adult daughter once said, "Mom, I don't remember the exact words that were on those notes. But they made me feel special and so loved. I kept them in my pocket the rest of the day."

Do you have a few words you could share with someone that would be multiplied into encouragement and love in their lives?

POOL MULTIPLICATION

"God blessed them and said to them, '
Be fruitful and increase in number; fill the earth and subdue it.
Rule over the fish in the sea and the birds in the sky
and over every living creature that moves on the ground.'"

Genesis 1:28

*R*ecently we spent the night in a hotel. On the way to breakfast the next morning, noise, clapping, and merriment came from the pool area. Curious, we stopped in.

The pool area and adjoining exercise room were packed with people of all ages, sizes, and colors. Looking beyond the crowd, we saw two white-robed figures and a young man with his arms crossed on his chest. He head was bowed, tears streamed down his cheeks, and he was smiling one of the brightest smiles I had ever seen. He was getting baptized!

As he went under the water and came up, his smile was radiant. The crowd cheered and clapped. Some wept. Some began to sing. There was an excitement in the air because the family of God had increased by another brother.

The same thing happened over and over as new believers were baptized in the pool of this large national hotel chain. And every time, the same joyful celebration.

God directed Adam and Eve to be fruitful and multiply and fill the earth. In our generation His directive is to be fruitful and multiply and bring people into His family to spend eternity with Him.

Have you had a chance to tell someone about Him lately?

ROADSIDE HELP

*"Let us not become weary in doing good,
for at the proper time we will reap a harvest if we do not give up."*
Galatians 6:9

Michelle had a blowout. Alone on a dark highway with a toddler, she didn't know what to do, so she called her husband. While she and three-year-old Kinzey waited as patiently as possible, a man in a red sports car pulled off the interstate.

"Need help, ma'am?" he asked.

Wary of strangers but grateful for the help, Michelle nodded. "I have a flat tire. I don't seem to have a spare, and my husband is on the way."

"Let me take a look."

By the time Michelle's husband arrived, this kind stranger named Max had the car jacked up and ready for the tire Michelle's husband brought. Max refused to let anyone else help and quickly had the tire replaced.

The young couple thanked Max and offered to pay him. "No, I'm just a roadie. Can't pass someone in trouble." With a wave, Max got back into his sports car and drove off.

Michelle pulled back into traffic with her husband following. Several miles later they spotted another disabled car. And what was in front of it? A bright red sports car. Max was already at the car lending a hand.

Max was a roadside "good Samaritan" looking for opportunities to help others. He spent his evening multiplying the gift of help God had given him. Do you have a gift you could use over and over again to bless others?

THE RIPPLE EFFECT

"But the word of God continued to spread and flourish."
Acts 12:24 NIV (2011)

Boats cruising on a lake usually have a wake behind them, small tight waves at first and then wider ones as the boat moves on. Slow wakes create soft, gentle waves, and faster wakes create high, strong waves that rock other boats. Even when the boat is out of sight, the water continues to ripple from its wake. Once the waves hit the shoreline, they reverse their direction and head back out to the main part of the lake. One boat can create waves that last a long time.

We don't usually think about that aspect of sharing God's love. But in a way it's like a boat on a lake. There is a ripple effect that goes on and on and on. When we touch one person's life in a way that makes an impact, it continues to the next person they touch and the next and the next.

One changed life touches another and changes it. The changed person can't wait to tell a friend, who receives a touch from God. Now those two folks seek out two more, and before you know it, ripples are everywhere. With the advanced technology of today, those ripples can be felt all over the world.

Think of someone who needs a special touch. Reach out and lend a hand or say a kind word. Start a ripple and watch the scope of its reach.

MULTIPLY THE MESSAGE

"I planted the seed, Apollos watered it,
but God has been making it grow."
1 Corinthians 3:6 NIV (2011)

*W*riting a book is often a solitary job. Writers sit in their tiny offices and create books, articles, poems, and more. But although the creation process is a one-person job, by the time the work is seen in print, many hands have worked behind the scenes to make it a reality.

Probably one of the jobs that touches the most manuscripts is the editor. He or she works on multiple manuscripts in a year. His or her name may never be in the byline or on the cover. But her work has been multiplied many times as she has made it possible for the writer's polished work to reach others.

Every manuscript that has been touched by a writing coach, editor, or critiquer and receives input from others has been made stronger. So for every person who was involved in that work, his or her influence has been multiplied.

That was kind of the way it was in biblical times. When it came to spreading the word about Jesus, it was a sort of teamwork. Someone introduced Jesus to those with whom he came into contact. Apollos came along and "watered" those words. Then God finished the job as He drew people to Him.

Have you been part of a team that multiplied God's message to the world? It could be through print or word of mouth that you introduce others to Jesus.

ABIDE

Abide is such a restful word. It can't be rushed or hurried, even in its pronunciation. Abide implies an invitation to stop. Restore your connection to the One who longs to have and hold your full attention. The Father who calls you by name. The Holy One who fills you with His power if you will just remain in His presence.

Retreat.
> *Refresh.*
>> *Renew.*
Abide.

ARE YOU MOVING?

"If you remain in me and my words remain in you,
ask whatever you wish, and it will be done for you."
John 15:7 NIV (2011)

The dictionary gives several definitions for the word *abide*. It can mean to continue, persist, live on, or remain. John was well aware of those definitions when he wrote chapter 15 of his gospel.

Remaining or abiding is necessary in your relationship with God. But how can you maintain a continuous state of closeness with your heavenly Father?

The easiest way is to remain. That means to get there and stay there. But is it that easy? If statistics were available, they would probably show that all Christians desire to stay close to God, but all would agree that staying close is one of the hardest things to do.

"If you feel far away from God, guess who moved." Have you heard that saying? God is all-knowing, all-powerful, and unmoving. That saying has truth to it.

When you feel you are not remaining or abiding in God, often it is because you have become so busy, so apathetic, so distracted, or so something else that you have diminished your quiet time and your prayer time with Him. It happens to everyone, even the most spiritual.

If you are feeling that way today, make sure you spend time with God. Let Him join you for your morning coffee as you read His Word. Remember, He is always with you. He wants to be your constant companion. He will never move.

STAY CONNECTED

*"Remain in me, as I also remain in you. No branch can bear fruit
by itself; it must remain in the vine. Neither can you
bear fruit unless you remain in me. I am the vine;
you are the branches. If you remain in me and I in you,
you will bear much fruit; apart from me you can do nothing."*

John 15:4–5 NIV (2011)

There is a stately oak tree standing in our backyard. The beauty of the tree is mesmerizing. Even in the winter with no leaves the tree commands its space, and it is easy to imagine how full and green it will be in the summer.

But the tree has developed a problem. Hit by lightning several times, the trunk, and the core are dying. Little by little the outer branches are also dying. Why? Because the source of nutrition and life, the trunk, is no longer able to supply what the branches need to survive and bear leaves.

If space allowed, we could provide a drawing of the Christian life "tree." God would be the trunk and each Christian would have a place on that tree. But if for any reason one of the Christians becomes separated from God, the Source of Life, if they neglect to abide in and with him, they begin to slowly die. In this case, it would be the branch that separates from the trunk (God), rather than the trunk causing the separation.

God is the Source of our salvation, strength, power, and love. Stay connected!

HOW'S YOUR
SPIRITUAL EYESIGHT?

"And now, dear children, continue in him, so that when he appears we may be confident and unashamed before him at his coming."
1 John 2:28

"Where are they now?" I said aloud as I walked through the house. I couldn't find my glasses anywhere.

Rounding the corner into the bedroom, I spotted the light reflecting off the lenses. There they were right where I had left them, on the bed where I had been reading.

As frustrating as it is to keep up with my glasses, I am thankful they are available to help me see. I enjoy reading much more when the words on the page are clear.

There are also some things that help my spiritual eyesight and keep me in close fellowship with God:

Prayer. God is readily available any time. In fact, He wants us to stay in touch and talk with Him about everything. He often speaks during quiet time alone with Him. Only when we are abiding in Him can we hear His still, small voice.

God's Word. God's wisdom is recorded for us in the Bible. I find it incredible that the words that were penned so many years ago could possibly be pertinent to me today. But there are answers to all of life's questions found on its pages. Constantly clinging to the truth in the Bible will keep you abiding in Him.

Godly counsel. When I have a problem or need to be accountable, I have two or three friends whom I know I can count on. God has blessed them with tremendous discernment. Find a good Christian friend and nurture that relationship.

These three things are key to an abiding and constant relationship with God. More important than keeping up with glasses is the blessing of good spiritual eyesight.

LET JESUS LIVE THROUGH YOU

"Whoever claims to live in him must live as Jesus did."
1 John 2:6 *NIV (2011)*

Several years ago there was a fad in jewelry, in writing, in preaching, and many books. These things included the letters *WWJD*. These letters were to serve as a reminder to ask yourself, *What would Jesus do?* in every situation. Many young people sported bracelets and necklaces with those letters. What would Jesus do? A good question then, and a good question for now.

When we accept Jesus Christ into our lives, our goal should be to live like Him. Galatians 2:20 reminds us we have been crucified with Christ and it is now Christ living in us. And in a perfect world that is what would happen.

Jesus will help us and guide us. But often in our humanness, we don't always know what is the right thing to do. Asking ourselves what Jesus would do is a good start to finding answers to our questions. But the real key to this kind of living is to abide in Him so that we are constantly aware of His presence in our lives. Start your day by reading the Word, praying to God, and asking Him to fill you in such a way that you can point others to Him.

The Bible is full of examples of Jesus loving, healing, and ministering to others. We can be His hands and feet on earth if we are constantly abiding in Him and allowing Him to touch others through us.

GOD'S ABIDING HAND

"By this we know that we abide in Him and He in us,
because He has given us of His Spirit."

1 John 4:13 NASB

Don pushed his letter of resignation across the desk. *Thank You, God, for my new job. I don't know exactly what this change will bring but I know I can rest in You.*

Working his two weeks' notice, Don was confident. Though he had been at this job a long time, Don's closeness to God assured Him it was time to leave. He would not look back.

A few days later, Don's telephone rang. "Don, Mr. Gilmore just died of a heart attack. Everyone is in shock."

Mr. Gilmore had been Don's boss. When Don had told Mr. Gilmore of his decision to change jobs, he was genuinely excited for him and had wished him the best.

Don successfully made the transition to his new job. Shortly thereafter, Don's former company closed the doors. Mr. Gilmore had been the company backbone, and it couldn't run without him. Those who still worked there were without jobs within six months of Don's leaving.

Don says, "I felt God's hand through this whole thing. I felt secure in trusting Him. Going to bed at night I never worried about the job or the job transition. I knew God saw the big picture and what was best for me and my family. Abiding in God's love, trusting in His plan, and resting in His peace is the way to go!"

Is there a situation in your life that has been hard to deal with? Talk to God about it, read His Word, and abide with confidence that you are in His hands today.

LEAD

There is nothing quite so reassuring as knowing that the one in charge can be trusted. As we follow Christ, our Great Shepherd, we can trust Him to lead us exactly where we need to go in His perfect timing. Following also helps us develop our own leadership. This week, as you think about what it means to lead, also consider what it means to follow.

FOLLOW THE LEADER

"Dear children, do not let anyone lead you astray.
The one who does what is right is righteous, just as he is righteous."
1 John 3:7

Our annual extended family beach trip includes a portrait. Just wear what Grandma says, smile for thirty seconds, and you are done. For those under twelve, this does not seem like the fun part of the trip.

"If you will all just smile right and not act silly, we'll be done and do something fun."

Excited about the prospect of fun, cooperation abounded and the picture was done quickly.

"Follow me," my daughter said. Everyone fell in line. Kris began to lead away from the beach, across the street, into the pool parking lot, and through the gate. She danced around the chairs and beautiful landscaping on the large pool deck.

The line arrived at the deep end. Suddenly, Kris jumped in, clothes and all! The children looked at each other, bewildered. Should they really take the plunge in the clothes Grandma had carefully chosen?

Elyse looked around, shrugged her shoulders, and jumped in. James hesitated but followed. Mae, already giggling, took a running leap in with all the others. Yes, this photo shoot had ended well.

Whom are you following? Can you trust the leader with no qualms? Are you sure that you can follow him or her like the children followed their mother, into creating a fun, if not unusual, activity?

Jesus is the only leader who will never lead you astray. Follow Him in all things.

THE FISHERMAN LEADER

"In everything set them an example by doing what is good.
In your teaching show integrity, seriousness."

Titus 2:7

Jeff loved to fish at his grandfather's farm. So his tenth birthday party was a fishing trip to the farm. Jeff's grandfather stocked his pond, so this was going to be an experience to remember!

The van was loaded with ten excited young men. Jeff's dad had prepared fishing poles, purchased hundreds of crickets, bought stringers, and enlisted teenagers to help.

The van stopped, the doors flew open, and ten excited boys exited.

"Where can I catch a big fish?" one asked.

"Show me where they are biting best."

The boys spread out and started fishing.

Hooks weren't in the water long when Ben let out a yell. "I've got one. He's really fighting. I hope I can land him."

Nine boys immediately swarmed around Ben.

"Hang on, Ben, you can reel him in."

"Wow! That fish must be a monster!"

Ben finally pulled in a beautiful four-pound bass.

The swarm wiggled excitedly. They had just started fishing and already one person had landed a whopper!

Slowly the swarm went back to their fishing poles. But one by one, they looked to see where Ben was fishing. And, one by one, they moved over to join him!

In many other areas of life, either we are looking to see who we want to emulate or someone is looking at us in the same way. Don't take either responsibility lightly!

WALK IN THE WAY

"Whether you turn to the right or to the left,
your ears will hear a voice behind you, saying,
'This is the way; walk in it.'"
Isaiah 30:21

Recently I looked out the front window. My neighbor and his dog, Lilly, were on their early morning walk.

When they came out of the carport, you could see Bob mouthing the words, "C'mon, Lilly!" His arm pulled on the leash, and Lilly came out behind Bob.

But you didn't have to watch the duo for long to see who was really walking whom! Bob started out in charge, and if you asked him, he'd say he was taking Lilly for a walk. But just a few seconds' observation made it pretty clear that Lilly was walking Bob. She chose the path. If she spotted something that looked interesting, off she went with Bob in tow.

Bob and Lilly walked for thirty minutes or so, creating a zigzag path around the neighborhood. Both enjoyed their time together no matter how many circles they went in.

When God is trying to teach me something and says, "Follow Me," I sometimes become headstrong and pull on the "leash" in my direction, thinking I know better. Even though I have learned God definitely knows best, there always seems to be a struggle. Next time I feel myself wanting to get out of line behind my Leader, I'll remember Lilly. But unlike Lilly, I think I'll do my best to fall back in line!

THE SHEPHERD'S VOICE

*"When he [the shepherd] has brought out all his own,
he goes on ahead of them, and his sheep follow him
because they know his voice."*

John 10:4

Caesarea is the city of the four *Ps*—Peter, Paul, Pilate, and Phillip. The largest Mediterranean seaport, it was built by Herod the Great and became the capital of the Roman government.

Near the theater entrance, there is a second-century statue of a man carrying a lamb on his shoulders. One of the most copied pictures in the world, it has been reproduced in many art forms. The original statue, unlike many copies, does not have facial features.

Strong-willed sheep often go astray, and the shepherd knows the other sheep will follow his lead. Shepherds are usually outnumbered by their sheep. So it is imperative that all the sheep stay with him.

Perhaps this is the message of the Caesarean statue. The sheep riding on the shoulders of the shepherd certainly was kept close, close enough to identify with the voice of the shepherd. After a certain amount of time, the sheep is so used to being close to the shepherd, he will not stray from his voice.

Are you so in tune with your Shepherd's voice that you will stay close to Him no matter what?

SEARCH ME, KNOW ME, LEAD ME

"Search me, O God, and know my heart;
test me and know my anxious thoughts.
See if there is any offensive way in me,
and lead me in the way everlasting."

Psalm 139:23–24

Psalm 139 stands as an all-time favorite for many people because of its personalized providential promises. It serves as a reminder that God knew us even before our tiny bodies were formed in our mothers' wombs. He knows the number of hairs on our heads and the number of days in our lives. He knows the words we are going to speak before we even think them. He knows when we lie down and when we go out, when we sit in darkness or when we travel or move far away. He knows everything and thinks about us day and night.

This portrait of intimacy creates a climate of trust. The psalmist feels confident and comfortable asking God to search and know his heart and his anxious thoughts. He asks God to pinpoint any offensive ways that might need to change. By humbling himself and asking the Lord for correction and direction, the psalmist can rest assured that the God who knows him so personally will provide a clear path for him to follow. And not just any path—he asks God to lead him in the way everlasting.

Take time to read Psalm 139 today. It will remind you of how much God loves and cares for you. And it will remind Him that you want to follow where He leads.

LOVE

*J*esus demonstrated the ultimate model of what it means to love by sacrificing His life that our sins may be forgiven and we may inherit eternal life with Him in heaven. The best way for us to love Him in return is to obey His command in John 13:34–35: "Love one another. As I have loved you, so you must love one another. By this all men will know that you are my disciples, if you love one another."

What better way to end our yearlong study of *Words to Live By* than with the greatest of all words— *LOVE*? As you consider the many ways God has demonstrated His love to you, may you see and seize opportunities to reciprocate by loving others in return.

BIRD EGGS MATTER

"I have loved you with an everlasting love;
I have drawn you with loving-kindness."

Jeremiah 31:3

My first mission trip experience was teaching Bible school in the abandoned coal mine areas of Kentucky.

At recess one day, one of my boys climbed a tree. A ruckus broke out at the trunk.

"Do something," one of the kids shouted. "Jake's gonna break them bird's eggs in the nest."

"Stop him," another said.

I looked up. "Jake, come down out of the tree." He ignored me. "Jake, come down please!" I gently tugged on his leg. Jake jumped from the tree and started swinging his fists. Children scattered.

My co-teacher took our class inside—everyone but Jake. I sat on the steps beside him.

"Jake, why would you want to do that? Those eggs will hatch into little birds and the mama bird will love them, just like your mama loves you." Jake looked away. "It's like God loves us since we are His children."

Jake turned to look at me. His dirty hand left a gray streak as he wiped a tear. "Nobody loves me. Ain't nobody who cares about me."

"Jake, I haven't known you long but I already love you."

Jake shrugged.

"God loves you. He cares about bird's eggs and He cares about you." I pulled him into a hug. "Let me show you this week how much I love you."

Do you have a Jake in your life who needs to know he is loved?

UNQUENCHABLE

"Many waters cannot quench love; rivers cannot wash it away."
Song of Songs 8:7

*H*uman love, even in its highest form of commitment, seems susceptible to change. Feelings and circumstances buffet the heart and may make even the sweetest saint snap and act or react in unloving ways. Even those in positions of leadership fall prey to the tempter's snare and betray relationships that should be held sacred and indestructible.

So, what kind of love cannot be quenched or washed away? Only that which flows from the perfect love of Christ—which knows no boundaries and springs from the Source of endless supply. The man or woman after God's own heart has access to this love and nothing can snuff it out. Whatever relationship or situation you are in where the devotion of true love is flooded daily by interruptions and inconveniences, unexpected expenses or illness, call on the Christ who demonstrated the ultimate sacrificial love—laying down His very life that we may have abundant life flowing in and through us.

Today, whether you care for little ones or elderly parents, whether you are flooded by work responsibilities or washed away by overcommitments in other areas, examine the source and see if you need to take another drink of living water from God's Word or spend time nestled in His presence. The love He supplies cannot be quenched or washed away; like His grace, it is sufficient for whatever you are called to do and whomever you are asked to love.

EASY FOR THEM, HARD FOR YOU

"Love is patient, love is kind. It does not envy, it does not boast,
it is not proud. It is not rude, it is not self-seeking,
it is not easily angered, it keeps no record of wrongs."
1 Corinthians 13:4–5

Susan had done her best to make it work. Over and over she offered options and alternatives, spending countless hours on phone calls and e-mails. The fun "girls only" weekend she tried to pull together just kept unraveling. Too many complicating variables. Too much aggravation. Too much changing and rearranging. Yet she never complained. She did not get angry. And she did not hold it against the two friends who just couldn't get it together. Smiling and shaking her head, she looked again at the last e-mail: "You made it easy for us, though it had to be hard for you. That is true love." Tomorrow morning she would change the reservations one last time—and hope!

Everyone has times when others cause inconvenience or concern. Not everyone responds the same way. The natural tendency is to get angry or aggravated and vow not to get caught in that kind of situation again. But true love keeps no record of wrongs. True love "always protects, always trusts, always hopes, always perseveres" (1 Corinthians 13:7). Even if her girlfriends hadn't 'fessed up at how they messed up, Susan determined to love them anyway.

Next time someone messes up, try loving them anyway. Make it easy for them, though it's hard for you. That's real love.

REACH OUT WITH LOVE

*"Dear children, let us not love with words or speech
but with actions and in truth."*
1 John 3:18 NIV (2011)

*O*nce again yesterday my pastor said, "There's a hurting heart on every pew."

I looked around. If I got very far away from my own personal pew space, did I really know what folks were going through?

The lady sitting four rows over sure looked like she had it all together. Dressed perfectly, makeup beautifully applied, and not a hair out of place. But I happened to know she had just buried her sister two weeks ago.

The gentleman in the side section worshiped with such fervor and joy. Unless you had been told, you would never know he was battling an incurable disease and his life expectancy was probably short.

The young lady on the front row struggled to keep her four children to minimum wiggles. Her shirt was crooked, and you wondered how long her hairbrush had been lost. Knowing she had to get four young, squirmy little ones ready to come to church gave you a clue to what everyday life was like.

How can we judge others based on their outward appearance? Can we possibly know what is behind a perfect smile or an unkempt appearance?

No. But we can refrain from judging others and reach out to them with the love of Jesus, no matter what the circumstances. Why not find someone today you can reach out to with the love of Jesus?

SHARE HIS PERFECT LOVE

"Be perfect, therefore, as your heavenly Father is perfect."
Matthew 5:48

Morning quiet time by the pool is my favorite time of the day. I have a spot that feels almost like holy ground.

On one of these mornings I looked over to the pool. The water was as shiny as a new mirror, and the image of the horizon was perfectly reflected in the smooth surface. The trees were green, and one lone, fluffy white cloud floated overhead. It was the kind of mesmerizing beauty that you can't take your eyes off of.

Looking at this beautifully reflected landscape, I couldn't help but think what a great picture this was of God's love living in us. When we are filled with the living water of Jesus Christ, we can reflect the perfect image of God.

We definitely can't be perfect. But God in us is perfect, and we can show that to a world that needs His love. We can be a reflection of our perfect God to the imperfect world around us.

Have you ever said something to someone and after you said it you surprised even yourself at how fitting it was for the situation? You had no idea exactly what was happening in their lives, yet you were able to make a difference. That was the reflection of God in your life to someone else.

Perhaps you know of someone who needs a glimpse of God. Visit them and let them feel His love through you.

THE OLD TESTAMENT

GENESIS

Genesis 1:28 "God blessed them and said to them, 'Be fruitful and increase in number . . .'" MULTIPLY

Genesis 35:10 "You will no longer be called Jacob; your name will be Israel." CHANGE

EXODUS

Exodus 20:12 "Honor your father and your mother, so that you may live long in the land the LORD your God is giving you." HONOR

Exodus 23:20 "See, I am sending an angel ahead of you to guard you along the way and to bring you to the place I have prepared." PREPARE

Exodus 33:12–13,17 "Moses said to the LORD . . . 'If you are pleased with me, teach me your ways so I may know you and continue to find favor with you . . .'" KNOW

LEVITICUS

Leviticus 19:9–10 "When you reap the harvest of your land, do not reap to the very edges of your field or gather the gleanings of your harvest. Do not go over your vineyard a second time . . ." SHARE

Leviticus 19:32 NIV (2011) "Stand up in the presence of the aged, show respect for the elderly and revere your God. I am the LORD." RESPECT

NUMBERS

Numbers 17:5 "The staff belonging to the man I choose will sprout, and I will rid myself of this constant grumbling against you by the Israelites." HONOR

Numbers 23:19 "God is not a man, that he should lie, nor a son of man, that he should change his mind. Does he speak and then not act? Does he promise and not fulfill?" RELAX

DEUTERONOMY

Deuteronomy 13:4 "It is the LORD your God you must follow, and him you must revere. Keep his commands and obey him; serve him and hold fast to him." OBEY

Deuteronomy 15:11 "There will always be poor people in the land. Therefore I command you to be openhanded toward your fellow Israelites who are poor and needy in your land." APPRECIATE

JOSHUA

Joshua 1:7 "Be strong and very courageous. Be careful to obey all the law my servant Moses gave you . . ." OBEY

Joshua 24:15 "But if serving the LORD seems undesirable to you, then choose . . ." CHOOSE

JUDGES

Judges 6:17–18 "Gideon replied, 'If now I have found favor in your eyes, give me a sign that it is really you talking to me. Please do not go away until I come back . . .'" SACRIFICE

Judges 6:26 "Then build a proper kind of altar to the LORD . . . Using the wood of the Asherah pole that you cut down, offer the second bull as a burnt offering." SACRIFICE

Judges 7:4 "But the LORD said to Gideon, 'There are still too many men. Take them down to the water, and I will sift them for you there.'" SACRIFICE

Judges 21:23 "So that is what the Benjamites did. While the girls were dancing, each man caught one and carried her off to be his wife . . ." DANCE

RUTH

Ruth 2:11–12 "Boaz replied, 'I've been told all about what you have done for your mother-in-law since the death of your husband—how you left your father and mother . . .'" RESPECT

1 SAMUEL

1 Samuel 1:27–28 "'I prayed for this child, and the LORD has granted me what I asked of him. So now I give him to the LORD. For his whole life he will be given over to the LORD.'" TRUST

1 Samuel 10:8 "You must wait seven days until I come to you and tell you what you are to do." WAIT

2 SAMUEL

2 Samuel 6:14 NASB "And David was dancing before the LORD with all his might, and David was wearing a linen ephod." DANCE

2 Samuel 7:20–21 "For you know your servant, O Sovereign LORD. For the sake of your word and according to your will, you have done this great thing and made it known to your servant." KNOW

1 KINGS

1 Kings 3:9 "So give your servant a discerning heart to govern your people and to distinguish between right and wrong." GIVE

I Kings 8:23 "'O LORD, God of Israel, there is no God like you in heaven above or on earth below—you who keep your covenant of love with your servants who continue wholeheartedly in your way.'" CELEBRATE

1 Kings 19:11–12 "Then a great and powerful wind tore the mountains apart . . . but the LORD was not in the wind. After the wind there was an earthquake . . ." WAIT

2 KINGS

2 Kings 10:27 "They demolished the sacred stone of Baal and tore down the temple of Baal, and people have used it for a latrine to this day." LAUGH

2 Kings 12:15 "They did not require an accounting from those to whom they gave the money to pay the workers, because they acted with complete honesty." COUNT

1 CHRONICLES

1 Chronicles 16:25, 27 "For great is the LORD and most worthy of praise . . . Splendor and majesty are before him; strength and joy in his dwelling place." PRAISE

1 Chronicles 28:19 "'All this,' David said, 'I have in writing from the hand of the LORD upon me, and he gave me understanding in all the details of the plan.'" KNOW

2 CHRONICLES

2 Chronicles 15:7 "But as for you, be strong and do not give up, for your work will be rewarded." PERSEVERE

2 Chronicles 29:5 "Consecrate yourselves now and consecrate the temple . . . Remove all defilement." CLEAN

2 Chronicles 29:30 "So they sang praises with gladness and bowed their heads and worshiped." SING

2 Chronicles 32:7–8 "Be strong and courageous. Do not be afraid or discouraged because of the king of Assyria and the vast army with him . . . With him is only the arm of flesh, but with us is the LORD our God." FIGHT

EZRA

Ezra 3:3–4 "Despite their fear of the peoples around them, they built the altar on its foundation and sacrificed burnt offerings on it to the LORD, both the morning and evening sacrifices. Then in accordance with what is written, they celebrated." OBEY

NEHEMIAH

Nehemiah 4:14–15 "'Don't be afraid of them. Remember the LORD, who is great and awesome, and fight for your brothers, your sons and your daughters, your wives . . .'" FIGHT

Nehemiah 9:6 "'You alone are the LORD. You made the heavens, even the highest heavens, and all their starry host, the earth and all that is on it . . .'" WORSHIP

ESTHER

Esther 9:28 NIV (2011) "These days should be remembered and observed in every generation by every family, and in every province and in every city. And these days of Purim should never fail to be celebrated . . ." CELEBRATE

JOB

Job 4:12–13 "A word was secretly brought to me, my ears caught a whisper of it. Amid disquieting dreams in the night." DREAM

Job 13:15 "Though he slay me, yet will I hope in him." TRUST

Job 33:14–15 "For God does speak—now one way, now another—though man may not perceive it. In a dream, in a vision of the night, when deep sleep falls on men as they slumber in their beds." DREAM

PSALMS

Psalm 9:10 "Those who know your name will trust in you . . ." TRUST

Psalm 20:4 "May he give you the desire of your heart and make all your plans succeed." COUNT

Psalm 27:13 NIV (2011) "I remain confident of this: I will see the goodness of the LORD in the land of the living." BELIEVE

Psalm 31:24 "Be strong and take heart, all you who hope in the LORD." PERSEVERE

Psalm 32:8 "I will instruct you and teach you in the way you should go . . ." CHOOSE

Psalm 34:8 NIV (2011) "Taste and see that the LORD is good . . ." TASTE

Psalm 37:4 "Delight yourself in the LORD and he will give you the desires . . ." DREAM

Psalm 39:1 "I said, 'I will watch my ways and keep my tongue from sin; I will put a muzzle on my mouth . . ." LISTEN

Psalm 46:10 "Be still, and know that I am God." STOP

Psalm 49:3 NIV (2011) "My mouth will speak words of wisdom; the meditation of my heart will give you understanding." TRANSLATE

Psalm 61:1–2 "Hear my cry, O God; listen to my prayer . . ." LISTEN

Psalm 71:8 "My mouth is filled with your praise, declaring your splendor all day long." TRANSLATE, WORSHIP

Psalm 77:11 "I will remember the deeds of the LORD; yes, I will remember your miracles of long ago." REMEMBER

Psalm 90:12 "Teach us to number our days aright, that we may gain a heart of wisdom." FOCUS

Psalm 91:4 "He will cover you with his feathers, and under his wings you will find refuge; his faithfulness will be your shield and rampart." SACRIFICE

Psalm 92:12–13 "The righteous will flourish like a palm tree, they will grow like a cedar of Lebanon; planted in the house of the LORD, they will flourish in the courts of our God." COUNT

Psalm 98:1 NASB "O sing to the LORD a new song, For He has done wonderful things, His right hand and His holy arm have gained the victory for Him." SING

Psalm 107:15 "Let them give thanks to the LORD for his unfailing love and his wonderful deeds for men." APPRECIATE

Psalm 118:24 "The LORD has done it this very day; let us rejoice today and be glad." REJOICE

Psalm 119:11 "I have hidden your word in my heart that I might not sin against you." REMEMBER

Psalm 119:103 "How sweet are your words to my taste, sweeter than honey to my mouth!" TASTE

Psalm 130:5 "I wait for the LORD, my whole being waits, and in his word I put my hope." WAIT

Psalm 133:1 NIV (2011) "How good and pleasant it is when God's people live together in unity." SING

Psalm 139:23–24 "Search me, O God, and know my heart; test me and know my anxious thoughts. See if there is any offensive way in me, and lead me in the way everlasting." LEAD

Psalm 144:1 "Praise be to the LORD my Rock, who trains my hands for war, my fingers for battle." FIGHT

Psalm 144:2 "He is my loving God and my fortress, my stronghold and my deliverer, my shield in whom I take refuge, who subdues peoples under me." FIGHT

Psalm 145:16 "You open your hand and satisfy the desires of every living thing." RELAX

Psalm 149:3 NIV (2011) "Let them praise his name with dancing and make music to him with timbrel and harp." DANCE

Psalm 150:4 NIV (2011) "Praise him with timbrel and dancing, praise him with the strings and pipe." DANCE

PROVERBS

Proverbs 1:5 "Let the wise listen and add to their learning . . ." LISTEN

Proverbs 3:5–6 "Trust in the LORD with all your heart and lean not on your own understanding; in all your ways acknowledge him, and he will make your paths straight." TRUST

Proverbs 13:4 NIV (2011) "A sluggard's appetite is never filled, but the desires of the diligent are fully satisfied." WORK

Proverbs 15:3 "The eyes of the LORD are everywhere, keeping watch on the wicked and the good." PLAY

Proverbs 15:13 "A happy heart makes the face cheerful . . ." LAUGH

Proverbs 17:22 "A cheerful heart is good medicine, but a crushed spirit dries up the bones." LAUGH

Proverbs 24:3 "By wisdom a house is built, and through understanding it is established." CLEAN

Proverbs 31:14 "She is like the merchant ships, bringing her food from afar." BARTER

Proverbs 31:27 "She watches over the affairs of her household and does not eat the bread of idleness." CLEAN

ECCLESIASTES

Ecclesiastes 3:1 "There is a time for everything, and a season for every activity . . ." CHANGE

Ecclesiastes 5:2 "Do not be quick with your mouth, do not be hasty in your heart to utter anything before God. God is in heaven and you are on earth, so let your words be few." LAUGH

Ecclesiastes 9:10 "Whatever your hand finds to do, do it with all your might." WORK

SONG OF SONGS

Song of Songs 8:7 "Many waters cannot quench love; rivers cannot wash it away." LOVE

ISAIAH

Isaiah 25:1 NIV (2011) "LORD, you are my God; I will exalt you and praise your name, for in perfect faithfulness you have done wonderful things, things planned long ago." TRANSLATE

Isaiah 26:3 NIV (2011) "You will keep in perfect peace those whose minds are steadfast, because they trust in you." FOCUS

Isaiah 30:15 "This is what the Sovereign LORD, the Holy One of Israel, says: 'In repentance and rest is your salvation, in quietness and trust is your strength . . .'" STOP

Isaiah 30:21 "Whether you turn to the right or to the left, your ears will hear a voice behind you, saying, 'This is the way; walk in it.'" LEAD

Isaiah 40:31 "Those who hope in the LORD will renew their strength . . ." STOP

Isaiah 43:2–3 "When you pass through the waters, I will be with you; and when you pass through the rivers, they will not sweep over you . . ." WORK

Isaiah 43:18–19 "Forget the former things; do not dwell on the past. See, I am doing a new thing! Now it springs up; do you not perceive it? I am making a way in the desert and streams in the wasteland." PUSH

Isaiah 50:4 "He wakens me morning by morning . . . to listen like one . . ." LISTEN

Isaiah 55:8 "For my thoughts are not your thoughts . . ." STOP

Isaiah 57:14 "Build up, build up, prepare the road! Remove the obstacles out of the way of my people." THINK

Isaiah 61:3 "A planting of the LORD for the display of his splendor." WORK

JEREMIAH

Jeremiah 1:6–8 "'Ah, Sovereign LORD,' I said, 'I do not know how to speak; I am only a child.' But the LORD said to me, 'Do not say, I am only a child.' You must go to everyone I send you to and say whatever I command you . . .'" ACCEPT

Jeremiah 23:24 NIV (2011) "'Who can hide in secret places so that I cannot see them?' declares the LORD. 'Do not I fill heaven and earth?' declares the LORD." COUNT

Jeremiah 29:11 "'For I know the plans I have for you,' declares the LORD, 'plans to prosper you and not to harm you, plans to give you hope and a future.'" WAIT

Jeremiah 31:3 "I have loved you with an everlasting love; I have drawn you with loving-kindness." LOVE

Jeremiah 31:4 NASB "Again I will build you and you will be rebuilt, O virgin of Israel! Again you will take up your tambourines, and go forth to the dances of the merrymakers." DANCE

Jeremiah 32:17 "Ah, Sovereign LORD, you have made the heavens and the earth by your great power and outstretched arm. Nothing is too hard for you." CELEBRATE

LAMENTATIONS

Lamentations 3:22 "Because of the LORD's great love we are not consumed . . ." CHOOSE

EZEKIEL

Ezekiel 36:26 "I will give you a new heart and put a new spirit in you." CHANGE

Ezekiel 44:23 "They are to teach my people the difference between the holy and the common." HONOR

DANIEL

Daniel 12:1 "There will be a time of distress such as has not happened from the beginning of nations until then. But at that time your people—everyone whose name is found written in the book—will be delivered . . ." THANK

HOSEA

Hosea 12:6 "But you must return to your God; maintain love and justice, and wait for your God always." RELATE

JOEL

Joel 2:23, 25 "Be glad, O people of Zion, rejoice in the LORD your God, for he has given you the autumn rains in righteousness. He sends you abundant showers . . ." REJOICE

AMOS

Amos 7:7 "This is what he showed me: The LORD was standing by a wall that had been built true to plumb, with a plumb line in his hand." LEAN

OBADIAH

Obadiah 15 "The day of the LORD is near for all nations. As you have done, it will be done to you; your deeds will return upon your own head." RESPECT

JONAH

Jonah 2:1–2 "From inside the fish Jonah prayed to the LORD his God. He said: 'In my distress I called to the LORD, and he answered me.'" PRAY

MICAH

Micah 7:7 "But as for me, I watch in hope for the LORD, I wait for God my Savior; my God will hear me." LEAN, WAIT

NAHUM

Nahum 1:7 "The LORD is good, a refuge in times of trouble. He cares for those who trust in him." LEAN

HABAKKUK

Habakkuk 2:20 "But the LORD is in his holy temple; let all the earth be silent before him." WORSHIP

Habakkuk 3:2 "LORD, I have heard of your fame; I stand in awe of your deeds, O LORD. Renew them in our day." RESPECT

Habakkuk 3:17–18 "Though the fig tree does not bud and there are no grapes on the vines, though the olive crop fails and the fields produce no food, though there are no sheep in the pen and no cattle in the stalls, yet I will rejoice in the LORD, I will be joyful in God my Savior." REJOICE

ZEPHANIAH

Zephaniah 3:17 NIV (2011) "The LORD your God is with you, the Mighty Warrior who saves. He will take great delight in you; in his love he will no longer rebuke you but will rejoice over you with singing." SING

HAGGAI

Haggai 2:9 "'The glory of this present house will be greater than the glory of the former house,' says the LORD Almighty. 'And in this place I will grant peace, declares the LORD Almighty.'" WORSHIP

ZECHARIAH

Zechariah 4:6 "Not by might nor by power, but by my Spirit, says the LORD Almighty." LEAN
Zechariah 8:5 "The city streets will be filled with boys and girls playing there." PLAY

MALACHI

Malachi 3:16 "Then those who feared the LORD talked with each other, and the LORD listened and heard. A scroll of remembrance was written in his presence concerning those who feared the LORD and honored his name." REMEMBER

THE NEW TESTAMENT

MATTHEW

Matthew 5:14–16 "You are the light of the world. A city on a hill cannot be hidden. Neither do people light a lamp and put it under a bowl. Instead they put it on its stand . . ." HONOR

Matthew 5:48 "Be perfect, therefore, as your heavenly Father is perfect." LOVE

Matthew 6:8 "Your Father knows what you need before you ask him." PRAY

Matthew 6:20 "But store up for yourselves treasures in heaven, where moth and rust do not destroy, and where thieves do not break in and steal." CHERISH

Matthew 6:27 NIV (2011) "Can any one of you by worrying add a single hour to your life?" PUSH, RELATE

Matthew 7:11 KJV "If ye then, being evil, know how to give good gifts unto your children, how much more shall your Father which is in heaven give good things to them that ask him?" GIVE

Matthew 9:20–22 "Just then a woman who had been subject to bleeding for twelve years came up behind him and touched the edge of his cloak. She said to herself, 'If I only touch his cloak, I will be healed . . .'" BELIEVE

Matthew 12:40 "For as Jonah was three days and three nights in the belly of a huge fish, so the Son of Man will be three days and three nights in the heart of the earth." CHANGE

Matthew 14:19–20 "And he directed the people to sit down on the grass. Taking the five loaves and the two fish and looking up to heaven, he gave thanks . . ." MULTIPLY

Matthew 18:4 NIV (2011) "Therefore, whoever takes the lowly position of this child is the greatest in the kingdom of heaven." BELIEVE

Matthew 25:40 NIV (2011) "Truly I tell you, whatever you did for one of the least of these brothers and sisters of mine, you did for me." SHARE

MARK

Mark 9:24 "I do believe; help me overcome my unbelief!" BELIEVE

LUKE

Luke 6:37 "Forgive, and you will be forgiven." FORGIVE

Luke 11:28 "Blessed rather are those who hear the word of God and obey it." CHERISH

Luke 12:22, 25 "Do not worry about your life. . . .Who of you by worrying can add a single hour to his life?'" ACCEPT

Luke 16:10 "Whoever can be trusted with very little can also be trusted with much . . ." BARTER

Luke 17:15–19 NIV (2011) "One of them, when he saw he was healed, came back, praising God in a loud voice. He threw himself at Jesus' feet and thanked him . . ." THANK

JOHN

John 3:16 "For God so loved the world that he gave his one and only Son, that whoever believes in him shall not perish but have eternal life." BARTER

John 10:4 "When he (the shepherd) has brought out all his own, he goes on ahead of them and his sheep follow him because they know his voice." LEAD

John 10:27–28 "My sheep listen to my voice . . ." LISTEN

John 14:1 "Do not let your hearts be troubled. Trust in God; trust also in me." TRUST

John 14:2–3 "In my Father's house are many rooms; if it were not so, I would have told you. I am going there to prepare a place for you. And if I go and prepare a place for you . . ." PREPARE

John 14:23 NIV (2011) "Jesus replied, 'Anyone who loves me will obey my teaching. My Father will love them, and we will come to them and make our home with them.'" OBEY

John 14:26–27 "But the Counselor, the Holy Spirit, whom the Father will send in my name, will teach you all things, and will remind you of everything I have said to you. Peace I leave with you; my peace I give you . . ." RELAX

John 15:4–5 NIV (2011) "Remain in me, as I also remain in you . . ." ABIDE

John 15:7 NIV (2011) "If you remain in me and my words remain in you . . ." ABIDE

John 15:12 NKJV "This is My commandment, that you love one another as I have loved you." REACH

John 15:16 "You did not choose me, but I chose you . . ." CHOOSE

ACTS (OF THE APOSTLES)

Acts 2:7–8 NIV (2011) "Utterly amazed, they asked: 'Aren't all these who are speaking Galileans? Then how is it that each of us hears them in our native language?'" TRANSLATE

Acts 9:13, 17 "'Lord,' Ananias answered, 'I have heard many reports about this man and all the harm he has done to your saints in Jerusalem' . . . Then Ananias went to the house and entered it. Placing his hands on Saul . . ." REACH

Acts 12:24 NIV (2011) "But the word of God continued to spread and flourish." MULTIPLY

Acts 17:27 NIV (2011) "God did this so that they would seek him and perhaps reach out for him and find him, though he is not far from any one of us." REACH

ROMANS

Romans 3:23 "For all have sinned and fall short of the glory of God." PUSH

Romans 8:16 "The Spirit himself testifies with our spirit that we are God's children." RESPECT

Romans 8:37 "No, in all these things we are more than conquerors . . ." APPRECIATE

Romans 10:14 "How, then, can they call on the one they have not believed in? And how can they believe in the one of whom they have not heard? . . ." THINK

Romans 12:1 NIV (2011) "Therefore, I urge you, brothers and sisters, in view of God's mercy, to offer your bodies as a living sacrifice, holy and pleasing to God—this is your true and proper worship." WORSHIP

Romans 12:2 "Do not conform any longer to the pattern of this world, but be transformed by the renewing of your mind . . ." RELAX

Romans 12:12 "Be joyful in hope, patient in affliction, faithful in prayer." PERSEVERE

Romans 12:18 "If it is possible, as far as it depends on you, live at peace with everyone." RELATE

Romans 14:19 "Let us therefore make every effort to do what leads to peace and to mutual edification." PLAY

Romans 15:7 "Accept one another, then, just as Christ accepted you, in order to bring praise to God." PRAISE

Romans 15:13 "May the God of hope fill you with all joy and peace as you trust in him, so that you may overflow with hope by the power of the Holy Spirit." HOPE

1 CORINTHIANS

1 Corinthians 1:31 "Therefore, as it is written: 'Let him who boasts boast in the Lord.'" CELEBRATE

1 Corinthians 2:9 "No eye has seen, no ear has heard, no mind has conceived what God has prepared for those who love him." PREPARE

1 Corinthians 3:6 NIV (2011) "I planted the seed, Apollos watered it, but God has been making it grow." MULTIPLY

1 Corinthians 6:19 "Do you not know that your body is the temple of the Holy Spirit?" KNOW

1 Corinthians 12:4 "There are different kinds of gifts, but the same Spirit." GIVE

1 Corinthians 12:31 "But eagerly desire the greater gifts." REACH

1 Corinthians 13:4–5 "Love is patient, love is kind. It does not envy, it does not boast, it is not proud. It is not rude, it is not self-seeking . . ." LOVE

1 Corinthians 14:33 "For God is not a God of disorder but of peace." CLEAN

1 Corinthians 16:13 NASB "Be on the alert, stand firm in the faith, act like men, be strong." PREPARE

2 CORINTHIANS

2 Corinthians 2:14–15 NIV (2011) "But thanks be to God, who always leads us as captives in Christ's triumphal procession and uses us to spread the aroma of the knowledge of him . . ." TASTE

2 Corinthians 4:18 "So we fix our eyes not on what is seen, but on what is unseen, since what is seen is temporary, but what is unseen is eternal." FOCUS

2 Corinthians 5:17 NIV (2011) "Therefore, if anyone is in Christ, the new creation has come: The old has gone, the new is here!" RELATE

2 Corinthians 9:15 "Thanks be to God for his indescribable gift!" GIVE

GALATIANS

Galatians 5:22–23 "But the fruit of the Spirit is love, joy, peace, patience, kindness, goodness, faithfulness, gentleness and self-control. Against such things there is no law." COUNT

Galatians 5:25 "Since we live by the Spirit, let us keep in step with the Spirit." EXERCISE

Galatians 6:2 "Carry each other's burdens, and in this way you will fulfill the law of Christ." LEAN

Galatians 6:9 "Let us not become weary in doing good, for at the proper time we will reap a harvest if we do not give up." MULTIPLY

EPHESIANS

Ephesians 4:12 NIV (2011) "To equip his people for works of service, so that the body of Christ may be built up." PUSH

Ephesians 4:25 "Therefore each of you must put off falsehood and speak truthfully to his neighbor, for we are all members of one body." APPRECIATE

Ephesians 4:26 "'In your anger do not sin': Do not let the sun go down while you are still angry." FORGIVE

Ephesians 5:2 NIV (2011) "And walk in the way of love, just as Christ loved us and gave himself up for us as a fragrant offering and sacrifice to God." SACRIFICE

Ephesians 5:15–16 "Be very careful, then, how you live—not as unwise, but as wise, making the most of every opportunity." BARTER

Ephesians 5:19 "Speak to one another with psalms, hymns and spiritual songs. Sing and make music in your heart to the Lord." PRAISE

PHILIPPIANS

Philippians 1:3 "I thank my God every time I remember you." APPRECIATE

Philippians 1:4 "In all my prayers for all of you, I always pray with joy." REJOICE

Philippians 1:6 "Being confident of this, that he who began a good work in you will carry it on to completion until the day of Christ Jesus." PERSEVERE

Philippians 1:20–21 "I eagerly expect and hope that I will in no way be ashamed, but will have sufficient courage so that now as always Christ will be exalted . . ." HOPE

Philippians 2:2 "Then make my joy complete by being like-minded, having the same love, being one in spirit and purpose." TRANSLATE

Philippians 2:4 NIV (2011) "Not looking to your own interests but each of you to the interests of the others." SHARE

Philippians 2:14–15 "Do everything without complaining or arguing, so that you may become blameless and pure, children of God without fault . . ." HONOR

Philippians 3:13–14 "Brothers, I do not consider myself yet to have taken hold of it. But one thing I do: Forgetting what is behind and straining toward what is ahead . . ." FORGIVE

Philippians 4:8 "If anything is excellent or praiseworthy—think about such things." STOP

Philippians 4:13 NIV (2011) "I can do all this through him who gives me strength." THINK

COLOSSIANS

Colossians 1:17 "He is before all things, and in him all things hold together." ACCEPT

Colossians 2:5 "For though I am absent from you in body, I am present with you in spirit and delight to see how orderly you are and how firm your faith in Christ is." CHERISH

Colossians 3:1–2 "Since, then, you have been raised with Christ, set your hearts on things above, where Christ is, seated at the right hand of God. Set your minds on things above, not on earthly things." THINK

Colossians 3:13 "Bear with each other and forgive whatever grievances you may have against one another. Forgive as the Lord forgave you." FORGIVE

Colossians 3:15 "Let the peace of Christ rule in your hearts, since as members of one body you were called to peace. And be thankful." THANK

Colossians 3:23–24 NIV (2011) "Whatever you do, work at it with all your heart, as working for the Lord, not for human masters . . ." WORK

Colossians 4:2 "Devote yourselves to prayer, being watchful and thankful." PRAY

Colossians 4:6 "Let your conversation be always full of grace, seasoned with salt, so that you may know how to answer everyone." TASTE

1 THESSALONIANS

1 Thessalonians 3:12 "May the Lord make your love increase and overflow for each other and for everyone else, just as ours does for you." CHOOSE

1 Thessalonians 5:11 "Therefore, encourage one another and build each other up, just as in fact you are doing." CELEBRATE

1 Thessalonians 5:16–18 "Be joyful always; pray continually . . ." PRAY

1 Thessalonians 5:25 NIV (2011) "Brothers and sisters, pray for us." PRAY

2 THESSALONIANS

2 Thessalonians 3:5 "May the Lord direct your hearts into God's love and Christ's perseverance." FORGIVE

2 Thessalonians 3:13 "As for you, brothers, never tire of doing what is right." PUSH

1 TIMOTHY

1 Timothy 4:4 "For everything God created is good, and nothing is to be rejected if it is received with thanksgiving." THANK

1 Timothy 4:8 "For physical training is of some value, but godliness has value for all things, holding promise for both the present life and the life to come." EXERCISE

1 Timothy 6:12 "Fight the good fight of the faith. Take hold of the eternal life to which you were called when you make your good confession in the presence of many witnesses." FIGHT

1 Timothy 6:17 "Command those who are rich in this present world not to be arrogant nor to put their hope in wealth, which is so uncertain, but to put their hope in God . . ." HOPE

1 Timothy 6:18 "Command them to do good, to be rich in good deeds, and to be generous and willing to share." SHARE

2 TIMOTHY

2 Timothy 1:7 NIV (2011) "For the Spirit God gave us does not make us timid, but gives us power, love and self-discipline. " REMEMBER

2 Timothy 1:12 "Because I know whom I have believed, and am convinced . . . " KNOW

2 Timothy 4:7 "I have fought the good fight, I have finished the race, I have kept the faith." PLAY

TITUS

Titus 2:7 "In everything set them an example by doing what is good. In your teaching show integrity, seriousness." LEAD

PHILEMON

Philemon 7 "Your love has given me great joy and encouragement, because you, brother, have refreshed the hearts of the saints." CLEAN

HEBREWS

Hebrews 3:1 NIV (2011) "Fix your thoughts on Jesus, whom we acknowledge as our apostle and high priest." FOCUS

Hebrews 3:13 NIV (2011) "But encourage one another daily, as long as it is called "Today," so that none of you may be hardened by sin's deceitfulness." RELATE

Hebrews 4:10 "Anyone who enters God's rest also rests from his own work, just as God did from his." RELAX

Hebrews 4:12 "For the word of God is living and active. Sharper than any double-edged sword, it penetrates even to dividing soul and spirit . . ." THINK

Hebrews 10:24–25 "Let us consider how we may spur one another on toward love and good deeds. Let us not give up meeting together . . ." BARTER

Hebrews 10:36 "You need to persevere so that when you have done the will of God, you will receive what he has promised." PERSEVERE

Hebrews 11:1 NIV (2011) "Now faith is confidence in what we hope for and assurance about what we do not see." HOPE

Hebrews 12:2 "Fixing our eyes on Jesus, the pioneer and perfecter of faith." FOCUS

Hebrews 12:14 "Make every effort to live in peace with everyone and to be holy; without holiness no one will see the Lord." ACCEPT

Hebrews 13:15 NIV (2011) "Through Jesus, therefore, let us continually offer to God a sacrifice of praise—the fruit of lips that openly profess his name." PRAISE

Hebrews 13:16 "And do not forget to do good and to share with others, for with such sacrifices God is pleased." SHARE

JAMES

James 1:2–5 "Consider it pure joy, my brothers, whenever you face trials of many kinds, because you know that the testing of your faith develops perseverance . . ." CHERISH

James 1:17 "Every good and perfect gift is from above, coming down from the Father of the heavenly lights, who does not change like shifting shadows." CHANGE James 5:10 "An example of patience in the face of suffering . . ." ACCEPT

1 PETER

1 Peter 1:3 "Praise be to the God and Father of our Lord Jesus Christ! In his great mercy he has given us new birth into a living hope through the resurrection . . ." PRAISE

1 Peter 2:3 NIV (2011) "Now that you have tasted that the Lord is good." TASTE

1 Peter 3:3–4 NIV (2011) "Your beauty should not come from outward adornment . . . Rather, it should be that of your inner self, the unfading beauty of a gentle and quiet spirit, which is of great worth in God's sight." REMEMBER

1 Peter 5:7 Cast all your anxiety on him because he cares for you." BELIEVE

2 PETER

2 Peter 1:4 "Through these he has given us his very great and precious promises." CHERISH

2 Peter 3:8–9 "With the Lord a day is like a thousand years, and a thousand years are like a day. The Lord is not slow in keeping his promise, as some understand slowness." DREAM

2 Peter 3:18 "But grow in the grace and knowledge of our Lord and Savior Jesus Christ. To him be glory both now and forever! Amen." EXERCISE

1 JOHN

1 John 1:7 "But if we walk in the light, as he is in the light, we have fellowship with one another, and the blood of Jesus, his Son, purifies us from all sin." SING

1 John 2:14 NIV (2011) "I write to you, dear children, because you know the Father." REACH

1 John 2:6 NIV (2011) "Whoever claims to live in him must live as Jesus did." ABIDE

1 John 2:28 "And now, dear children, continue in him . . ." ABIDE

1 John 3:7 "Dear children, do not let anyone lead you astray . . ." LEAD

1 John 3:18 NIV (2011) "Dear children, let us not love with words or speech but with actions and in truth." LOVE

1 John 4:4 "You, dear children, are from God and have overcome them, because the one who is in you is greater than the one who is in the world." EXERCISE

1 John 4:13 NASB "By this we know that we abide in Him and He in us, because He has given us of His Spirit." ABIDE

1 John 4:18 "Perfect love drives out fear." PLAY

1 John 5:3 "This is love for God; to obey his commands. And his commands are not burdensome." OBEY

1 John 5:14 "This is the confidence we have in approaching God: that if we ask anything according to his will, he hears us." THANK

2 JOHN

2 John 8 "Watch out that you do not lose what you have worked for, but that you may be rewarded fully." LAUGH

3 JOHN

3 John 2 "Dear friend, I pray that you may enjoy good health and that all may go well with you, even as your soul is getting along well." EXERCISE

3 John 4 "I have no greater joy than to hear that my children are walking in the truth." DREAM

3 John 5 "Dear friend, you are faithful in what you are doing for the brothers, even though they are strangers to you." GIVE

JUDE

Jude 20–21 "But you, dear friends, build yourselves up in your most holy faith and pray in the Holy Spirit. Keep yourselves in God's love . . ." PREPARE

Jude 24 "To him who is able to keep you from falling and to present you before his glorious presence without fault and with great joy." REJOICE

REVELATION

Revelation 3:7–8 "These are the words of him who is holy and true, who holds the key of David. What he opens no one can shut, and what he shuts no one can open . . ." HOPE

ABOUT THE AUTHORS

Linda Gilden is an experienced writer, speaker, editor, writing coach, and word lover. Author of many books, including *Personality Perspectives* and *Called to Write*, Linda also writes magazine articles and is a regular columnist for Just18summers.com, presidentialprayerteam.com, and thewriteconversation.com. As a member of the CLASSeminars training staff, Linda enjoys helping others polish words to enrich their speaking and writing ministries. She and her family live in South Carolina, where words can often be long and drawn out.

Dalene Parker, Ed.D., works with words daily as she teaches English, creative writing, journalism, and public speaking to high school students. It brings her great joy to assist teen writers in getting their work published. With a doctorate in education from Bob Jones University, Dalene's passion for biblical literacy fuels her desire to use God's Word as a way of optimizing her life, her work, and her relationships. Author of *Christian Teachers in Public Schools* and faith-based articles in numerous magazines, Dalene makes her home in South Carolina with her husband, Pat, and children, Daniel and Susanne.

IF YOU ENJOYED THIS BOOK, WILL YOU CONSIDER SHARING THE MESSAGE WITH OTHERS?

Mention the book in a blog post or through Facebook, Twitter, Pinterest, or upload a picture through Instagram.

Recommend this book to those in your small group, book club, workplace, and classes.

Head over to facebook.com/worthypublishing, "LIKE" the page, and post a comment as to what you enjoyed the most.

Tweet "I recommend reading #WordsToLiveBy
by Linda J Gilden and Dalene V Parker // @worthypub"

Pick up a copy for someone you know who would be challenged and encouraged by this message.

Write a book review online.

Visit us at worthypublishing.com

twitter.com/worthypub

worthypub.tumblr.com

facebook.com/worthypublishing

pinterest.com/worthypub

instagram.com/worthypub

youtube.com/worthypublishing